11/21

US POL/HEALTH

NEW

The Enablers

The COVID-19 pandemic will forever be remembered as a pivotal event in American history. Written by one of the world's foremost experts on leadership and followership, this book centers on the first six months of the pandemic and the crises that ran rampant. The chapters focus less on the former president, Donald Trump, than on his followers: on people complicit in his miserable mismanagement of the crisis in public health. Barbara Kellerman provides clear and compelling evidence that Trump was not entirely to blame for everything that went wrong. Many others were responsible including his base, party, administration, inner circle, Republican elites, members of the media, and even medical experts. Far too many surrendered to the president's demands, despite it being obvious his leadership was fatally flawed. The book testifies to the importance of speaking truth to power, and a willingness to take risks properly to serve the public interest.

Barbara Kellerman was founding Executive Director of the Harvard Kennedy School's Center for Public Leadership and a member of the Kennedy School faculty for over twenty years. She is author, co-author, and editor of many books on leadership and followership, including *Leaders Who Lust*, *Followership*, *Bad Leadership*, *The End of Leadership*, and *Professionalizing Leadership*.

Other Leadership Books by Barbara Kellerman

- *Leaders Who Lust: Power, Money, Sex, Success, Legitimacy, Legacy* (Coauthor with Todd Pittinsky), Cambridge University Press, 2020
- *Professionalizing Leadership*, Oxford University Press, 2018
- *Hard Times: Leadership in America*, Stanford University Press, 2015
- *The End of Leadership*, HarperCollins, 2012
- *Leadership: Essential Selections on Power, Authority, and Influence* (Editor), McGraw-Hill, 2010
- *Followership: How Followers are Creating Change and Changing Leaders*, Harvard Business School Press, 2008
- *Women and Leadership: State of Play and Strategies for Change* (Coeditor with Deborah Rhode), Jossey-Bass, 2007
- *Bad Leadership: What It Is, Why It Happens, How It Matters*, Harvard Business School Press, 2004
- *Reinventing Leadership: Making the Connection Between Politics and Business*, State University Press of New York, 1999
- *The President as World Leader* (Coauthor with Ryan Barrilleaux), St. Martin's Press, 1991
- *Leadership and Negotiation in the Middle East* (Coeditor with Jeffrey Rubin), Praeger, 1988
- *Political Leadership: A Source Book* (Editor), University of Pittsburgh Press, 1986
- *Women Leaders in American Politics* (Coeditor with James David Barber), Prentice-Hall, 1986
- *The Political Presidency: Practice of Leadership*, Oxford University Press, 1984
- *Leadership: Multidisciplinary Perspectives* (Editor), Prentice Hall, 1984
- *All the President's Kin: Their Political Roles*, New York University Press, 1981
- *Making Decisions* (Coauthor with Percy Hill et al.), Addison-Wesley, 1979

The Enablers

How Team Trump Flunked the Pandemic and Failed America

BARBARA KELLERMAN

CAMBRIDGE
UNIVERSITY PRESS

CAMBRIDGE
UNIVERSITY PRESS

University Printing House, Cambridge CB2 8BS, United Kingdom

One Liberty Plaza, 20th Floor, New York, NY 10006, USA

477 Williamstown Road, Port Melbourne, VIC 3207, Australia

314–321, 3rd Floor, Plot 3, Splendor Forum, Jasola District Centre,
New Delhi – 110025, India

103 Penang Road, #05–06/07, Visioncrest Commercial, Singapore 238467

Cambridge University Press is part of the University of Cambridge.

It furthers the University's mission by disseminating knowledge in the pursuit of
education, learning, and research at the highest international levels of excellence.

www.cambridge.org
Information on this title: www.cambridge.org/9781108838320
DOI: 10.1017/9781108974417

First published 2021

Printed in the United Kingdom by TJ Books Limited, Padstow Cornwall

A catalogue record for this publication is available from the British Library.

Library of Congress Cataloging-in-Publication Data
Names: Kellerman, Barbara, author.
Title: The enablers : how team Trump flunked the pandemic and failed
America / Barbara Kellerman, Harvard University.
Description: Cambridge, United Kingdom ; New York, NY : Cambridge
University Press, 2021. | Includes index.
Identifiers: LCCN 2021009540 (print) | LCCN 2021009541 (ebook) | ISBN
9781108838320 (hardback) | ISBN 9781108974417 (ebook)
Subjects: LCSH: COVID-19 (Disease) – Political aspects – United States. |
COVID-19 (Disease) – Psychological aspects – United States. | Leadership. |
Followership. | Organizational behavior. | BISAC: PSYCHOLOGY / Applied
Psychology | PSYCHOLOGY / Applied Psychology
Classification: LCC RA644.C67 K45 2022 (print) | LCC RA644.C67 (ebook) |
DDC 362.1962/414–dc23
LC record available at https://lccn.loc.gov/2021009540
LC ebook record available at https://lccn.loc.gov/2021009541

ISBN 978-1-108-83832-0 Hardback

For Susan Ray, my sister
For Rachel Bratt, my friend

When somebody is the President of the United States, the authority is total, and that's the way it's got to be.

Donald Trump

My philosophy is very simple. When you see something that's not right . . . stand up, say something, and speak out.

John Lewis

Contents

Acknowledgments   *page* ix

Author's Note   x

Prologue – Enabler   1

    PART I TRUMP'S TRIBE   17

1. Base   19

2. Party   36

3. Administration   54

4. Inner Circle   71

    PART II VIRUS CRISIS   91

5. Prequel to the Pandemic   93

6. Sequence of the Pandemic   109

7. Science of the Pandemic   130

8. Politics of the Pandemic   149

    PART III TRUMP'S TEAM   169

9. Vice President, Cabinet   171

10. Senior Advisors   189

11. Senators, Governors, Media   209

12. Medical Experts   234

Epilogue – Enabler Effect   261

Notes   279
Index   314

Acknowledgments

For the second time over Will Imbrie-Moore was an invaluable forager. Jessica Greenwald was another, in her case a first timer who went on the hunt with the skill of a seasoned professional.

Now, as before, Ashley Davis was there when I needed her.

Kenneth Dana Greenwald made the book better. Makes me better. Thomas Dana Greenwald made the book better. Makes me better.

Thank you.

Author's Note

This book is centered on an event in American history that will be remembered as pivotal – the pandemic. "We have therefore made the assessment that COVID-19 can be characterized as a pandemic," declared the World Health Organization on March 11, 2020.

The Enablers: How Team Trump Flunked the Pandemic and Failed America was written in real time, contemporaneously, so it cannot constitute an historical record. What it can be, and is, is a mosaic. A mosaic that consists of numberless pieces, each a person who played a part in the pandemic at a particular time in a particular place.

President Donald Trump was, of course, one of these pieces – in the United States of America he was the central piece. But Trump was not, I repeat *not*, the only piece. Which is the reason for this book. For to see what happened, to grasp what happened, a single piece will not suffice. The mosaic is the whole not just as it pertains to the pandemic but to the entirety of the Trump administration, from its first day to its last.

Prologue – Enabler

This book centers on what happened during the first six months of the coronavirus crisis – from approximately January 1, 2020 to July 1, 2020 – first as it hit and then as it impacted the United States of America more widely. During this time of what within months was declared a pandemic, Americans were fixated, as they are inclined anyway to be, on their leader, President Donald J. Trump. Some credited him with handling the crisis well. Others faulted him for handling it less well – much less well, or even inordinately badly. The point is that Trump was the country's national fixation, even more of a fixation during the fourth year of his presidency than he was during the first three.

The present book deviates from this pattern. Here the lens is trained not on Trump, the leader, but, primarily, on his followers. Specifically, on Trump's enablers, on those who made it possible for the president to lead as he did during the inception of the pandemic and then during the months immediately subsequent – during which, in the USA, the virus crisis went from bad to far worse. As I use the word here, e*nablers are followers who allow or even encourage their leaders to engage in, and then to persist in behaviors that are destructive.* Given the enabled are leaders, their destructions have implications not only for them but, crucially, additionally, for others, sometimes for many, even millions of others. What we have then are not only bad leaders, but bad followers. The implications of this are not minor, they are major. Especially if the leader has great power, enablement can and often does have ramifications as pernicious as they are ubiquitous.

Writing about followers is devilish business. First, people seem not much to care. What they care about more, infinitely more, are leaders. Second is the matter of semantics. Always the semantics. What exactly is a follower? And do followers necessarily, by definition, follow? Or do leadership and followership imply something different? Relationships that are complex, not obvious? And behaviors that are nimbler, more nuanced?

First the evidence. The evidence that people do not care, or at least not much, is overwhelming. For all the many programs on leaders and leadership, almost none of them deal with the topic of followers and followership, and in comparison to the countless books and articles on the subject of leadership, there are very few specifically on followers and followership. Similarly, unlike the amount that is spent on leader training and development, the investment in follower training and development is meager at best. Followers and followership are, in sum, poor, pathetic, hangers-on. They are never at the center of what I call the leadership industry – they are always at the margin.

Second the semantics. The semantics are a problem, and for good reason. Curiously, while the words "leader" and "leadership" suffer from too many definitions, the words "follower" and "followership" suffer from too few. There are, literally, hundreds of definitions of the former; there are hardly any of the latter. Even in the smattering of books directly on the topic of followers and followership, clear, consistent definitions of what exactly is being discussed are hard to find. The truth is that the word "follower" makes us squirm. Being a follower conjures images of "docility, conformity, weakness and the failure to excel."[1] It conjures images of "subordination, submissiveness, passivity."[2] And these images are the opposite of those we have of leaders: leaders are strong, followers weak; leaders are active, followers passive; leaders are successful, followers not so much.

Most of the experts avoid the semantics by avoiding the topic. They focus laser-like on leaders; they steer clear of followers. But there is a problem with this approach – an insurmountable one. For leadership, like followership, is a relationship. Leaders and followers are inextricably bound, the one to the other. So, the problem of language remains. Now as before the only antonym of leader is follower, the only antonym of leadership is followership. *This does not, however, mean that followers always follow, any more than it means that leaders always lead.*

I first focused on followers in 2008, in a book titled *Followership: How Followers are Creating Change and Changing Leaders.* Then as now my argument was deceptively simple: that to fixate on the person at the top at the expense of those in the middle and at the bottom is misguided and misleading – a mistake. It explains nothing, it distorts everything. If leaders are key determinants, followers are no less.

- Followers are subordinates who have less power, authority, and influence than do their superiors and who therefore usually, but not invariably, fall into line.
- Followership implies a relationship (rank) between subordinates and superiors, and a response (behavior) of the former to the latter.[3]

Defining followers by rank, as opposed to behavior, allows us immediately to see that while followers, subordinates, usually follow, they do not always follow. Sometimes, in fact, they refuse to follow, refuse to go along with what their leaders want and intend. The same applies to followership. Implying a relationship between leaders and followers that is determined by rank, the latter subordinate to the former, does not extrapolate from this rank the nature of the response. *The ways in which followers respond to their leaders' directives vary. They range from blind obedience to deliberate disobedience, from abject loyalty to outright disloyalty.*

Followers who are enablers enable then by choice – some of the time. Not all the time, not for example in situations in which they are threatened with physical harm if they refuse to enable. But while in the United States refusing to enable President Donald Trump might have put a very few of his followers at professional or political risk, the risk was not to life or limb. Therefore, had a highly placed administration official such as, say, Secretary of Health and Human Services Alex Azar, or for that matter a Republican Party stalwart such as, say, South Carolina Senator Lindsey Graham, decided not to follow where Trump led, decided not to enable him, it would have put them at risk – but not in a way that came close to life-threatening. Professionally or politically impairing? Possibly, maybe even probably. But life-threatening? Certainly not.

Which raises the question of what should followers do? Take orders from on high even if these orders are seriously misguided? Pay deference to their leader even if their leader is evidently incompetent and demonstrably corrupt? Or should followers follow the dictates of their conscience? Should followers who want to be good refuse to follow leaders who obviously are bad?

HISTORY

The great leadership literature has always taken followers into account. But go back thousands of years and you will find then what we find now: leaders in the foreground, followers in the background. Leaders as leading actors, followers as second bananas. This is not to say that followers were unimportant, rather it is to say that they were not important in and of themselves, as worthy of dignity. Rather their role was a supporting one: their task was to support, or even to enable, their leaders, ideally not because they had to but because they wanted to. In other words, the great leadership teachers taught how to lead with a light hand.

Lao Tsu: "If the sage would guide the people, he must serve with humility. If he would lead them, he must follow behind. In this way when the sage rules, the people will not feel oppressed." Confucius: "Lead [the people] by political maneuvers, restrain them with punishments; [they] will become cunning and shameless. Lead them by virtue ... they will develop a sense of shame and a sense of participation." And though Machiavelli is usually thought to have taught that it was better for a prince (a leader) to be feared than loved, fear was to be the last arrow in the leader's quiver, used only if all else failed. The prince "should think to avoid those things that make him hateful and contemptible."[4]

But if the great leadership literature that was earliest has a familiar ring – followers as supporters – the great leadership literature that came later was different. Now followers were individuals with their own rights and privileges. For the ideals and ideas of the Enlightenment signaled a major shift. A shift that redressed, in theory if by no means always in practice, the balance of power between leaders and followers. To be sure, there were precursors to the Enlightenment, prominent among them Athenian democracy. But the impact of the Enlightenment was expansive, and it was enduring.

In the late 1600s John Locke provided moral and legal grounds for a system of governance that distributed power between leaders and led. "There remains still in the people," Locke wrote, "a supreme power to remove or alter the legislative, when they find the legislative act contrary to the trust reposed in them." Imagine that – power to the people! Similarly, in the mid and late 1700s, the revolutionary firebrand Thomas Paine raged against control of the American colonies by Great Britain, declaring that even "brutes do not devour their young, nor savages make war upon their families." By the mid-1800s women's voices surfaced or, if you will, resurfaced, among them Elizabeth Cady Stanton's, urging women to rise against the "history of repeated injuries and usurpations on the part of man toward woman." And little more than a century later Nelson Mandela declared in a South Africa courtroom that, "the ideal of a democratic and free society" was one for which he was "prepared to die."[5]

The Enlightenment, then, signaled a sea change. Followers were no longer expected to be, or even supposed to be mere appendages – appendages to leaders who had a right to control them as they saw fit. Rather those who ranked lower than leaders were themselves a force to be reckoned with. Not for nothing those revolutionary references to life, liberty, and the pursuit of happiness; to liberty, equality, and fraternity. They sent a signal that ideally anyway things now were different – that ideally power now was to be shared.

The history of followership is not, though, either in theory or practice, only about ideals and ideas. It is also about facts and figures. Which is where war comes in – specifically World War II. For it was primarily in the wake of World War II that followers became not just objects of abstract intellectual exercises but subjects of scientific studies. How, historians and social scientists wondered, had it happened that followers had followed bad leaders, enabled leaders so bad they were evil? Enabled a leader such as Adolf Hitler, a genocidal dictator who, notwithstanding his malevolence, was able nonetheless to get his most of his followers to do most of his bidding, and to do so of their own volition.

For most of the immediate postwar period the explanations for what happened in Germany between 1933 and 1945 centered primarily on Hitler. He was held personally as well as politically responsible for everything that had gone calamitously wrong: from the horrors of the Holocaust and the massive numbers of Europeans and Americans dead and wounded, to the destruction of large swaths of the European continent. More to the point, perhaps, it was Hitler who was the explicator. For example, though so far as we know Hitler personally never killed a single Jew, it was he who was held responsible for the murder of six million.

But before long, attention shifted and by the time the postwar period was over, Germans during the Nazi era were the most carefully studied followers ever. The first academic treatise on the subject was published in 1950, titled *The Authoritarian Personality*.[6] The lead author was Theodor Adorno, a philosopher and social scientist whose impetus was the Holocaust. How could it possibly have happened, he wondered, that in a country as cultured as Germany many millions of people were ready, willing, and even eager to follow where Hitler led? This profoundly important question was repeatedly raised thereafter, notably by other experts who sought similarly to explain what Hannah Arendt famously (infamously) called "the banality of evil."[7]

Two other studies – also of followers, also triggered by what happened during World War II – were of seminal importance. The first, on "obedience to authority," was based on Yale University psychologist Stanley Milgram's work in the 1960s, which centered on the single most famous social science experiment ever. The experiment was designed to shed light on why followers were willing to obey people in positions of authority who ordered them to do something they never normally would do: inflict pain, obvious physical pain, on another human being. Again, Milgram sought to answer the question raised by the Nazis: how do people get to the point of behaving so "callously and inhumanely"?[8] The second seminal study of followers during the Nazi period was Christopher Browning's 1992 book, *Ordinary Men: Reserve Police Battalion 101 and the Final Solution in Poland.*[9] As the title makes clear, the book is about men who before the war were "ordinary." Nevertheless, with only a very few exceptions, during the war they did what they were told to do, no matter how cruel, how treacherous, or murderous. Within months or even weeks they went from being ordinary men to enabling Hitler to implement "the final solution" – to eradicate, or try to eradicate, European Jews.

The history of followership has been curiously cyclical. Thousands of years ago followers were thought of rather as they are now: they were part of the action, but not central to the action. In the interim, however, were several periods during which followers came to the fore. In the wake of World War II certainly it was well understood that without followers there are no leaders, that without followership there is no leadership, and that while leaders matter so do followers – just as much. More recently though, there has been a retreat, a retreat to a time when followers were afterthoughts, sidebars, bit players. This book takes exception to what is now again the conventional wisdom. It reaffirms in no uncertain terms the power of the follower, and that subordinates determine outcomes – not just superiors.

THE LEADERSHIP SYSTEM

As it became apparent that it was impossible to understand what happened in Nazi Germany without accounting for the German people, so also it was recognized that this required understanding Germany itself – its history and culture, its geography and demography, and the country's political transformation and rampant inflation. To take an obvious example: Hitler was appointed chancellor in 1933. How this happened cannot be understood separate and apart from Germany in the ruinous wake of World War I and the devastating vortex of the Great Depression. In short, context matters.

The presidential leadership of Donald Trump cannot then be understood separate and apart from the event that constitutes the context of this book – *the pandemic as it unfolded in a particular place at a particular time, the United States during the first six months of 2020.* We need to understand what I call the "leadership system" – which consists of three parts: leaders, followers, and contexts.[10] I have argued, in other words, that it is impossible to understand leaders without their followers, or followers without their leaders, or to understand either leaders or followers without understanding the contexts within which they are situated.

The six-month period covered in this book – January through June 2020 – might seem arbitrary in that the pandemic persisted well beyond it. But for the purposes of this book the timeframe is apt. First, most of Trump's enablers – including Trump's team – had long since signed on and they chose during the half year to stay rather than go. Second, six months into the virus crisis was a marker. By then the facts and the figures had made clear just how bad was the pandemic – especially in the United States. Third, and most important, the first half year of the virus crisis set the template for what came subsequently. Whatever the patterns of leadership and followership as they pertained to the pandemic during Trump's presidency by then were set in stone.

By the end of June, though the USA had only 4 percent of the world's population, it had almost 25 percent of new coronavirus cases. On one particular day in early July, Germany (population 80.2 million) had 159 new cases; the state of Florida (population 21.5 million) had 15,300.[11] Six months into the virus crisis, more Americans had been infected with and died from COVID-19 than any other people in any other country in the world.[12] By October there was evidence that the pattern continued. A report in the *Journal of the American Medical Association* found that in the five months preceding, per capita deaths in the USA, both from COVID-19 and from other causes, were far greater than in 18 other high-income countries. An expert at the University of Pennsylvania, Dr. Ezekiel Emanuel, found the comparisons shocking. "The United States really has done remarkably badly compared to other countries. I mean remarkably badly."[13] Some states, such as Arizona, Florida, and Texas, fared particularly poorly: in early July, the Sun Belt was declared "the global virus capital."[14]

In short, by every objective measure, during the first half of 2020 and beyond, under the leadership of President Trump, the federal government's management of the pandemic was woefully, humiliatingly, bad. George Packer, an astute observer of the American scene, wrote that the USA had reacted as if it were Pakistan or Belarus, "like a country with shoddy infrastructure and a dysfunctional government whose leaders were too corrupt or stupid to head off mass suffering."[15] During this same six-month timeframe, the public health crisis was not the only crisis America faced. Two others also occurred: the economic crisis that was a direct result of the pandemic, and the social and political crisis that developed in the aftermath of the killing of George Floyd by a police officer in late May. Neither of these two crises are at the center of this book, but nor are they at the margins. As I always tell my students, everything is connected to everything else.

As the title of this book makes clear, my focus is on followers who were enablers. Specifically, it is on those who enabled President Donald Trump during the first half year of the coronavirus crisis, in some cases primarily as members of groups, in others primarily as individuals. However, since followers who are enablers cannot be divorced either from their leaders or from the contexts within which they and their leaders are situated, Trump is never far from center stage. Additionally, that which takes place on center stage, the pandemic, is itself of utmost consequence. This then is the story of a president who presided over a certain place at a certain time. It is also the story of a new coronavirus that became a pandemic in this place at this time. *But at the center of this story are the president's enablers – followers who allowed or even encouraged Trump to engage in, and then to persist in behaviors that were destructive.* Some were in the president's orbit before the pandemic was ever imagined, others were brought in as the pandemic came to pass. Every enabler chose in any case for his or her own reasons – such as family fealty, group loyalty, ideological affinity, party identity, professional anxiety, political expediency, personal preference, promise of reward, or fear of punishment – to remain in the president's fold.

ENABLERS

This book has a large cast of characters all of whom were followers. But was every follower an enabler? For example, Trump's base was composed of hardcore supporters who were critical to his presidency. But most of these supporters, however dedicated, never came close to the White House nor, obviously, were they involved in the president's management of the pandemic. Nevertheless, no matter what Trump did or said as it pertained to the new coronavirus; no matter how mistaken, misguided, or misleading his leadership; no matter how bad the pandemic during the first half of 2020, they continued to give him their undiminished, unconditional support. Included in this book as well are men and women who were close to the president – for example, Stephen Miller, a key aide, especially on immigration, and Melania Trump, his wife – but who played only a small part or even no part in managing the pandemic. Nevertheless, they played a large part in Trump's presidency.

They were then – both his base and a large cast of significant others – not just followers, but enablers. They allowed and even encouraged President Donald Trump to engage and then to persist in behaviors that were destructive. The best way to think about enablers is as along a continuum, depending on their level of engagement. Enablers at a distance, such as Trump's base, were, albeit only indirectly, important to his management of the pandemic. For their continued support throughout 2020 – despite growing evidence of White House callousness and ineptitude – explains why significant others, such as virtually every Republican senator, remained for the duration silent to the point of being complicit. However, enablers who were proximate, such as, for instance, son-in-law and senior advisor Jared Kushner, and director of the Centers for Disease Control and Prevention, Dr. Robert Redfield, were much more important. In fact, these enablers, members of Trump's *team*, were critical determinants of what exactly happened in America during the pandemic and what did not.

Trump's team was a management team. In one way or another its members were involved, deeply involved, with the president's management of the pandemic. These are the followers on whom I finally focus, enablers who were critical in the context of the virus crisis. They remained not only in the president's fold but under his thumb. Specifically, day in and day out they did more or less what Trump wanted them to do as it pertained to the pandemic – even after it became apparent that his management of the pandemic was highly problematical, if not even irrational. By choosing to stay rather than go, sign on rather than speak out, support rather than oppose the president during the first half of 2020, members of Trump's team were almost as responsible as was Trump himself for everything that went wrong. Let me be as clear as I can. I maintain that *members of Trump's team were almost as responsible as was the president himself for so many Americans dead, for so many Americans sick, for so many Americans out of a job, for so many American lives destroyed, displaced, and disrupted.* I argue that members of Trump's team explain almost as much as does the president himself about why, in comparison with other countries such as Germany, South Korea, and Canada, as it pertained to the pandemic the United States performed abysmally poorly.[16]

The book is in three parts. Part I – "Trump's Tribe" – is about enablers at a distance. Chapter 1, for example, is about Trump's base, his hardcore supporters. It was they who were the foundation on which the president stood during his four years in the White House. Part I has three additional chapters, each of which is devoted to another group in Trump's tribe: his party, his administration, and his inner circle. Part II – "Virus Crisis" – is about the pandemic that constituted the context. About the new coronavirus that felled and killed so many Americans, as it insinuated itself into the United States during the period January through June 2020. Part II also has four chapters: the first about the prequel to the pandemic; the three subsequent about the sequence, science, and politics of the pandemic.

Part III – "Trump's Team" – is about enablers who were up close and personal. Some had direct responsibility for managing the virus crisis, like Kushner. Others, like Attorney General William Barr, were less directly involved, but they nonetheless were key. Each enabler remained for the duration under Trump's thumb, day in and day out deviating little or not at all from doing what the president wanted when he wanted it. Part III also has four chapters, each about a group that constituted Trump's team as it pertained to the pandemic: (1) the vice president and four members of the Cabinet; (2) eight senior advisors; (3) two legislators, two governors, and four members of the media; and (4) members of the White House Coronavirus Task Force along with, separately, five medical experts, each a physician. The list of enablers is not definitive, it is representative. Each of these people enabled the president to lead and manage in ways that failed the American people. The people whose health and welfare, safety and security, President Donald Trump had sworn to uphold.

ENABLEMENT IN A PANDEMIC

Though I have long been interested in bad (as well as good) leadership, I am in the minority.[17] Moreover, those of us with an interest in bad (as well as good) followership are an even smaller minority. Which brings us to *The Enablers: How Team Trump Flunked the Pandemic and Failed America.* It is impossible to write a book such as this one, with such a title and subtitle, without taking a stand on who in this instance was a bad leader, and on who in this instance was a bad follower – a bad follower to the point of being an enabler. Ironically, though I was anything but a fan of President Trump, what prompted me to write about his followers was the ceaseless, merciless, brutal bashing of him as a leader. When it became clear that the coronavirus had become a crisis, and when it became clear that our obsession with Trump was becoming more crazed and consuming, I began to ask, "Is that all there is? Is President Trump the only one to blame for what went wrong?" The only one who can be tagged as being both incompetent and unethical in addressing America's greatest public health crisis in over a century?

That things went wrong in the USA during the first six months of 2020 seems to me an assertion beyond dispute. But, of course, it is not. Not at all. Trump and his followers have always maintained that during the months immediately before the pandemic was officially declared, and in the months immediately thereafter, they did nothing wrong and everything right. To be fair, the USA is not the only country in the world in which the pandemic was handled badly by people in positions of authority. Britain's Prime Minister, Boris Johnson, for example, was roundly criticized for his handling of the virus crisis. In July, the *Financial Times* claimed that Johnson's management of the pandemic had consisted of, "months of mistakes, fatal delays and episodes of incompetence at the heart of the British state."[18] Still, for the last 70 years or so the USA has had a reputation not only for unparalleled military and economic might, but also for unparalleled competence and capacity. For being at the front of the global pack in virtually every area of human endeavor. Now though, according to a study by Columbia University if the USA had locked down just one week earlier in March, some 36,000 fewer Americans would have died in the immediate wake of the virus outbreak.[19]

There is widespread agreement among medical and scientific experts that if the US government had moved more smartly and swiftly to contain COVID-19, Americans would have been spared the worst not only of the public health crisis but of the economic crisis. For what transpired during the first half of 2020 was exceedingly costly measured not only by the nation's physical health but also in terms of its economic health. In mid-2020 the US Labor Department reported that since the start of the pandemic 42.6 million people had filed for unemployment.[20] Additionally, though it will take years to know for certain, some estimates were that approximately 42 percent of the layoffs would result in job losses that were permanent.[21] By October it was apparent that the pandemic was the "greatest threat to prosperity and well-being the U.S. had encountered since the great depression."[22]

No wonder that by mid-June fully eight out of ten voters were telling pollsters that "things are out of control in the United States." A large majority of Americans were concerned about the spread of COVID-19 and pessimistic about the economy's returning to normal any time soon. Furthermore, in the wake of the massive demonstrations following the killing of George Floyd, it was reported that a large majority of Americans were "down on President Donald Trump's ability to unite the nation."[23] Floyd's death led to one of the largest and longest-lasting demonstrations against racism in America there has ever been. But, instead of choosing to empathize and unite, President Trump chose to denigrate and divide. Early on he denounced some of the demonstrators as "terrorists," and threatened to send the military to places where, as he assessed it, state and local leaders were either unwilling or unable to maintain law and order.[24]

Which brings us to the sorts of questions that are at the heart of this book:

- Given his complete lack of relevant experience and expertise, why was Donald Trump initially able to attract, and then to hold in his fold legions of ardent admirers? Why was there even such a thing as Trump's base?
- When it became apparent that a virus crisis was likely, what did members of Trump's team do to sound the alarm and, subsequently, to confirm what the president heard?

- When it became apparent that Trump was refusing to respond to fact-based evidence, what did members of Trump's team do first to stave off and then to mitigate the virus crisis? Should they have done differently?
- If members of Trump's team should have acted differently – should, for example, have in some way objected, intervened, resisted, or countermanded – but did not, does this make them bad followers? Are bad followers necessarily enablers?

How to make meaning of being bad? And what does the meaning we make of being bad tell us about who or even what is a bad follower? Here I turn to my earlier analysis of a related topic – bad leadership. Not bad leaders – bad *leadership*. For as earlier indicated, leadership, and followership, imply a relationship.

Bad leadership falls into two categories: bad as in *ineffective* and bad as in *unethical*. Ineffective leaders, in tandem with their followers, fail to accomplish what they want and intend. Unethical leaders, in tandem with their followers, fail to distinguish between right and wrong or, worse, they make the distinction but pay it no attention. The same can be said about followers. Which is to say that bad followership falls into two categories: bad as in *ineffective* and bad as in *unethical*. Ergo, ineffective followers, in tandem with their leaders, fail to accomplish what they want and intend. And, unethical followers, in tandem with their leaders, fail to distinguish between right and wrong or, worse, they make the distinction but pay it no attention.[25] It is possible, then, for followers to be (1) bad as in ineffective; or (2) bad as in unethical; or (3) bad as in both. It is also possible for leaders to be ineffective and/or unethical, but followers not – *that is, for followers to be good even if their leaders are bad.*

It is possible, in other words, for followers, defined here by rank, *not* to follow, to, instead, break with leaders who are bad. To do something other than what their leaders want them to do, ask them to do, tell them to do, order them to do. What I am arguing, then, is that members of Trump's team – followers who knew full well that he was not responding to the virus crisis as cogently, coherently, competently, or even as ethically as he could have – should have distanced themselves from him. Even broken with the president publicly, by refusing, publicly, to follow where he led. For in the end every one of Trump's followers, including members of his team, was an independent agent. Had these independent agents failed to follow their leader they might have been demeaned, demoted, or fired, or they might not have been reelected. But they would not have been shot.

It is in some ways better and in others worse that in liberal democracies especially, relations between followers and leaders have changed in recent decades. In general, followers have been empowered, and leaders have been enfeebled.[26] The reasons for this shift in the balance of power and influence include changes in culture, such as a decline in respect for authority; and changes in technology, social media especially, media that give voice to anyone and everyone no matter their status or station. This does, or it should, make it easier than it used to be for subordinates who have good and sound reason to oppose their superiors actively to resist them. First from within. Then, if necessary, from without. But, as we will see, there is evidence that opposing a leader, even like Trump, who demonstrably was bad, is a task followers resist.

Again, as I use the word here, *enablers are followers who allow or even encourage their leaders to engage in, and then to persist in behaviors that are destructive.* By focusing on enablers, I am, then, taking a stand. I am saying that Trump was a bad leader who depended completely and absolutely on his bad followers – his enablers. For though America's fixation on the president during the first year of the pandemic was complete, not for a moment was he the only actor in the drama. President Trump gets blamed, properly so, for his administration's feeble, feckless, incompetent, and immoral leadership during the first several months of the coronavirus crisis. But he was not alone. His enablers made it possible for Trump to do what he did – and not to do what he did not.

PART I   **Trump's Tribe**

I Base

Though occasionally he played at politics, it still seemed that Donald Trump came out of nowhere. He had never held political office. He had never had government experience. And he had never served in the military. What he was instead was a New York City real estate developer – a man who touted himself as a mega mogul, a man who promoted himself a television reality star, and who boasted of his bad-boy ways and got away with it. He got away with it because for many years he had confined himself to his playpens, one in New York City, where he wined and dined and knew everyone who was anyone; the other in Palm Beach, Florida, where he garrulously hosted, regularly golfed with, and relished hobnobbing with the very rich and not so very famous.

Trump was so far out of the realm of consideration as president of the United States that when it first became apparent that he was toying with the idea of running it seemed – he seemed – unserious. He appeared instead to be engaged in just another publicity stunt, able by standing on the national stage as a putative candidate for the Republican nomination for president, to secure even more visibility for the Trump brand than it had before. Moreover, when the Republican primary kickstarted in 2015 there already was a slate of candidates most of whom were much more plausible presidential contenders. Among them were some well-known Republican heavyweights such as Jeb Bush, former governor of Florida and scion of one of the best-known families in American politics, and Senators Ted Cruz and Marco Rubio. Each of these, along with several experienced and establishment others, appeared better qualified – far better qualified – to be president of the

United States than the rambunctious, almost buffoonish, political novice out of New York.

But from the start candidate Trump was a surprise. He was a surprise particularly when he got in front of a large audience and excited it, energized it, in a way that was extraordinary. Tim Alberta, author of *American Carnage*, wrote that beginning on day one Trump's bombast was not only *not* off-putting, to many Americans – who already knew him from his successful, long-running television show, *The Apprentice* – it was hugely appealing. "He was a larger than life character," Alberta writes, "someone with whom Americans of all ages had become familiar … He was universally recognized and, increasingly on the right, seen as a kindred spirit, his rants against political correctness resonating more with each passing day." Crowds across the country gave the billionaire businessman standing ovations. "We can make this country great again," Trump would shout to the crowd, the audience hooting and hollering in response.[1]

His audiences loved it, ate it up. They – those who saw him in person and became converts and those who saw him on television and became converts – were the seeds of his candidacy and then of his presidency. *It was they who constituted the core of his base, that unshakable base on which he stood during his entire time as president.* That support persisted long after it became apparent to the rest of America that he was in every way – personally, professionally, temperamentally, and characterologically – ill-equipped to be the nation's chief executive. Which raises the question of why – especially given that Trump's immediate presidential predecessors, George W. Bush and Barack Obama, were reasonable and restrained – Trump's rants against political correctness were so resonant.

The main reason Trump's voice resonated was because the country had become deeply polarized, and he appealed, strongly, to a particular segment of the population. "The master story," wrote expert and pundit Ezra Klein, "the one that drives almost all" American divides is polarization. The logic is this. To appeal to a more polarized public, political actors "behave in more polarized ways." These, in turn, further polarize the public, which sets off a feedback loop in which polarization becomes not only more extreme but more entrenched.[2]

If Donald Trump's surprisingly strong base was the effect of polarization, what was the cause? Why did polarized politics emerge when it did? Klein concluded the reason was change. The two mainstream American parties, Republicans and Democrats, used to consist of both liberals and conservatives. But the success of the civil rights movement and its alliance with mainstream Democrats ended that equilibrium. It "triggered an era of party sorting" with Democrats becoming overwhelmingly liberal and Republicans much more conservative. This led to Obama's presidency – "the younger, more diverse coalition taking power." Which in turn led to Trump's presidency – "the older, whiter coalition taking it back."[3]

This is the soil to which I refer – the fertile soil in which Trump's base took root. Of course, Americans who comprised Trump's base – Americans who loved his politics and persona and were quick to forgive his transgressions – had reasons for their preferences. While to many Americans Trump's supporters seemed somehow deviants – at a 2016 New York City fundraiser Hillary Clinton said that "half of Trump's supporters belong in a 'basket of deplorables'" – they were not. They were ordinary people who because of who they were and the circumstances in which they were situated believed they had good cause for strongly supporting Donald Trump. For strongly believing that he would be the best possible person to be the best possible president.

TRUMP'S APPEAL

Precisely because Trump was such a puzzle, seemed so outlandish a Republican nominee, his supporters were of interest to the experts from the start. In March 2016 a Brookings Institution demographer, William Frey, concluded they were "a nonurban, blue-collar, and now apparently quite angry population." They are "not people who have moved around a lot," he continued, "but they live in areas that feel stagnant in a lot of ways."[4] Not long after, there was another study, this one by The Democracy Fund, which dispelled the idea that Trump's supporters were part of a single, monolithic bloc. Instead researchers identified "five types of Trump voters." The first type, "Staunch Conservatives," were loyal Republicans, fiscal traditionalists with traditional values, who worried about immigration, tended to be older, more often male than female, and likely members of the National Rifle Association. The second type, "Free Marketers," were free traders who favored small government, and were inclined to vote against any candidate who was a Democrat. The third type, "American Preservationists," were the "core group that propelled Trump to the nomination." They were not the largest of the five groups, but they were the most eager and enthusiastic. They were not just favorably disposed to Trump but very favorably. The most striking thing about the fourth type, "Anti-Elites," is the degree to which they voted for Trump not because they loved him but because they hated her – his opponent in the 2016 presidential election, Hillary Clinton. Finally, the fifth type, "Disengaged," were those who voted for Trump but did so more out of apathy than enthusiasm.[5]

Though references to "Trump's base" were numberless, only rarely was it precisely defined. For the present purpose I define Trump's base as consisting of men and women who remained for most or even all of Trump's time in American politics, up to and including Election Day 2020, loyal to him particularly – personally and politically. Additionally, to be a member of Trump's base meant to be fierce and fervent, to back him with special intensity. Sometimes Trump's base was called a "cult." While the word "cult" is not exactly accurate, it does suggest the fervor of Trump's supporters, especially those who started to attend his rallies in 2015 and then continued throughout his time in public life to be among the faithful.

In 2018 there was another study of Trump's base which found it divided not into five groups but six: (1) white evangelicals; (2) white men; (3) white non-college; (4) white over age 50; (5) white with an income over $50,000; and (6) white rural. This confirmed what had long been obvious: overwhelmingly Trump's base was white. Race had always been a subtext, sometimes even an explicit text, and his views on race were part of his political appeal to a number of American people. (Trump had been a prominent "birther," claiming years before he entered politics that Barack Obama was not born in the United States and was not, therefore, eligible to be president.) The study also confirmed just how many in Trump's base were evangelicals. "If you want to know one thing that will tell you whether a white person voted for Trump, ask them if they were born again."[6]

From the time he first declared himself a candidate for the Republican nomination for president, Trump played to his audience, which often meant pandering to white racial fears and resentments. He described Mexican-American immigrants as criminals and rapists; he promised repeatedly to build a wall along the Mexican border; he proposed deporting millions of immigrants who were undocumented; he alleged, falsely, that thousands of Muslims in New Jersey cheered on 9/11 when the World Trade Center was attacked; and he charged massive voter fraud especially in communities that were African American – a tactic that years later was repeated.[7]

Trump's pandering to white fears about blacks and people of color was reiterated and exacerbated throughout his presidency. In the wake of the 2017 violence in Charlottesville, Virginia, associated with the white supremacist and neo-Nazi "Unite the Right Rally," Trump outraged millions of Americans when he asserted "fine people" were on both sides. Speaking (also in 2017) to law enforcement officers in the state of New York, he encouraged them not to use less force, but more. "Like when you guys put somebody in the car and you're protecting the head," he said, "you can take the hand away, OK?" And in 2020, in the wake of the killing by police of George Floyd, the president was insensitive and insulting, tweeting that protesters in Minneapolis, where Floyd was killed, were "thugs," and warning darkly that when "the looting starts, the shooting starts."[8] Each of these themes was reiterated again and again, especially during the 2020 presidential campaign. It was no great surprise then that the theme of white supremacy was threaded through the attack on the US Capitol on January 6, 2021.

Trump's base further consisted, to a considerable degree, of "those who felt that they were on the losing end of a newly global economy." Beginning in the early 1970s there was an explosion of positions that required college degrees. Around the same time, the number of traditional jobs, especially in manufacturing, dwindled, and disappeared from central cities. This left those who lacked the education they needed to prosper in the new economy with little choice but either not to work at all, or to take jobs in the service sector which was growing, but significantly less secure. Wages in the service sector were notably lower than in manufacturing, and there were far fewer benefits. Finally, manufacturing jobs that were moved from urban to rural areas were moved again – this time offshore. Effectively, then, for much of the American labor force these jobs vanished. Thus, the years that preceded the 2016 presidential election gave "Americans who were ill suited for the global economy good reason to feel neglected. Trump appealed to them directly ... with an agenda that merged white nationalism and economic protectionism."[9]

Finally, findings were released in 2020 that showed that Trump had tapped into a strain of authoritarianism in the American electorate that had been there for years, but that he was able to surface. Authoritarian personalities are characterized in part by their anti-democratic beliefs. As described by the authors of a 2020 book on the subject, John Dean and Bob Altemayer, titled *Authoritarian Nightmare: Trump and His Followers*, Trump's most fervent followers tended to be "submissive, fearful, and longing for a mighty leader who will protect them from life's threats." They further inclined to "divide the word into friend and foe, with the latter greatly outnumbering the former."[10] As we saw in the Prologue, the idea of the authoritarian personality goes back to the 1950s, when in the wake of World War II studies were conducted of Germans who were Nazis, followers of Hitler. This is not to compare Trump to Hitler. It is, however, to suggest that findings relating to "authoritarian" personalities are plausible. And that evidence of such personalities among some of Trump's strong supporters was probably not hard to find by anyone who looked carefully.

TRUMP'S ACOLYTES

On the surface, why some people follow leaders whom other people judge bad is a puzzle. Bad as in obviously ineffective and bad as in obviously unethical, maybe even bad in both. To an extent, of course, this puzzlement reflects our differences – our different preferences, and different values. But scratch the surface and there is more, which is why bad leaders trailed by bad followers are, in the end, easy enough to explain, if not necessarily easy to understand.

In my book *Bad Leadership*, I wrote that followers follow bad leaders for two basic reasons. First, bad leaders, though they are unethical, or ineffective, or both, can and often do fulfill followers' needs as individuals – for example, their needs for safety, simplicity, and identity. Second, bad leaders often satisfy followers' needs as members of groups – for example, their needs for cohesion and affiliation, and for a designated someone who gets the group's work done.[11] In her book *The Allure of Toxic Leaders*, Jean Lipman-Blumen asserted, as did, not incidentally, Sigmund Freud, that on some level, conscious or unconscious, we all want leaders. We want leaders because they satisfy certain psychological and physical needs. But what about bad leaders? Why are we attracted to bad leaders, ever? Lipman-Blumen wrote that many people are ready to follow even bad leaders so long as they promise to provide them with certain benefits, such as a reassuring relationship with an apparently powerful person.[12] Think, for example, of Donald Trump, who during his time in public life – as real estate mogul, as television reality star, as candidate running for the nation's highest office, and finally as president of the United States – exuded nothing so much as supreme confidence. After all, in his most recent incarnation, as politician,

Trump's claim was that he, and he alone, could and would "make America great again."

To be clear: Trump was not just a psychological phenomenon. He was a political player as well, a president who did, after all, have a few policy preferences that resulted in some political successes. On the domestic front, first, he delivered a significant tax cut. The Tax Cuts and Jobs Act of 2017 reduced tax rates for businesses and individuals and increased the standard tax deduction and family tax credits. Second, by 2020 he had appointed and the Senate had confirmed more federal judges (a total of 194) than any chief executive since Jimmy Carter.[13] Third, in keeping with conservative Republican orthodoxy, Trump to an extent at least dismantled the federal government, deregulating industries, defunding regulation agencies, and depopulating bureaucracies. Finally, he catered to the Christian right by, to take one example, appointing to the nation's highest court conservatives such as Neil Gorsuch, Brett Kavanaugh, and, at the end of his time in office, Amy Coney Barrett. Trump had some foreign policy successes as well: for example, during his administration ISIS effectively vanished as a menace. All this while continuing to feed his base its regular diet of red meat: Trump tirelessly trying to ban non-white people from entering the country; Trump regularly introducing tariffs ostensibly to protect US industries; and Trump reliably trying to roll back whatever his predecessor, Barack Obama, had enabled or enacted, the Affordable Care Act highest on the list.

Still, Trump's base was not so deeply devoted just because of his politics and policies. Among other reasons, he was anything other than an ideologue: most of his life he had been a Democrat, not a Republican. His base was also attracted by his persona and personality. The aspects of Trump that drove many Americans up a wall were precisely those that drove many other Americans into his waiting arms. Above all, perhaps, what drew the base to the man was his complete brazenness and total shamelessness. Donald Trump always did have, and he continued during his candidacy and presidency to have, an attitude that can best be described as F-you. Michigan congressman Justin Amash put it this way: "I think Trump is one of a kind – you can't replicate what he is doing. It requires you not to feel shame … The president feels comfortable … going to a rally and saying one thing and then holding a press conference and saying another. Most people aren't comfortable doing that. But because he is, it gives him this superpower that other people don't have."[14]

More than anything else, Trump's "superpower" explains why those who made up his base, especially but not exclusively white men, were so extremely devoted to him. Trump was amoral; to all appearances he lacked a moral compass. Counterintuitively, perhaps, it was precisely this amorality that was at the core of what Amash called Trump's superpower. There was never the slightest evidence that Trump cared if he was blatantly lying, or outlandishly exaggerating, or crassly insulting, or irresponsibly defaming, or deliberately distorting, or smashing the china. To the contrary, he did so loudly and proudly, an outlier who all his life got away with behaving in ways for which the rest of us seem promptly to get nailed and then properly punished. To the end of his time in office, Trump was an outlaw, he was the cowboy who wore the black hat not the white one, galloping into the distance with the authorities one step behind. Some Americans – not all Americans, but many of them – ate it up, especially those who were fed up.

Donald Trump's appeal as an outsider was, of course, not only because of how he behaved but also because of who he was. Trump was the real thing – he was anything other than a member of the Washington establishment. While some were put off by the mere idea that someone could become president of the United States without any experience or expertise whatsoever – why would we hire as our most important single political leader someone exceptionally ill-prepared and inordinately ill-equipped? – others found Trump's outsider status downright appealing. Who better than an outsider to speak for an outsider? Trump was unqualified to be president only if "qualified" was conventionally defined. But it turned out that those who made up Trump's base measured his qualifications by yardsticks other than the traditional ones. To them his deviations from the norm were not traits and behaviors to be derided but admired.

TRUMP'S INTRODUCTION

Shortly before Election Day 2016 and two days before the second presidential debate, the *Washington Post* posted a video from 2005 featuring Trump and television host Billy Bush. They were heard having "an extremely lewd" conversation about women. The two men were on a bus, on their way to film an episode of *Access Hollywood*, when Trump told Bush that he once tried to sleep with one of his cohosts. "I moved on her and I failed. I'll admit it. I did try and fuck her. She was married. And I moved on her very heavily." Later in the conversation Trump effectively said his trying to seduce women without their consent was, at least for him, behavior as usual. "I don't even wait. And when you're a star, they let you do it. You can do anything ... Grab them by the pussy. You can do anything." In response to what was widely presumed a politically lethal revelation, Trump issued a statement in which he semi apologized, describing what he had said as no more than "locker room banter." But his main response was to deflect attention away from himself and toward the husband of his opponent in the race for the White House, Hillary Clinton. Bill Clinton, Trump claimed, had "said far worse" to him on the golf course.

The reaction to the recording was immediate and dramatic, though also, predictably, varied. Democrats of course pounced. Hillary Clinton tweeted, "This is horrific. We cannot allow this man to become president." Her running mate, Tim Kaine, said the tape made him, "sick to my stomach ... I'm sad to say that I'm not surprised." Reactions from Republicans, on the other hand, were mixed. A few, such as, most prominently, Republican stalwart and former presidential nominee John McCain, promptly withdrew his support.[15] But while most of the rest were critical – such as Trump's running mate, Mike Pence, and Senate Majority Leader Mitch McConnell – they stayed the course. Notwithstanding the scandal they did not withdraw their support for the Republican candidate for president.

The result in any case was a major brouhaha just days before a presidential debate, and just weeks before Election Day. In the meantime Trump continued to display his usual bravado – he was, after all, all man. Moreover, Trump the counterpuncher punched. Less than two hours before the start of the October 9 debate, he put on what Tim Alberta called "a surprise pregame show." Without advance warning, Trump held an impromptu press conference "alongside a group of women who had publicly accused Bill Clinton of sexual misconduct."[16] Imagine that! Instead of Trump's sexual misconduct in the spotlight, now front and center of the spectacle slated to draw millions of eyeballs, it was Bill Clinton who was getting all the attention; his accusers, the women, sitting right there, present for the occasion. Who else but Trump would be so outrageous? So combative? So instinctually ready, willing, and able to go for Hillary's jugular?

The story matters because Trump not only survived the battle, he won the war. While for a couple of weeks after the scandal Trump's numbers went down, they soon climbed back up. And then they climbed some more. "Teflon Don" had done it again – survived a bruising fight without so much as an apparent scratch.

When Election Day was over it was clear that whatever the slings and arrows, whatever the fiascos and firestorms, whatever the detours and deviancies, it didn't matter. Trump had triumphed. Voters had stood by him. Above all those who made up his base, notwithstanding that many were from the Christian right which, presumably, was mortified by the candidate's vulgarity and philandering ways. To be sure, some evangelical leaders did as was expected: they spoke out against the candidate and against those on the Christian right who stood by him. Russell Moore, for example, head of the Southern Baptists Convention's political arm, was demonstrably upset that in the wake of "Pussygate" most of his peers remained unmoved. "How any Christian leader is still standing behind this," Moore tweeted, "is just genuinely beyond my comprehension." But Moore was the exception who proved the rule. Jerry Falwell, Jr., who a few years later was embroiled in a sex scandal of his own, spoke for most on the Christian right when he said, "We're never going to have a perfect candidate until Jesus Christ reigns forever on the throne."[17]

Why did the base stay in place? Several reasons come to mind, including the demographics to which I referred earlier. There are two more: first, the base was enthralled not only by Trump's persona but by his promise. Particularly perhaps by his promise to install in the courts – as he did – strictly conservative judges who would hue to a strictly conservative agenda. Second, was Trump's opponent, Hillary Clinton, who on the right was as disdained and even detested as Trump was admired and adored. I cannot offer here an extended exegesis of why Clinton evoked such antipathy in so many people for so many years. Suffice to say that during the 2016 presidential election all that vitriol served her opponent well.

Nowhere was this venom more in evidence than at his campaign rallies, performance pieces at which King Trump reigned while his faithful subjects cheered him on. It was for good reason that Trump held 323 rallies during the 2016 presidential campaign. These generally enormous, rambunctious gatherings were feasts and festivals for Trump supporters, inside-the-tent events in which everyone who was in was an ally, and everyone who was out an enemy. Chants of "Lock her up, lock her up, lock her up," references of course to Clinton, were the rallying cry. And those MAGA hats, those bright red "Make America Great Again" trucker hats, were the uniform. The chants and the hats both were intended to solidify Trump's base even further – effectively to swear his followers to fidelity. The hats or caps themselves were a beacon, almost an icon, a stroke of branding genius associated in an instant with the big man himself. The most loved, and the most hated, symbol of the election, they were at the same time comic and serious, symbolic in any case of the middle Americans the liberal elites were said to disdain.[18]

TRUMP'S TENURE

Donald Trump's presidency was tumultuous. Not only was he impeached; his character was assailed, relentlessly, and his competence questioned, regularly. He shattered norms at home. And he shattered them abroad. He palled around with the likes of Russia's Vladimir Putin and North Korea's Kim Jong-un, while he distanced himself from Germany's Angela Merkel and France's Emmanuel Macron. His physical persona was mocked and derided. His psychological stability was scrutinized from day one. His staff turned over at an unprecedented rate. His inner circle included as central players one of his daughters and her husband. He was a constant butt of numberless jokes – as he regularly triggered high anxiety. All this even before 2020 – the first half of which is the focus of this book and which witnessed not one crisis but three simultaneously.

Withal, President Trump's base held firm. As he stood his ground, so did his base. Notwithstanding the difficulties of his presidency, or the crises that characterized his tenure, especially during the pandemic, Trump and his base shifted hardly a whit. In fact, Trump doubled down on everything he was and everything he stood for which, in the short term, paid off. In June 2020 Trump's approval ratings among self-identified Republicans remained high – well over 90 percent. In fact, the level of party support for Trump was not only high, but it was unusually, atypically, high. Whereas recent Republican presidents had on average the backing of approximately 84 percent of Republicans, Trump's numbers were nearly ten points higher.[19] None of this, obviously, is to say that playing to the base was a winning strategy. Rather it is to point out how remarkably loyal were Trump's most fervent followers – notwithstanding the virus pandemic, the economic turmoil, and the social and political unrest.

To be sure, to the above numbers should be added some caveats. Such as, throughout Trump's presidency his critics felt more strongly about opposing him than his defenders about supporting him. A poll conducted in fall 2019 found that only about 24 percent of registered voters strongly approved of Trump's performance, while 44 percent strongly disapproved. More to the point, Trump never gained much traction beyond his base – and his base was not large, only about a third of American voters.[20] But these were the people who remained fiercely loyal: those who continued to attend Trump's rallies and who continued to wear those bright red trucker hats and shout gleefully if menacingly from the rafters, "Lock her up, lock her up" – even years after Hillary Clinton had exited the political stage. (In 2020 Michigan's Governor Gretchen Whitmer replaced her as primary political punching bag.) In other words, though their numbers as a percentage of American voters were not a majority, people who made up Trump's base compensated by being singularly steadfast, ardent, and fervent.

Their fervor extended into 2020, the president's base still willing, even eager, to turn out in support, even when doing so could be dangerous to their health. Because of COVID-19 the American people had been repeatedly told by medical experts to avoid large gatherings, and to wear masks and socially distance. But Trump's rallies saw no such thing. In summer and fall 2020, even after he himself had contracted COVID-19, Trump continued right up to Election Day to attract large crowds of adoring supporters to a long string of campaign rallies, most of which evidenced the deliberate eschewing of mask-wearing and social distancing. (This is not even to mention their defiance of state and local ordinances prohibiting outdoor gatherings of more than 50 people.[21]) It turned out, however, that the price paid by some was dear. A group of researchers at Stanford University estimated that in direct consequence of 18 campaign rallies held by President Trump between June and September 2020, there were at least 30,000 infections and 700 deaths.[22]

Notwithstanding the exigencies and contingencies, *it was Trump's base more than anything else that explains the president's iron grip throughout his tenure.* He had an iron grip on American politics generally and on the Republican Party specifically – including almost every Republican member of Congress. This grip held even during the dark days of 2020, when most of the country turned against Trump, including a few of the highest-ranking and most widely respected members of the American military, such as Admiral William McRaven. Still, despite Americans being beleaguered by three crises simultaneously, Republican members of Congress remained securely in the president's pocket, in small part because they were afraid of him and in large part because they were afraid of his base. They believed that Trump's hard-core supporters would punish them – by, for example, voting in a primary for a candidate more feverishly devoted to him than they – if they left the reservation, even after he lost the November election. In sum, so long as President Trump had a stranglehold on his base, he had a stranglehold on his party.

Trump's supporters lived mainly in sections of the country that were described as abundant with "white working-class pain." They sensed "the indifference or disdain of the winners on the prosperous coasts and in the innovative cities" – and they reciprocated.[23] Which to a considerable degree explains why, notwithstanding the failures of Trump's presidency, and notwithstanding his own personal and polit-ical flaws, his base still stood. Even in 2020, during the pandemic, when so many Americans were severely tested and badly afflicted, Trump's supporters continued to support, Trump's followers con-tinued to follow, and Trump's enablers continued to enable.

Of all the indicators of how thoroughly Trump rewrote the rules, broke past patterns, and tossed aside longstanding norms, the single most telling was Trump's relationship to truth. After all, most Americans are taught from an early age not to lie. First at home and then in school they are told that telling a lie is bad and that telling the truth is good. In fact, one of the most cherished fables in American history – the one about George Washington and the cherry tree – is about the various virtues of not lying, of truth telling. One would think, then, that an American president who lied repeatedly, habitually, out-rageously, would have been run out of town. Wrong. President Donald J. Trump's relationship to the truth was weak. From the beginning of his presidency to mid-July 2020 he told an astronomically high number of lies: over 20,000 were documented.[24] So not only was Trump not a truth-teller, but "misinformation, disinformation, and outright lies were always central to his politics."[25] Additionally, in 2020 Trump's ubiquitous Twitter feed became even angrier, darker than it was before, the president regularly reiterating conspiracy theories and frequently attacking his enemies. Notwithstanding, the base as well as the Republican establishment continued to toe the line. No matter how far from the truth their leader strayed and no matter how often, his followers continued to follow.

How did it happen that President Trump flagrantly violated this most fundamental of American principles, truth telling, and got away with it? Where else can we look as we seek to explain why Trump's base remained for the duration essentially intact? Psychologists use terms such as "entrapment" and "escalation of commitment" to explain why people who face increasingly negative outcomes – such as a pandemic that worsens – in consequence of a decision they made nevertheless persist. Instead of changing their direction or even their opinion in response to negative feedback, they go on. They go on to do in the present what they did in the past even if what they did in the past was disappointing. The reasons for persisting even as the costs of doing so are escalating are psychological, social, and structural. The point is that the commitment continues – despite growing evidence that it is doing more harm than good. We should, however, be clear. The damage done to democracy by incessant lying, especially when the incessant liar is president, is enormous. The great Yale historian Timothy Snyder has warned that "post-truth is pre-fascism" and that "Trump was our post-truth president."[26]

In this book I argue that Donald Trump was a bad leader. That during the first half of 2020, certainly as it pertained to the pandemic, he was both unethical and ineffective. Does this mean that those who remained in his fold throughout, who continued to constitute his base, were bad followers? At this point I will say simply that whatever virtues President Trump might have had, moral rectitude was not among them. This leaves us with two possibilities. Either some reasonable level of moral rectitude in an American president is less important to a considerable segment of the American people than it used to be. Or, if it as important as it used to be then a president who lacks this attribute must be, by definition, a bad leader. What seems most plausible in the case of President Trump is that most of those who comprised his base knew perfectly well that truth telling was not his strong suit. But they considered this failing – assuming they even deemed it a failing – to be of minor not major importance. Their willingness to look past Trump's flaws was, in any case, critical. Critical to enabling him first to sustain his candidacy – and then to maintain his presidency.

2 Party

During the first impeachment trial of President Donald J. Trump, it was pointed out that just four years earlier almost all Republican leaders had reacted to Trump "with horror." But now they were making "a different calculation." Now they were deciding to stand by Trump no matter what.[1] Moreover, they seemed to believe that even if he went down in November 2020, on Election Day, Trumpism itself might well not only survive but thrive.

Trump's relationship to the Republican Party, especially to its most prominent members, had changed over the years: from fear and loathing in 2015 to co-existing in 2020. At no point was there any love lost on either side. Not on Trump's side – after all, up to his own run for political office some 80 percent of his political donations had been to Democrats, not Republicans. Nor on the side of party stalwarts most of whom continued to find him personally unappealing if not repellent, and certainly politically wanting.[2] But as it turned out, precisely because of Trump's fiercely devoted and reliably steadfast base, party regulars concluded they had no choice. To get along they had to go along. Go along first with the Republican nominee for president, and then with the president himself. For by the time Trump was impeached the first time in 2019 his hold over his party was unshakable.

Which inevitably raises the question of why. Why were prominent Republicans, from public officials to wealthy donors, so loyal to a man for whom they had so little regard and less love? The most obvious answer is that it was in their personal, professional, and political interest to follow where Trump led. Which is true. But given the present is always a product of the past, the recent history of the Republican Party additionally explains how it came to pass that Donald Trump got to the White House – and stayed in the White House.

The Republican base had long been whiter and older, more male, more rural, and more fervently Christian than the United States as a whole. It was also, as we have seen, more conservative than it used to be, its ideology having hardened over time to the point of excluding those who fell outside its ideological parameters. By 2016, Republicans were more eager to contract for the sake of homogeneity than to expand for the sake of heterogeneity. But, then, the Republican Party was always centered on a "core constituency of people who are regarded by themselves and others as typical Americans, but who are not by themselves a majority of the electorate."[3] It was presidential candidate and renegade Barry Goldwater who got the Republican Party to move away from the center of American politics to the right. He did not "use the standard, reassuring lexicon of the big tent and the mainstream." Instead, at the Republican convention in San Francisco in 1964 he "embraced extremism" and denounced Republican regulars, introducing a phrase that soon became a mantra, "Moderation in pursuit of justice is no virtue."[4]

Goldwater was not himself an original thinker. But William F. Buckley, who preceded him on the national scene, was. His conservative journal (founded in 1955), the *National Review*, was the ideological foundation on which Goldwater, and later Ronald Reagan, came to stand. During the second half of the twentieth century Buckley provided the American conservative movement with grist for its mill. As one historian of American conservatism put it, for an entire generation, he "was the preeminent voice of American conservatism."[5] In consequence, then, of both men, Buckley and Goldwater, there was a 16-year period during which the conservative movement and the Republican Party came increasingly to converge. This convergence culminated ultimately in the presidency of the widely liked and, in time, widely admired Ronald Reagan.

Though the term "Reagan Revolution" was for a time a common one, Reagan had neither the ideological inclination nor the personal disposition of a revolutionary. In contrast, Newt Gingrich, Speaker of the House of Representatives from 1995 to1999, did. Gingrich, known for his lust for power, was a rebel who spoke about overthrowing the existing Republican Party – and any of its leaders who smacked of the establishment. He went low, mentoring Republican candidates for office by instructing them on how to demonize their opponents, by, for example, describing them as "traitors." Gingrich in turn was followed by the Tea Party, a modest movement maybe, but, still, a movement.[6] The Tea Party was a loosely organized amalgam of libertarians, right-wing populists, and conservative activists, from inside government and out, who drove Republican moderates, such as Speaker of the House John Boehner (2011–2015), to distraction. If by the third decade of the twenty-first century the Tea Party had effectively disappeared, which it did, the reason seems clear. It was coopted. The erstwhile Tea Party was coopted, inadvertently more or less, by Donald Trump who came in short order to personify it. He personified the ideas the Tea Party had stood for and, more importantly, the feelings it had expressed: feelings of anger, paranoia, hostility, frustration, and of being at the margin of America not at the center.

However improbable it was that an upstart like Trump, an outsider and a newcomer, could, and would, effectively take over the Republican Party, this is, of course, exactly what happened. A "hostile takeover" it was called. Hostile or not, Trump came to dominate the Republican Party not only because of his wholly unanticipated appeal to those who became the bedrock of the Republican base, but also because of his wholly unanticipated relationships to Republican elites. These fell broadly into two groups. First were Republican political elites who had initially viewed Trump with horror – Ted Cruz had called Trump "utterly amoral"; Rick Perry had said Trump's candidacy was a "cancer on conservatism"; Marco Rubio had warned that Trump was "dangerous" – but then changed along with the changing winds because it was in their political interest to do so.[7] Second were the Republican financial elites, those described by *New Yorker* writer Evan Osnos as "the executive class of the Republican Party." Unlike most of the base, those who belonged to the executive class were wealthy, or relatively so. Additionally, they were more conservative and politically active than their establishment forebears. Notwithstanding the differences, the Republican financial elites joined with the Republican political elites to help Trump reach the White House; to navigate a tumultuous four-year term; to survive his first impeachment; and, finally, to run for a second four-year term. As Osnos put it, understanding how Trump retained the overwhelming support of Republicans requires an "accounting of not only what he promised Americans at the bottom" but also what he provided "Americans at the top."[8] Those at the top got an anti-tax, more or less libertarian agenda that left them free further to grow their wealth largely unimpeded.

This shift in attitude, notably among Republican elites, is key to understanding how Trump's base came to hold such sway. In the past, party elites would have stopped a Trump-type in his tracks – long before the choice was narrowed to him or Hillary Clinton. But that was then, when candidates were decided on in back rooms by party bosses who prioritized power over ideology or for that matter over money. Now the success of presidential candidates no longer depends on winning over party officials, but on winning over the party faithful, "the intense minority of party supporters who turn out to vote in primaries" and those who enter with them into an alliance of convenience.[9] Trump was not then slapped onto an empty canvas. He was a creature of the Republican Party – the party's past, the party's present. In 2012 political scientists Thomas Mann and Norman Ornstein wrote that the Republican Party had become "ideologically extreme." It was "contemptuous of the inherited social and economic policy regime; scornful of compromise; unpersuaded by conventional understanding of facts, evidence and science; and dismissive of the legitimacy of its political opposition, all but declaring war on government."[10] They were prescient.

Trump was outlandish from the outset. But, to many people it was precisely his crassness and coarseness, his pugilism and populism,

his oafishness and outrageousness that were appealing. Not for nothing had candidate Trump cut his teeth on TV. As it turned out, by the
2016 presidential campaign he was an old hand at mastering not only
old media but new, at playing to the crowds with the seasoned skill of
an experienced performer, and at tweeting to the crowds with the
frequency of someone who chronically was energized or, if you prefer,
angry and agitated. But what distinguished him more than anything
else, certainly as a mainstream candidate, was his willingness to do,
without apparent shame or contrition, that which no other politician,
of either major party, would have dared. Above all was his willingness,
even eagerness to attack his opponents not only politically, but personally. Hillary Clinton was a "monster" (as was Kamala Harris four
years later). Rick Perry should be "forced to take an IQ test." Marco
Rubio was "soaking wet and sweating." Ben Carson had
a "pathological temper." Carly Fiorina was demeaned for being
plain. "Look at that face," Trump said of her. "Would anyone vote
for that? Can you imagine that, the face of our next president?" Ted
Cruz's father was said somehow to be involved in the assassination of
John Kennedy. Democrat Elizabeth Warren was scorned as
"Pocahontas." War hero John McCain was not a war hero because he
had the temerity to be captured and Trump "liked people who weren't
captured." And broadcaster Megyn Kelly, who dared to ask candidate
Trump a few tough questions, was hauled into the court of public
opinion because of her body fluids. "You could see there was blood
coming out of her eyes, blood coming out of her – whatever."[11]

Who before had used such language? Who before had behaved
that way – during a mainstream political campaign no less? No matter. Contrary to all expectations, Donald J. Trump vanquished his
Republican opponents, thereby seizing control of the Republican
Party, lock, stock, and barrel. Experts were left scratching their
heads, trying to explain the inexplicable. One opined, "If Republican
voters hadn't been so disillusioned by their usual leaders, Trump
would have remained a fringe candidate. Instead ... he was able to
present himself as the heir to the Tea Party revolution ... He was also

able to tap into many Republicans' anger, some of it tinged with racism … and into broader fears of terrorism and economic decline, and into a general disgust with professional politicians."[12]

PARTY MEDIA

Donald Trump candidate and Donald Trump president made great copy. He made great copy even before he opened his mouth. His physical self – his oversized body and oversized suits and oversized tie and oversized hair – itself sufficed. His hair alone, which ranged in color from orangutan orange to baby blond, and in style from frozen perfection to obvious comb-over, was a cartoonist's dream. To be clear, by the time he ran for public office Trump was no longer young or especially good looking. But he was, somehow, eye-catching. It was hard for many if not most Americans to take their eyes off him. Whether on a debate stage, or at one of his raucous rallies, or watching him shout over the noisy whir of a nearby helicopter, he was not boring to look at.

Nor was he boring to listen to. Tedious was not in his lexicon – outrageous yes, but tedious no. He was an exaggerator and liar. He was scandalous and slanderous. He was remarkably ignorant of facts and remarkably fond of fantasy. When he spoke, he turned a lot of people off, but he turned the media on. The media, old and new, could never, ever get enough of Donald Trump. To paraphrase Winston Churchill, their appetite grew with eating.

Withal, the media's love/hate relationship with Donald Trump – Trump as great copy is not synonymous with Trump as an object of affection – was not reciprocated. At least not the love part. While Trump was in love with media that loved him, Fox News the most obvious example, his loathing of what he called "fake news" was unrelenting and unmitigated. Trump hated the mainstream media – if only because he was sure they hated him – with a passion and venom that has rarely if ever been replicated. Trump's administration stepped up prosecutions of news sources, interfered in the businesses of media owners, and empowered foreign leaders to restrict their own media.

But his most effective ploy by far was destroying the credibility of the press, dangerously undermining objective truths as well as any attempt at achieving national consensus. Even during the pandemic, he called the mainstream media – his special targets were the *New York Times*, the *Washington Post*, and CNN – "disgraceful and false." The press is "very dishonest," he would repeat, over and over again, adding for good measure that journalists "truly do hurt our country."[13] One way Trump solved his problem with mainstream media was by bypassing them – in good part by taking to Twitter, tirelessly. On a weekend in May 2020, President Trump tweeted hundreds of times; the following Monday almost 60 times; and the Tuesday after some 30 times – the last all before 9 a.m.[14] (One month later, for the first time ever, Twitter finally stepped up to the plate, labeling a video that Trump had tweeted "manipulated" – as, in other words, a distortion of the truth.)

Trump's most reliable and powerful media ally by far was, of course, that longtime staple and stalwart of the Republican Party, Fox News. Under the legendary if controversial leadership of the late Roger Ailes, who himself served under the equally legendary and controversial leadership of Australian-American media mogul Rupert Murdoch, Fox News had become a powerhouse. In the late 1990s and into the 2000s it had grown into the proverbial 800-pound gorilla, the top-rated cable network that dwarfed its competitors in importance and influence. The relationship between Fox News and those at the highest levels of the Republican Party was widely understood to be symbiotic. Each depended absolutely on the other, and though Fox had once claimed to be "fair and balanced," by the time of Trump's presidency the network was widely seen, especially during prime time, as an administration mouthpiece. Moreover, while liberals had no single media outlet on which they overwhelmingly depended, conservatives did – Fox News. Pew Research Center surveys conducted in 2020 found about two-thirds of Republicans and Republican-leaning independents (65 percent) said they trusted Fox News for political and election news. Pew concluded that Fox News holds a "unique place in the American media landscape, particularly for those on the ideological right."[15]

If Fox News helped Donald Trump to get to the White House, which it did, the first impeachment process confirmed yet again that the network would do everything it could to keep him there. To be clear, other media outlets, most conspicuously MSNBC, tried their hardest, especially during the trial, to do the opposite, to get Trump tossed out. No surprise then that Fox, like nearly every one of its counterparts, on the right and the left, was only too eager to engage in what was an all-out, no holds barred political brawl. Fox's opinion shows behaved according to script. They mocked the impeachment hearings as "alternately biased and pointless," as being tedious and time-wasting. Similarly, Fox's evening shows proceeded as expected – "according to the stereotype." One of the network's leading lights, Tucker Carlson, called the hearings not only "dumb" but "boring." Another Fox prime time player, Laura Ingraham (and her guests), made fun of the various players, at least those on the Democratic side of the aisle, such as California Congressman Adam Schiff. Schiff chaired the House Intelligence Committee and was the Democrats' point person on impeachment. He was described by Ingraham as having a "very priggish presentation," while Val Demings, African American Democratic congresswoman from Florida, was derided for her pronunciation of the word "irregular."[16]

Of course, Fox News was not the Republicans' only prominent, rock solid media ally. There were others, for example, Breitbart, and, most conspicuously, the star of *The Rush Limbaugh Show*, that long-time loudmouth party stalwart and reliable man of the right, Limbaugh himself. (Limbaugh died in February 2021). He was something of a media phenomenon, famous for his remarkably durable and successful radio show (it started in 1988), as well as for his supremely confidently held, but highly controversial and combative Manichean political opinions. A case in point is Limbaugh labeling the media, the scientific community, academia, and the government, "the four corners of deceit."[17] He and Trump were, in any case, two of a kind, which is why in the

Washington Post Paul Waldman wrote it was "not an exaggeration to say that Limbaugh made the Trump presidency possible." Limbaugh is credited with communicating to an enormous national audience some of the ideas that later became central to Trump's rhetoric, including making whiteness core to his conservative constituency. Moreover, well before Trump ever ran for office, Limbaugh had already primed members of his radio audience, telling them there was no such thing as truth, and that if any of them did not like what they heard, including on the national news, they should ignore it.[18]

To be sure, the relationship between the two men went both ways. Trump depended absolutely on Limbaugh's support, but Limbaugh was unwilling to lend his unless Trump toed Limbaugh's hardliner line. When Trump briefly retreated from an all-out push for the border wall between the USA and Mexico, Limbaugh, along with other Republican media operatives such as Ann Coulter, was furious. Millions of Limbaugh's listeners were told, "Trump gets nothing and the Democrats everything."[19] Still, Trump and Limbaugh were bedfellows. In a surprise announcement made during the 2020 State of the Union Address, the former bestowed on the latter the Presidential Medal of Freedom. The award, Trump declared, was being given to Limbaugh for his "decades of tireless devotion to our country."

The fact that Fox News and like-minded fellow travelers were so unswervingly loyal to Trump was of consequence especially during the pandemic – a point that will be further explored later. Suffice now to say there is evidence that Americans who relied on Fox News or similar right-wing sources were duped as the new coronavirus started to spread. "Dangerously duped." Studies made of the Fox effect painted a picture of a "media ecosystem" that amplified misinformation, entertained conspiracy theories, and discouraged "audiences from taking concrete steps to protect themselves and others."[20]

Though this section is called "Party Media," and though neither Facebook nor Twitter is party media, it should be added, and emphasized, that both played, along with other social media, an important role in the spread of false information and even encouraging violence

particularly as they pertained to American politics. This was especially true during election years, when "fake news" peaked online. It
was only in January, 2021, subsequent to the attack on the US Capitol
and just weeks before the end of President's Trump's time in office,
that Facebook and Twitter finally suspended him from posting to their
platforms.[21]

PARTY MONEY

Despite his own very considerable wealth, both Donald Trump's
presidential campaigns depended on the kindness of strangers. Well,
not strangers exactly, not necessarily anyway, but contributors other
than himself. In 2016, Trump raised approximately $957.6 million, of
which just $66 million was his.[22] (The 2016 campaign spent 99 percent
of what it brought in.) This in sharp contrast to other extremely rich
men who ran for president, such as, for example, Democrat Tom
Steyer, who during the 2020 campaign raised $343.9 million, 98 per-
cent of it out of his own pocket. And Democrat Michael Bloomberg,
who in 2020 spent over half a billion dollars on ads alone, every dime
of which was, though, from his own funds.

At first Trump insisted he would accept no outside money at all. In
2015, when he and Melania descended that Trump Tower escalator to
announce his longshot bid to become president of the United States, he
announced his run would be self-funded. "I'm using my own money,"
Trump declared. "I'm not using the lobbyists. I'm not using donors.
I don't care. I'm really rich."[23] But, things change. By 2020, the degree
to which his presidential campaigns depended on, and aggressively soli-
cited, the money of others had become clear. It was clear as could be that
if it were not for the munificence of Republican donors, Trump would
not have run for president in 2016 and would not have run again in 2020.
As Michela Tindera pointed out in *Forbes*, approximately six months
before Election Day 2020 "the richest president in American history"
had received campaign donations from nearly one in ten US billionaires.

By mining the database of the Federal Election Commission for
information on Trump's richest donors, *Forbes* was able to access

a trove of relevant materials. Moreover, if money is the "mother's milk of politics," then the information is important. It is important to know that among Trump's followers were some among the mega rich who, as suggested, were strongly, materially, incentivized first to get Trump to the White House and then to keep him there. After all, who better for their pocketbooks: a chief executive who was a Democrat or a chief executive who was a Republican? More than half of Trump's wealthiest donors lived in just three states: New York, Florida, and Texas. Most were self-made, many got rich in finance, investments, and real estate, and some who did not give to Trump in 2016 did so in 2020. Because by law no single individual can donate more than $5,600 to a presidential campaign, most of the money that came to Trump from billionaires was funneled through one of two separate so-called joint fundraising committees. According to *Forbes*, some 45 billionaires put more than $100,000 each into Trump's coffers.[24] Of course, among Trump's donors a few stand out. Some stand out because of the nature of their relationship to Trump; some because of who they are; still others because of the immenseness of their largesse.

There is, for example, Isaac "Ike" Perlmutter, who was CEO and remains chair of Marvel Entertainment. Perlmutter is worth $4.5 billion. He is also a Trump neighbor and friend, and a member of his club, Mar-a-Lago. Perlmutter is famously reclusive. But because of his relationship with Trump, to whom he gave (at last count) nearly three quarters of a million dollars in contributions, Perlmutter became not only better known, but more controversial, especially after his inappropriate intrusions into the Veteran's Administration.[25] Then there is Stephen Ross, billionaire chair and majority owner of The Related Companies, a global real estate firm, who is also owner of the Miami Dolphins. Ross had long donated to Republican candidates and causes, making no exception for Trump, for whom, in summer 2019, he hosted a multimillion-dollar fundraiser that itself was politically controversial. There are also the Mercers: strongly conservative Robert and his daughter Rebekah, who were among Trump's original supporters and financiers. During the 2016 campaign Robert funneled millions of dollars into supporting Trump's run, while Rebekah had ties to Breitbart News and to Steve Bannon, at the time among Trump's closest advisors. In February 2020 Robert Mercer resurfaced, contributing $355,200 both to the Trump campaign and to the Republican National Committee.[26]

There was also Sheldon Adelson, who for years was neither shy nor reclusive, and who was only too glad to tell anyone who cared to listen what his political priorities were and what he would do to realize them. Initially Adelson and his wife, Miriam, were skeptical of Trump. But by 2018 they had emerged as among his biggest donors. The reason of course was simple: they found much to like in a Republican-controlled government that aligned almost perfectly with several of their most important goals. These included foreign policies that were unflinchingly pro-Israel, and domestic policies that were dedicated to deregulation and lower taxes.[27] During the 2018 midterm elections the Adelsons were among the Republican Party's most prolific donors, giving over $100 million to various conservative groups and causes, and a combined $10 million to America First Action, the principal pro-Trump super PAC (political action committee).[28] In early 2020 it was reported that their intention was to donate to President Trump specifically and the Republicans more generally at least $100 million. (Sheldon Adelson died in January 2021.)

In January 2020, Bernie Sanders, Democratic candidate for nomination for president, announced that he had raised $34.5 million in the fourth quarter of 2019 – an impressive amount. More impressive, however, was that by then his campaign could claim fully five million individual contributions. In other words, Sanders's remarkably successful campaign for president – though he did not of course ultimately secure the nomination – was fueled by an enormously high number of single donors, most of whom gave small sums. In the 2020 campaign cycle, the average contribution to Sanders's campaign for president was $21.[29] This, obviously, is in contrast to what transpires in the Republican Party – Trump being exhibit A – which is the converse. That is, Republican candidates for office depend much more heavily on a small number of contributors – supporters, followers, enablers – who give them large sums of money. Adelson, for example, gave to Republican causes and candidates well before the advent of Trump. In 2012 he supported the presidential ambitions of Newt Gingrich to the tune of $20 million.

The impact of large and important donors on political campaigns can be traced to a 2010 Supreme Court ruling on campaign finance. Generally referred to as "Citizens United," the divisive decision transformed the political landscape. It meant that "one donor could now single-handedly sustain a candidate with millions of dollars in super PAC-spending," thereby potentially at least empowering wealthy individuals as they had not been previously.[30] Given that the Republican Party is more associated with immensely wealthy Americans than the Democratic Party, the decision was immediately seen for what it was: on its face advantageous to Republican candidates running for political office; disadvantageous to Democratic candidates running for political office. Which is why Republican Mitch McConnell commended the decision, while Democratic Barack Obama condemned it.[31] No question: it was to the immense benefit of a politician such as Trump who warmly welcomed the generous support of a very small number of very rich people.

It is important to add, however, that as 2020 crawled on, there was ample evidence that these small numbers of rich people were quite aware of the president's sagging fortunes. In consequence of Trump's declining popularity, and his erratic, divisive, and incompetent management of the pandemic, by summer it was clear that some of the nation's wealthiest Republicans had decided to delay, divert, or diminish their replenishment of his coffers.[32] By fall it was even clearer: in a major reversal from earlier in the year, when Trump had a "seemingly unbeatable fundraising head start" against his Democratic opponent for president, Joe Biden, six months later it was he who was in the catbird seat. Democrats' campaign cash reserves beat those of Republicans by nearly $200 million.[33] Diminished enthusiasm for Trump, combined with mismanagement of his campaign coffers, had led to a cash crunch as remarkable as it was revealing.

PARTY FEALTY

Most striking about Republican leaders during President's Trump's time in the White House was the consistency with which they fell into line – toed whatever line that Trump drew nearly without dissent. Though Republican senators were the most stunningly, and consequentially, subservient, other prominent Republicans were little different, for example, Republican governors. They too were almost always in lockstep with a leader who in many, if not in most instances they privately derided.[34] If Trump did indeed, as it is often claimed, conquer the party in a "hostile takeover," it was remarkable how quickly he received from self-identified Republicans, on every rung of the political ladder, their near unanimous support.[35]

After the pandemic hit, things changed, though only slightly. After it became clear that guidance on the virus from the White House was irregular and unreliable, if not occasionally downright dangerous, a few Republican governors took matters into their own hands. Among them was Ohio Governor Mike DeWine, who unlike a handful of other Republican governors who also deviated from the president's line, notably Maryland's Larry Hogan and Massachusetts's Charlie Baker, was leader not of a blue state but of a red one. But, even as Trump continued to dismiss the dangers of the pandemic, DeWine acted to the contrary. In fact, he was the first governor in the country to shut down schools across the state. This despite pressures to the contrary from business leaders, conservative activists, and Republican colleagues, all of whom questioned the costs of imposing what quickly became a statewide quarantine. The wisdom of what became a national lockdown is not, of course, here the point. The point is that Governor DeWine did what previously was nearly unheard of. Instead of automatically following where Trump led, he made a deliberate decision not to follow.

Interestingly, Ohioans' response to DeWine's independence from the White House was overwhelmingly positive. Not only did they not punish him for his deviation from what by then was the political norm, his popularity soared. In a statewide poll in April 2020, 89 percent of respondents reported trusting DeWine as a source of information, and three out of four said that so far as the virus crisis was concerned, their governor was doing a better job than their president.[36]

DeWine was, though, the exception that proved the rule. For months, only a handful of other leading Republicans deviated from the party line, though by late June they were joined by a few others, such as Florida Senator Marco Rubio, who finally admitted that, "Everyone should just wear a damn mask." Withal, the single explanation for why President Trump was sustained and supported in office throughout 2020, from the impeachment trial straight through the pandemic, despite his being clearly ineffective and just as clearly unethical, was the abject loyalty of high-ranking members of the Republican Party. The degree to which Trump was able to maintain his iron grip on Republican members of Congress, and on Republican governors, was an unending source of astonishment and, depending on your point of view, either an abomination or an admirable demonstration of party loyalty.

Republican senators (and certainly some governors) especially were so crucial to the president's survival that they must be labeled enablers. After the president was impeached for the first time by the Democratic-controlled House of Representatives, Republican senators could reasonably have held a relatively fair and open trial. It would have been the most obvious way, the way the Founders wanted and intended, to rid the American people of a bad, both incompetent and unethical, American president. But with the single exception of Utah Senator Mitt Romney, every Senate Republican opted instead to hunker down, to vote against having a trial at which even a single witness would be called to testify. Hence the president's acquittal.

The first impeachment trial of President Donald Trump began in the US Senate on January 16, 2020; it ended on February 5. It did not take long in other words for Republican senators to decide to refuse to hear any evidence at all against the president on either of the two charges: abuse of power and obstruction of justice. The outcome of the proceedings was never really in doubt. While Trump had not inspired among Republican officeholders the same cultish devotion as among Republican voters, his hold on his allies in the Senate remained nevertheless ironclad. It was why they sought not truth and justice but instead "to ensure that Trump not be removed from office under any circumstances."[37]

In 2020 Trump's standing in the polls began somewhat to erode. How could it have been otherwise? By then the virus crisis, the economic crisis, and the social and political crisis were in full flow. Still, through it all, through the first six months of 2020, Trump held on to the support of nearly all Republican officials and officeholders. To be sure, in the recent past there had been some exceptions, a small number of Republicans who were Trump critics – such as South Carolina Representative Mark Sanford and Senators Jeff Flake of Arizona, Bob Corker of Tennessee, and Kelly Ayotte of New Hampshire. But by 2020 each had been driven into retirement. Additionally, there were a handful of sitting Republicans in Congress who dared from time to time to challenge the president, such as Romney, Nebraska Senator Ben Sasse, Alaska Senator Lisa Murkowski, and Wyoming Representative Liz Cheney. But at least three of these did so from positions of unusual political strength. Because their colleagues were not, by and large, nearly so politically secure, they kept their mouths shut.

Trump's continuing to be the beneficiary of virtually complete party fealty was arguably the single greatest astonishment, and disappointment, of his presidency. As he was evidently incompetent, certainly as it pertained to the pandemic, and obviously corrupt, the question was repeated – why? Why, given this man and this circumstance, was unswerving party loyalty a hallmark of Trump's presidency? Some answers to this question may be proposed.

- *Polarization*: As we have seen, Ezra Klein pointed out that American politics have changed. Americans "are so locked into our political identities," identifying so strongly with their party, that Donald Trump, the outlandish outlier, was "ultimately treated as if he were just another Republican" – which, clearly, he was not, and never was.[38]

- *Base*: For the duration of Trump's presidency his base remained essentially fixed firmly in place. It was the foundation on which he stood at the start of his political career and on which he continued to stand throughout. During his time in the White House Trump remained extremely popular among those who identified as Republicans. In the 2020 presidential election, former Vice President Joe Biden got some 7 million more votes than did President Donald Trump. Still, Trump's more than 74 million votes were the second highest tally in American history.
- *Media*: Once Trump became Republican nominee for president, reliable right-wing Republican media rushed to his side. Whatever he did and did not do, whatever he said and did not say, they never left.
- *Money*: Until he was not, Trump was the chosen one. Chosen by Republican bigwigs and fat cats as their candidate. Though by fall 2020 his significant fundraising lead over Biden had evaporated, in spring 2020 Trump still was the beneficiary of Republican largesse.[39]
- *Punishment*: Trump always thought that anyone who doubted him was traitorous. Therefore, he thought that anyone who doubted him merited his unmitigated wrath. He and his supporters went on a vendetta against whoever was deemed an enemy, weapons ranging from being tweeted to being "primaried." Not for nothing did Bob Woodward title his 2018 book about Trump in the White House, *Fear*.
- *Reward*: Conversely, Republicans who loudly and seemingly proudly supported President Trump were rewarded for their loyalty, goodies ranging from money in their coffers to tweets singing their praises.
- *Policy*: Trump delivered on what Republicans considered some important campaign promises. They ranged from appointing at least 200 like-minded federal judges to minimizing what the administration called "unnecessary regulatory burdens."
- *Personality*: Trump always was and became in time more so, a loose cannon. The president, a self-described "very stable genius," was by no means a genius and he was decidedly not stable. Woodward described the first two years of the Trump administration as "a nervous breakdown of the executive power of the most powerful country in the world." All this strongly suggested a president so tempestuous he was dangerous.[40]

Does this list of good and sound reasons fully explain what happened? Why respectable Republicans, especially Republican officeholders and specifically Republican senators, became complicit in supporting and sustaining so poor a president and so damaging and destructive a presidency? Became without question among the most important of Trump's enablers?

Not really, not fully anyway. For here in part is the oath that all members of the US Senate take when they are sworn into office: *I do solemnly swear (or affirm) that I will support and defend the Constitution of the United States against all enemies, foreign and domestic . . . and that I will well and faithfully discharge the duties of the office on which I am about to enter: So help me God.*

3   Administration

Never let it be said about Donald Trump that he did not trumpet who he was and how he would govern. To his credit, as it were, he never pretended to be someone he was not, nor did he ever suggest that governing wisely and well was his special strength. We knew, therefore, or we should have, from the beginning what we were getting. Nevertheless, the American people voted Trump in. Voted in as president of the United States a man without any of the qualifications traditionally associated with being the nation's chief executive. This meant among many things that anyone who signed on to join the Trump administration signed on to be subordinate to a superior who had no relevant experience or expertise.

At the inauguration, and in its immediate aftermath, there were already signs of what Americans were in for. President Trump's inaugural address was atypically dark, dour, depicting what he described as the current "carnage," and reciting a litany of calamities including gangs, drugs, poverty, and unemployment. He indicted the Washington establishment for profiting at the expense of the people and promised that from here on in things would be different. "Today," said the newly minted president, "we are transferring power from Washington, D.C. and giving it back to you, the people." While his populist message was certain to gladden the hearts of some, it was also sure to be seen as a shot across the bow of Washington's political elite. Trump warned, in effect, that he did not come to the White House to conduct business as usual. To the contrary: he was a disrupter, a newcomer to the nation's capital, who had come to break with its past, to question if not even to upend its previous patterns and processes.

As soon as the festivities were over, came the first such disruption. A flat-out, bald-faced lie about, of all things, crowd size – the size of the crowd that attended the president's inauguration. Still wet-behind-the-ears White House press secretary Sean Spicer was instructed to tell the press that the new incumbent had drawn "the largest audience ever to witness an inauguration period, both in person and around the globe."[1] Everyone who was there knew this was not true. No matter. Soon it was confirmed that at Trump's personal request a White House photographer had edited pictures of his inauguration "to make the crowd appear bigger."[2]

On the surface it was a small lie. Beneath the surface it was a precursor of what was to come. First, a president whose presentation of self was pockmarked by false or misleading claims – outright lies. A president who, as Anne Applebaum wrote, "effectively ordered not just his supporters but also apolitical members of the government bureaucracy to adhere to a blatantly false, manipulated reality."[3] Second, an administration blanketed by blatant exaggerations, flagrant distortions, and narcissistic fabrications. Over time, Trump's narcissism became more obvious and onerous, testifying to a president disposed not to democracy but to autocracy. The indicators – for instance his early and then systematic attempts to intimidate the media, to politicize the civil service, to reward supporters while punishing opponents, and to rig the system – were clear.[4] As virtually every close observer of the Trump administration has testified, his preference was completely to control, and his tendency was aggressively to self-aggrandize.

Among the most important tasks conducted by every president-elect is selecting the Cabinet and high-ranking members of the administration. Inevitably then, those chosen by Trump to be his close advisors, initially as well as subsequently, revealed a great deal about him not only personally and politically, but also professionally. In other words, was professionalism and everything that this implied, especially character and competence, the leading criterion? Or did other criteria take preference?

The early signs were not heartening. For example, the evidence suggested that one standard for service in the Trump administration was money. Within a few weeks of his election, he had already appointed six of his big donors to important jobs. It was not unusual for a president (president-elect) to choose high-level funders to fill high-level posts –such as, for example, ambassador to France. What was unusual was for a president to appoint to his Cabinet so many whose chief asset was they were major donors.[5] Along similar lines were Trump's selections of oil-industry allies for plum positions, such as Rex Tillerson for Secretary of State and Rick Perry for Secretary of Energy. Secretary of State is, it should be added, traditionally considered the highest ranking of the Cabinet posts. Yet whatever Tillerson's previous accomplishments, and they were considerable – before joining the Trump administration he retired as chair and chief executive officer of ExxonMobil – a track record of government service was not among them. Among Trump's early calls were also several to members of the military. Before November 2016 was over, he had appointed retired Marine General James Mattis as his Secretary of Defense, retired Marine General John Kelly as his Secretary of Homeland Security, and retired Army Lieutenant General Michael Flynn as his National Security Advisor.

Finally, there was the president's family. Though Trump's wife, Melania, remained in the background, other members of his family did not. His two oldest sons, Donald Jr. and Eric, were immediately appointed members of his transition team. His oldest daughter, Ivanka, was immediately positioned to play a prominent part in her father's administration. And her husband, Jared Kushner, who also had zero government experience (like Trump he was primarily a New York area real estate developer), was immediately slated to be as deeply involved in his father-in-law's presidency as he had been in his presidential campaign.

Though Donald Trump ran for president, it is widely agreed that he never expected to win. No surprise, then, that when it came time to pick high ranking members of his administration, he was entirely unprepared not only for what he should do, but even for what he wanted to do. Not only did he lack experience and expertise in public service, he had no apparent political or ideological agenda. In other words, Trump had no clear idea of what he wanted to accomplish. He was moreover mercurial and superficial. From the earliest days of the administration "the entire operation was guided by Trump's instincts and whims." Which also meant that from the earliest days of the administration his choice of advisors was based not so much on competence as on more superficial qualities, for instance, "the ability to present well on television."[6]

Given all this – everything from Trump's personal proclivities and preferences to his total lack of an expansive and well-honed political network – it was probably predictable that Trump's administration was quickly perceived to be a sharp break from those that recently had preceded it. His Cabinet was notably homogeneous – it was overwhelmingly white (85 percent) and male (75 percent), and mostly it was rich.[7] His appointments were alarmingly capricious – Trump's first National Security Advisor, Michael Flynn, was forced to resign after just 22 days in office. His management was singularly inefficient – by summer 2017 Trump's team was still "riddled" with vacancies. (Some 354 of the 577 top administration jobs remained open six months after the inauguration.[8]) And though he denied it – "This administration is running like a fine-tuned machine," he insisted – the early evidence was that Trump's team was dysfunctional.[9] Some of his longtime allies, such as Attorney General Jeff Sessions and White House lawyer Don McGahn were stressed out from day one, irritated by the constancy of his demands and intimidated by the regularity of his intrusions. Those less familiar with their difficult and domineering boss were quickly ground down by his manner, which behind closed doors was not only not ingratiating, it was intimidating. Long before he become president, Trump was known for his short fuse. He lost his temper easily and often and, given he was a large presence even when calm, it is easy enough to see why he was described by a former Trump Organization executive as "scary."[10]

ADULTS IN THE ROOM

Several of those who joined the Trump administration early on, quickly came to be called "the adults in the room." The phrase was coined by *Politico*, which after the December 2016 appointment of James Mattis as defense secretary declared that finally there was "an adult in the room." Similarly, the following month, when Rex Tillerson was confirmed as Secretary of State, the chair of the Foreign Relations Committee, Senator Bob Corker, told his colleagues, "To me, Mr. Tillerson is an adult who's been around." And when Tillerson and John Kelly (then Secretary of Homeland Security, later White House Chief of Staff) went with Trump a month later to visit Mexico, the *Financial Times* referred to the two former, but not to the latter as "the adult wing of the new regime."[11]

Who were these "adults" and why were they so tagged? In their brief prime they consisted importantly of these four: Tillerson, Mattis, Kelly, and National Security Advisor H. R. McMaster. Three had been in the highest ranks of the American military, one in the highest ranks of American business. This had at least two important implications: first, all four had been exceptionally successful and were therefore beholden to no one; second, none of the four was overtly political. The three military men were virtually by definition apolitical, and while Tillerson had in the past contributed to the Republican Party, he had not donated to Trump's presidential campaign. In any case, he was not seen, any more than the others, as Trump's toady.

But, of course, to speak of the "adults in the room" is to say something not only about the adults but also about the children. Clearly the phrase was a slap in the face of President Trump. It suggested that the American people depended on the adults to save the nation from a man whom many even in the center of American politics, not to speak of the left, determined early on was unfit to be chief executive – unfit intellectually, temperamentally, and characterologically.

The trouble was that none of the four lasted long. We can assume that each took the job in the first place not only because they were asked, but also because they thought they could serve. Three had a lifelong history of public service; Tillerson, in turn, had been extremely successful in the private sector, so being Secretary of State probably appealed to him personally as well as professionally. It appears, then, that each of the "adults" made the decision to join the Trump administration with high hopes and equally high ambitions – if not necessarily to change the world for the better then to forestall it from getting worse. Whatever the red flags they saw, they would not have agreed to be Trump's subordinates had they not assumed a best-case scenario or, at least, one that was good enough.

Rex Tillerson was Secretary of State from February 2017 to March 2018. H. R. McMaster was National Security Advisor from February 2017 also to March 2018. John Kelly was White House Chief of Staff from July 2017 to January 2019. Secretary of State James Mattis lasted longest of the four – from January 2017 to January 2019. What happened? How did it happen that the adults in the room made their departure in such remarkably short order? Of course, each of their stories is in some ways different. But in other ways they are the same. For the purposes of this book, suffice to sum up their situation this way: none of the four was willing in the end to be an enabler.

Given that Tillerson was Trump's first choice as Secretary of State, his departure from the post was startlingly swift, almost without historical parallel. To be sure, there is no evidence that Tillerson was a standout as secretary of state. There is even less evidence that during his brief tenure Tillerson's relationship with the president was anything better than testy. But, however difficult Trump was to work with during his first few months in office, in short order he became more difficult. In the beginning it was obvious he was a novice, so there was no choice but for him to listen at least some of the time to some of his advisors. But, as the weeks went on, the president became more unpleasant, erratic, and demanding. Just six months into his job Tillerson thought for the first time about resigning. He was unhappy in his post and angry at his boss.

Around that time Tillerson attended a White House meeting that was summed up by a senior administration official as follows: "The president proceeded to lecture and insult the entire group about how they didn't know anything when it came to defense or national security. It seems clear that many of the president's senior advisors, especially those in the national security realm, are extremely concerned with his erratic nature, his relative ignorance, his inability to learn, as well as what they consider his dangerous views." It was after this meeting that Tillerson famously told one of his colleagues that Trump was "just a moron." (The president got wind of the insult a few months later, when it was reported by NBC News.) Little more than six months after the "moron" remark, Trump summarily fired Tillerson – by tweet. The president never confronted the ranking member of his Cabinet personally or told him face to face that he was being replaced, effective immediately, by Mike Pompeo. It was left to Chief of Staff Kelly to tell Tillerson what had happened. Trump did, however, speak to reporters, telling them on the White House lawn that, "Rex and [I] were not really thinking the same ... It was a different mind-set, a different thinking."[12]

Because President Trump was effectively forced to fire his first national security adviser, Mike Flynn (formally Flynn resigned), post haste, pressure was on the White House to replace Flynn, also as quickly as possible. Though at no point in the process was there any evidence of any chemistry between the president and Army Lieutenant General H. R. McMaster, Trump nevertheless chose him as Flynn's replacement. It was a choice that played well – publicly. "The media saw McMaster was an adult. There would be no more crazies. The president basked in the positive stories."[13] But given McMaster had written a book, *Dereliction of Duty*, about how under certain circumstances subordinates had an obligation to stand up to their superiors, it was no wonder he did not last long.[14] Like Tillerson, it was not long before McMaster was summarily dismissed. Trump told him on the phone that he was done – that he should be gone the very next day.[15]

John Kelly served as Trump's Secretary of Homeland Security for a half year before taking over from Reince Priebus as White House Chief of Staff. Priebus had lasted six months in the job. Like Tillerson he discovered he was fired when Trump tweeted he was fired or, more precisely, when Trump tweeted that Kelly would be his, Priebus's, successor. Kelly hung on and hung in as Chief of Staff for about 18 months. Initially Trump and Kelly were said to get on well. But initially in this case meant several weeks, not even several months, before the honeymoon was over. It was not long before Kelly described the president as "unhinged."[16] It was also not long before Kelly was said to have nearly "killed himself on the job."[17] Before long, the president and his chief of staff were on nothing so much as a collision course. In December 2018 Trump told reporters that Kelly was leaving – even though "he's a great guy." They were a miserable mix of oil and water but, as Philip Rucker and Carol Leonnig wrote in their book, *A Very Stable Genius*, at least "Trump afforded Kelly a graceful exit compared with how he had dismissed Tillerson, Reince Priebus, H. R. McMaster, and other senior advisors."[18]

General James Mattis is one of America's most deeply admired, even revered, members of the military. He is known for his supreme professional competence and his deeply serious, even sober personal demeanor. His reason for agreeing to join the administration was that he was asked. Mattis was asked by the president of the United States to serve his country and so Mattis said yes. But as is by now well known, his tenure as Trump's Secretary of Defense was difficult throughout. It came then as a shock but not as a surprise when less than two years after he took office Mattis concluded, as he put it later, he "had no choice but to leave."[19]

What pushed him over the edge was President Trump's decision (quickly reversed) to pull American troops out of Syria. Mattis believed the decision was badly misguided; it made him feel, according to one of his confidants, "like he was becoming complicit."[20] Soon thereafter Mattis called Kelly and told him, "I need an hour with the boss." The next day Mattis met with Trump to make his case for keeping the troops in place. The president rejected the argument, whereupon Mattis told the president that he would have to get the "next secretary of defense to lose to ISIS." Mattis continued, "I'm not going to do it," and then handed the president his previously prepared letter of resignation.[21]

The letter was made immediately public. It remains one of the most important documents of the Trump administration. The letter was entirely respectful. Additionally, it was a model of professional independence and personal integrity. Mattis wrote in part, "Because you have the right to have a Secretary of Defense whose views are better aligned with yours on these and other subjects, I believe it is right for me to step down from my position." If Mattis had worried he was becoming "complicit" – he was becoming an enabler – with this letter he made certain he need worry no longer.

TURNOVER

Even a year into the administration of President Donald Trump it was apparent that while his tenure was in many ways highly unusual, one of the ways in which it was unusual to the point of being unprecedented was the high turnover rate among his staff. High staff turnover is never a good sign, especially when it is the staff of the president of the United States. First, as noted by Harvard professor Guatam Mukanda, high levels of senior staff turnover are difficult for any organization to absorb; inevitably there are disruptions and inefficiencies. Second, when the White House loses a member of its senior staff it is additionally impaired by the complexity of the hiring process, and the steepness of the learning curve.[22] Yet by January 2018, just one year into Trump's tenure, it was already clear that heavy staff turnover was going to be one of the hallmarks of his administration.[23] By April 2018 Trump had replaced a shockingly high 48 percent of those who worked in the Executive Office of the President. Comparative numbers for Ronald Reagan were 17 percent; for George H. W. Bush 7 percent; for Bill Clinton 11 percent; for George W. Bush 6 percent; and for Barack Obama 9 percent. Trump professed, of course, to be undisturbed. In March he tweeted, "People will always come & go. I still have some people that I want to change (always seeking perfection). So many people want to come in. I have a choice of anybody."[24]

According to a study by Brookings, by October of 2018 "turnover within the most senior level of White House staff members bumped up to 83 percent."[25] The numbers of departures included several other "adults in the room," such as White House Counsel Don McGahn, and chair of the National Economic Council, Gary Cohn. There were also famous, or infamous, dismissals, such as FBI Director James Comey, whom Trump was determined to dismiss, once Trump learned he had the legal right to do so. Additionally, also ignominiously, was Attorney General Jeff Sessions, who while he was still Senator from Alabama was one of Trump strongest and most prominent supporters. In fact, Sessions was the first Senator publicly to back Trump for president and, in April 2016, it was Sessions who helped candidate Trump craft his first major foreign policy speech.

But, as Rucker and Leonnig pointed out, "In Trump World, people's fortunes can rise and fall based on the president's changing moods." Which explains how Sessions went "from confidant to persona non grata" in the political equivalent of a heartbeat.[26] For his devotion and loyalty to Trump Sessions had been amply rewarded: Trump named him to his Cabinet. But once Trump decided that Sessions was less than slavishly loyal, he was done. From the president's perspective Sessions had turned traitor. Why? For excusing himself from overseeing the Russia investigation. It was a decision for which Sessions would never be forgiven, and for which he would be abused by the president, in private and in public, until finally he got out. Or, more precisely, was pushed out. Immediately after the midterm elections, President Trump demanded and received yet another letter of resignation, this time from his erstwhile acolyte, Sessions.

By the fourth year of Trump's tenure, the high level of administration turnover was among its most striking and suggestive characteristics. It was striking because it was so astronomically high. It was suggestive because it reflected the theme of this book: *the only ones who remained on Trump's train for the duration were those willing to serve as enablers.* Here are a couple of quotes from an article by Brookings expert Kathryn Dunn Tenpas on staff turnover and vacancies:

- "Just 32 months into the Trump administration, the rate of turnover had exceeded his five predecessors' full first terms."
- "It is undeniable that the churn in the Trump White House is unlike anything that other presidents have experienced."[27]

The "churn" to which Tenpas referred was for two reasons. Reason number one was that Trump dismissed many of his subordinates. Reason number two was that many of his subordinates ditched Trump. They were two sides of the same coin.

LOYALTY TESTS

Why did President Trump dispose of so many of his subordinates? Why did so many of President Trump's subordinates dispose of their superior?

First: why did the president push so many people out? Of course, occasionally, there were some obvious reasons, such as they were ineffective or inefficient, or they were incompatible or uncooperative, or they were misaligned or mismatched. But even one year into Trump's tenure it was clear that the usual reasons did not explain, or at least not fully explain, what was going on. In January 2018 Tenpas wrote another piece that pointed out that years earlier she wrote that "presidents want aides with substantive policy knowledge who are sensitive to the bargaining interests of other 'Washingtonians.'" It was true, she went on, at the time. But it was not true now. By early 2018 it was clear that President Trump did not "prefer these traits," her way of saying that he valued other traits over professional competence and political temperament. There was of course a single trait that stood out: "the president's focus on loyalty over qualifications."[28]

Loyalty was an obsession. President Trump was fixated on whether a subordinate was unfailingly, deeply, and passionately, loyal. His perception was, moreover, unnuanced in the extreme: unless he or she was totally loyal, unswervingly loyal, it meant they were, ipso facto, *dis*loyal. This obsession was not something that emerged over time. To the contrary, it was there from the start. Even as president-elect he was consumed by the issue, his doubts about the fealty of those he was considering hiring already amply in evidence. As names were being vetted Trump asked, repeatedly, "Is he loyal? Is she loyal?"[29] And just a week after his inauguration, seated for a dinner at a small table in the Green Room of the White House, he said to FBI head James Comey, signaling what was to come, "I need loyalty. I need loyalty." Of course, as his biographer, Tim O'Brien, later wrote, what Trump was talking about was not "allegiance to the flag or allegiance to the country," it was "allegiance to Trump."[30]

The president's insistence on subservience persisted throughout his time in the Oval Office and it impinged, inevitably, on his capacity to do the work that needed to be done. In fact, the president's premium on subordinates who prioritized his interest over the national interest explains much of what went wrong, sometimes calamitously, during his time in the White House – especially as it pertained to the pandemic. It also explains why several federal agencies lacked the medical and scientific experts required during what quickly became America's greatest health crisis in over a century. For Trump's hostility to expertise – diplomatic, military, scientific, and medical – was related to his insistence on loyalty. The former, expertise, was, quite simply, sacrificed at the altar of the latter, loyalty.

The president never brought on board anyone he thought would be insufficiently loyal. And he never kept on board anyone he thought was insufficiently loyal. An article in the *Washington Post* dryly described how the Presidential Personnel Office had been "reorganized to focus on rooting out dissenters." Qualified officials were removed from their posts, while potential new hires were required to take political litmus tests.[31] At the same time, the demands on most who served in the administration were enormous; on many they were additionally onerous.

There was a constant demand that people prove not just their loyalty to the president, but their admiration of him, and their willingness publicly as well as privately to pay him homage. An example was that much-mocked, high-level meeting in June 2017 when one by one (Mattis was the exception) participants praised Trump – out loud and extravagantly. Priebus thanked Trump for "the opportunity and blessing that you've given us to serve your agenda." Sessions said, "It's an honor to be able to serve you." Labor Secretary Alexander Acosta volunteered that he was "privileged to be here, deeply honored." Health and Human Service Secretary Tom Price told Trump that he could not thank him "enough for the privileges you've given me and the leadership that you've shown." And, not to be outdone, Transportation Secretary Elaine Chao chose to express her boundless gratitude to Trump for having visited her department, adding that "hundreds and hundreds of people were just so thrilled."[32]

It is no surprise that not everyone in the administration was able or willing to stomach such obligatory adoration. Moreover, managing up was itself a challenge, a game of sorts that not everyone was disposed to play, at least not for long. A year or so into Trump's presidency it became clear that working for him was a trial every which way, personally, professionally, politically. Books such as Woodward's *Fear*, Rucker and Leonnig's *A Very Stable Genius*, and Michael Wolff's *Fire and Fury: Inside the Trump White House* testified in abundance to how hard it was to be a subordinate when Donald Trump was the superior.

These were supplemented by numberless articles documenting the day-to-day grind, the endless stress, the relentless fatigue, all to satisfy the self-aggrandizing, self-interested demands of this one difficult man. For instance, from an Associated Press article written in July 2018, titled "Life in Trump's Cabinet: Perks, Pestering, Power, Putdowns," we get this: "Welcome to the Trump Cabinet, where broad opportunities to reshape government" come with "everyday doses" of presidential "adulation" and "humiliation."[33] From Woodward's book we are told that Gary Cohn and Rob Porter (for a time close presidential advisors) "worked together to derail what they believed were Trump's most impulsive and dangerous orders ... It was no less than an administrative coup d'etat."[34] And from one-time national security advisor John Bolton's book, *The Room Where It Happened*, we hear that "I am hard-pressed to identify any significant Trump decision during my White House tenure that wasn't driven by reelection calculations."[35]

SUBORDINATES

The word "subordinate" can mean different things. Usually it is a descriptor, a noun, that refers simply to rank. Subordinates in organizations are lower in rank than their superiors, which in theory though not always in practice means that subordinates are under the control of their superiors, as well as under their authority. To be *a* subordinate, therefore, also suggests a behavior, one in which the subordinate typically defers to the superior. When, however, subordinate is a verb it means something somewhat different. "To subordinate" is to indicate that Person A is deliberately treating Person B as if he or she had less value, was of less importance than Person A. In this situation leader and followers are in a relationship in which Person B is, even independent of rank, subject to, subservient to, Person A. An example is the just mentioned Cabinet meeting. Participants such as Priebus and Chao were not just subordinate to President Trump in rank, which they clearly were. More interestingly, more tellingly, they were subordinate to him in their behavior, which was strikingly, atypically, subservient. The president was, in other words, subordinating his underlings, implicitly demanding they show him inordinate deference. They, in turn, got the message. They understood what he expected – and they delivered.

By April 2020 there was an 85 percent turnover in "Trump's A Team" – the team that worked with the president on close to a daily basis. Who, then, were the few that managed for over three years to hold on? They fell into two groups. In the first were members of what in the following chapter I call "Donald Trump's Inner Circle." In the second were a handful of others who either were policy experts, or had jobs that kept them out of the public eye.[36] In sum, because Trump's demands, above all for deference, were so extreme, and because he was otherwise so difficult to work for, and because only a few were willing to be completely under his thumb for any length of time, the turnover among members of Trump's A Team was sky high.

The damage done by Trump's insistence on subservience was not, however, confined only to those who worked with him in the White House – it was wide ranging and far reaching. An example: the speed with which federal workers, eager to accommodate the president, "internalized" his "antagonism for climate science." Things went so far that many of those working at the Environmental Protection Agency believed that one or more of their managers "had interfered with or suppressed the release of scientific information," especially as it related to climate change, a subject to which Trump was famously hostile.[37] Another example: by Trump's fourth year in office the executive branch was "riddled with vacancies." These included important posts that were filled temporarily by those serving in an "acting" capacity. There was, for example, an acting director of the Office of Management and Budget and an acting director of national intelligence.

But, as public service expert Max Stier pointed out, acting officials are "substantially hampered." They "don't see themselves as the real authority, nor are they perceived as the real authority."[38] Another example is President Trump's hostility to the federal government's internal watchdogs, inspector generals, fully five of whom were fired during a six-week span in spring 2020. A case in point was Michael Atkinson, inspector general for the intelligence community, who was sent packing for making the fatal mistake of alerting Congress to a whistleblower complaint about Ukraine. As the *New York Times* editorialized in May 2020, "For Mr. Trump, there may be no greater betrayal than being the bearer of unflattering news about his administration ... The president has been working to cleanse his administration of officials he considers insufficiently loyal."[39] A final example is the Pentagon. By June 2020 it faced a "hemorrhage of talent." Senior officials resigned in large numbers "amid continued efforts to purge those perceived as political foes." (Among them was Lt. Col. Alexander Vindman, who, to Trump's immense displeasure, had testified, as the president perceived it, against him, in the House impeachment hearings.) Which left Defense Secretary Mark Esper with the unenviable task of trying to manage external, White House, pressures on the one hand, while trying to address internal, Pentagon, concerns, on the other.[40] (For his troubles, Esper was summarily fired, by White House tweet, within days after Trump lost the 2020 election. Why? Though no reason was given, it was well known that for months the president thought him less than unflinchingly loyal.)

Among those who worked closely with the president – though not usually daily – were, of course, a few high-level survivors. A few who had managed to stay the course while straddling the line between being wholly loyal to Trump while at the same time retaining a modicum of independence. Treasury Secretary Steven Mnuchin was such a person – he did his job mostly as he saw fit while rarely if ever breaking with Trump, certainly not in public. But the few members of the administration who had the temerity openly to challenge Trump, such as, briefly, before he was fired, FBI director James Comey and, until fall 2018, White House counsel Don McGahn, were gone.[41] So were those who did not directly defy the president but did insist on retaining their independence while trying to serve as moderating influence – national intelligence director Dan Coates comes to mind. Finally gone also were those who stayed almost to the end but who close to that point were so fed up they got out. An example was assistant secretary of state for legislative affairs, Mary Elizabeth

Taylor. Taylor, the only African American senior official at the state department, had been a loyal aide to the president since the start of his administration. But what motivated her in June 2020 finally to quit was his dismissive response to the widespread demands for racial justice in the wake of the death of George Floyd. In a letter to Secretary of State Mike Pompeo, Taylor wrote that "moments of upheaval can change you, shift the trajectory of your life." She went on to criticize the president's "comments and actions" during this trying time, concluding that for her a tipping point had been reached. I must, she wrote, "follow the dictates of my conscience and resign."[42]

As 2020, the year of living dangerously, unfolded, it is safe to say that those who remained in the administration, especially if they worked closely with the president, were willing, with effectively no exceptions, to be subordinate. Everyone else had by then either been canned or themselves had checked out, unwilling to submit to a superior who insisted on submission, who forbade dissent, and who severed dissenters. This explains as well as anything else why when the new coronavirus insinuated itself literally and figuratively into the American body politic, the White House was miserably ill-equipped to manage it. President Trump had starved his administration of independent experts, had forced it instead to subsist on a diet heavy with subservient enablers.

4 Inner Circle

The first thing to be said about Donald Trump's inner circle is that he did not have one. Or, at least, not much of one, not one that had, among other virtues, longevity. If inner circle implies a small group of family and/or friends and associates with whom a person connects on a close and consistent basis over a long period of time, most of Trump's ties do not qualify. If, on the other hand, inner circle implies a small group of family and/or friends and associates who are at or near the center of power over a long period of time, then Donald Trump did have one, though only after a fashion. Only after a fashion for, among other reasons, members of leaders' inner circles typically have some influence, which in Trump's case was exercised on rare occasions. Not only was Trump unusually isolated as a person, and as a president, he was unusually impervious to the input of others. In fact, this was the case even in those areas and on those issues about which he knew little or nothing. Such as the new coronavirus.

Donald Trump was a loner lifelong. As a teenager at the New York Military Academy, he was known to disappear into his room after dinner. Years later his military school classmates did not remember anyone "that he was particularly close to." As one put it, "I was not a confidant as to his personal thoughts. No one was." At Fordham University, where Trump spent his freshman and sophomore years of college, his experience was no different. A classmate with whom he carpooled, Brian Fitzgibbon, described them as being "friendly," but not "friends." "I can't recall any real friendships he had at Fordham," Fitzgibbon later remembered. It was the same in Philadelphia when Trump was at the Wharton School. He did not

participate in campus life, returning instead to New York every weekend to work for his father. Another classmate later recalled, "I don't
think he had any best friends. I never saw him pal around with *anyone*,
quite frankly." Decades after that, when Trump was known as
a wealthy and successful Manhattan real estate developer, he was
asked by an interviewer, "Is there somebody that you really confide
in?" No, Trump replied, "I ... tend not to confide ... I don't trust
people, I'm a non-trusting person." His biographer Tim O'Brien captured the consensus: "One of the loneliest people I've ever met. He
lacks the emotional and sort of psychological architecture a person
needs to build deep relationships with other people."[1]

Early in Trump's presidency the *New York Times* described his
"advisors." They were from "family, real estate, media, finance and
politics, and all outside the White House gates – many of whom he
consults once a week." The names included millionaires and billionaires such as Thomas Barrack, Carl Icahn, and Steven Schwartzman;
conservative strategists such as Corey Lewandowski and Roger Stone;
Republican politicians such as Chris Christie and Newt Gingrich; Fox
News host Sean Hannity; and a few members of his family. Each of
Trump's confidants was white, most were male, and many were older.
All were chosen according to "two crucial measures: personal success
and loyalty to him."[2] Just a few years later, however, most of these
names, not all, but most, had gone by the board. They had peeled away,
their relationships with the president of the United States soured, or
enfeebled, or evaporated. In fact, of the names just listed, other than
family the only one who was in his inner circle for the duration of
Trump's presidency was Hannity. (Former New York City mayor
Rudy Giuliani was an exception to this rule; but while he remained
tied to Trump, he was not a friend. Theirs was, so to speak, a business
relationship.) Some of the others were occasionally around, but by no
means were they the president's intimates.

The fact that most of Trump's closest associates tended to
disappear into the ether is testified to by several men who, notwithstanding their proximity to him for a time, were gone, most long gone,

by the time his tenure in the White House was over. *Politico* described the banishment of Tom Barrack, for example, in an article from 2019 titled, "Trump Cuts Off One of his Closest Friends."[3] Though they had known each other for decades (Barrack reportedly comforted Trump during the funeral of his father, Fred), and though during the early months of Trump's time in Washington they were said to have spoken almost daily, and though Trump had named Barrack chair of his inauguration fund, once there were questions about how Barrack had handled the fund, their relationship was over.

In some ways similar was the case of Steve Bannon. Bannon was a right-wing populist and nationalist, a firebrand and media man who had run the equally right-wing populist and nationalist news site, Breitbart. To everyone's surprise, including his own, Bannon played a large part first in Trump's election as president, then in Trump's transition to president, and finally, briefly, in Trump's presidency. Trump was of course a political novice whose campaign, especially in the early days, was run by other political novices. Enter Steve Bannon, a brawler and blowhard who was clever and cunning. In August 2016 Bannon was named chief executive officer of Trump's presidential campaign. And in January 2017 Bannon was appointed Trump's "chief strategist." But, by August he was out. He was out because Trump came quickly to chafe against his powerful personality, and because Trump came quickly to consider his influence and imprint overbearing and outsized. Trump resented it when *Time* magazine put Bannon on its cover and referred to him as "The Great Manipulator." And Trump was aggrieved when *Saturday Night Live* depicted Bannon as the Grim Reaper, making presidential decisions behind the Resolute Desk, while Trump sat alongside, small, tucked behind a tiny kiddie desk, playing with an inflatable toy.

Then there was Trump's erstwhile lawyer, Michael Cohen. We now know that for years Cohen was eager to do what others might have thought an awful job: he cleaned up the messes, the many, many messes, that Trump left behind. Cohen was one among several of Trump's lawyers – more importantly he was

Trump's first fixer. It was said that Cohen was "closer to the president than anyone else," and that he had "the best understanding of how Trump thought."[4] And reputedly Cohen was the "keeper of Trump's secrets and executer of his wishes, from business deals to personal affairs."[5] But, when Cohen ran into legal trouble for what he had done at Trump's behest, the worm turned. Initially Trump lent weak support, describing Cohen as a "fine person." But it was not long before Trump dumped Cohen – hung him out to dry. Cohen, in turn, ultimately testified against Trump. Moreover, by admitting to paying Stormy Daniels hush money – she claimed she was one of Trump's former lovers – "in coordination with" and "at the direction of" a "candidate for federal office" he implicated President Trump publicly in a federal finance crime.[6] So much for Trump's relationship with the man, Cohen, who for some ten years was said to be closer to him than anyone else, and who, when he wrote a book about his tie to Trump, titled it, *Disloyal*.[7]

Notwithstanding his isolation at the deepest level, President Trump did have something that can reasonably be considered an inner circle. The best way to think of it is as having three rings: outer, middle, and inner. The outer ring of the inner circle contained those who were the least close among those closest to the president. The inner ring contained those who were closest to the president. And the middle ring contained those who fell somewhere in between. Because every member of the inner circle was, comparatively at least, close to the president, every member of his inner circle was an enabler. In different ways and to different degrees every member of Trump's inner circle enabled him to do what he did – sustain first his candidacy, then his presidency.

OUTER RING OF THE INNER CIRCLE

Three people were in the outer ring of the inner circle. All three were in different ways unusually close to the president, and all three remained close to the president throughout his time in the White

House. They were Stephen Miller, Hope Hicks, and Kellyanne Conway.

Early in his tenure President Trump called Stephen Miller and Steve Bannon, "my two Steves." But Steve Bannon did not last, while Stephen Miller did. Miller's ascent up the slippery slope of Washington politics was astonishing. He was young, in his early thirties; had worked mainly in the office of Senator Jeff Sessions; and focused on a single issue, immigration. But even in 2016 it was evident that Miller had several qualities that candidate Trump and then president-elect Trump prized.[8] Miller was unswervingly loyal. He was an extremely hard worker. He could speak and write for Trump in "strikingly complete and adamant sentences." He was connected closely to several powerful Republican insurgents, notably Sessions and the right-wing Breitbart media machine. And Miller's expertise was on an issue, immigration, that became for Trump paramount. Miller was, in sum, a fierce, fervent, and clever underling.[9]

Early on Miller gained favor with the man who quickly became the "president's most indispensable advisor," son-in-law Jared Kushner.[10] Like Trump, Kushner found Miller to be clear, cogent, and fluent in the language of grievance. Miller was so skilled in peddling populism and nationalism that just a month into Trump's tenure he was already at the "epicenter of some of the administration's most provocative moves," border wall and travel ban included.[11] Others fell off Trump's train, but his "Right-Hand Troll," Miller, never did.[12] In fact, he was so deeply entrenched in the president's psyche, in his politics, and in his policies, that he, Miller, was "untouchable."[13]

For Donald Trump and Stephen Miller, the pandemic, which came upon the nation during Trump's fourth year in office, was in one way a perfect storm. It provided what *Slate* called an "excuse" for the administration to issue an executive order temporarily suspending immigration into the United States.[14] Given that Miller's fingerprints were on every one of Trump's declarations on immigration, and given that Miller believed absolutely in the absolute power of the president, it was Miller who was responsible for the executive order issued on

April 22, 2020. It read in part: "[In March] I declared that the COVID-19 outbreak in the United States constituted a national emergency ... I have [therefore] determined that the entry, during the next 60 days, of certain aliens as immigrants would be detrimental to the interest of the United States."[15] So, far from in any way fracturing the special relationship between Donald Trump and Stephen Miller, the coronavirus crisis further secured it.

White House aides Hope Hicks and Kellyanne Conway belonged in the outer ring of President's Trump's inner circle because they were important to the president personally and professionally; they were unflinchingly loyal to the president, never publicly dissented from what the president preferred, and remained in or close to the administration for its duration.

Hicks joined the Trump Organization in 2014. In 2015, at age 26, she was asked by Donald Trump to be his press secretary for a potential presidential campaign. Given she had no political experience whatsoever, her qualifications for the position were unclear. But, as Bob Woodward pointed out, she did have "two qualities important to Trump – loyalty and good looks."[16] Given she additionally had some skill in public relations, after Trump was elected president she was offered and she accepted the newly created role of White House director of strategic communications. Nine months later she was promoted, and given a new title. In March 2018 she resigned. Though she insisted for the record that she had been intending to leave the White House for some time, her departure was almost certainly hastened by her having to testify before the House Intelligence Committee. (Her name was mentioned more than 180 times in Robert Mueller's report on Russian election interference and possible obstruction of justice.) Still, by early 2020 she was back working in the White House, this time, formally, as an aide to Jared Kushner and counselor to the president.

What exactly did Hope Hicks do in the White House? From the beginning her responsibilities were unclear. Though she held a lofty title, she operated outside any organizational chart. Instead, in the president's world of rival power centers, she was protected by the "deep bond" she shared with the man at the top. He sometimes referred to her affectionately as "Hopester."[17] She, in turn, became the president's "de facto therapist."[18] Others came to rely on her for managing his moods, reading his mind, and, occasionally, preventing him from acting on his impulses. She had easy access to the Oval Office for good reason – she pleased the president and served him with loyalty, affection, and discretion. When she returned to the White House after her time away, Kushner said, "We are excited to have her back on the team." No doubt he meant it. By every account she was a somewhat stabilizing influence on the man who self-described as "a very stable genius." Her proximity to the president persisted virtually to the end of his tenure. Perhaps unsurprisingly in October, within days of each other, Hicks and Trump each tested positive for COVID-19.

When Kellyanne Conway and Donald Trump first crossed paths, she was already a person of substance, a highly accomplished woman who was well known, especially in Republican circles, as a successful pollster and commentator. Trump hired her in mid-2016 to help run his campaign. Just a few months later – after the resignation of the later-disgraced Paul Manafort – she was put formally in charge. (Informally, Jared Kushner was in charge.) Not long after, Conway could claim to be the first woman ever successfully to run a presidential campaign. But, if her responsibilities were clear before Trump became president, afterwards they were less clear. Conway's formal title was counselor to the president. But what exactly her new job consisted in remained opaque.

Conway was like Trump. Bold and brassy, quick on the trigger, quick to mouth off, quick to land in the thicket of one or another controversy. She was, moreover, akin to her boss in that she was wed not to the truth but, rather, to "alternative facts" whenever such "facts" were convenient.[19] (It was Conway who coined the phrase, "alternative facts" – an Orwellian confection if ever there was one.) Though her tasks were never clearly delineated, Conway found her niche. The president continued to enjoy her company, to value her ability to perform the rhetorical contortions required to defend him and, of course, to love her loyalty. So far as it was possible to tell, her primary task was to be a media foil, which usually meant media punching bag. However, over time her act wore thin. The press tired of her high spirits and high jinks and even Trump was somewhat put off.

What put him off? It is safe to assume in part it was Kellyanne Conway's husband, George T. Conway III. For by the fourth year of Trump's presidency George Conway was not simply anti-Trump, he was co-founder of the Lincoln Project, a group that had but one goal, "to defeat Donald Trump and Trumpism." So, was Kellyanne Conway toward the end of the administration where she was at the beginning – in the outer ring of Trump's inner circle? Not so much. But until late summer 2020 she was still a member of Trump's administration and, husband notwithstanding, she remained fiercely loyal to the man who was her boss. When she finally resigned, in August, she said it was for purely personal reasons, for her four children, who would now have "less drama, more mama." In her case, however, to resign from her formal position did not mean resigning from her informal one. She remained for the duration of the Trump administration relatively close to the White House. Conway was among those who prepped the president for his first debate with Joe Biden. And she was among those who contracted COVID-19 at about the same time as did dozens of others close to the president. These included the president's wife, Melania, and their son, Barron, as well as the president himself.

MIDDLE RING OF THE INNER CIRCLE

In the middle ring of President Donald Trump's inner circle were four men. Each was close to the president – though only within the limits set by Trump. He was, after all, a loner, more disposed to push people away than to invite them in. Two of the men in the middle ring were the president's older sons, Donald Jr. and Eric. One was his stalwart pal from Fox News, Sean Hannity. And the fourth was the vice president, Mike Pence.

Donald Trump has five children, three with his first wife, Ivana Trump, who is the mother of Don Jr., Eric, and Ivanka (about whom more below). All three were all their lives involved in the family business, as adults in official capacities under the banner of the Trump Organization. However, unlike Ivanka – who, together with her husband, Jared Kushner, became involved in politics as soon as her father did so, and moved to Washington when Trump did – Don Jr. and Eric were not, to start with, as tightly tied to their father as a political figure. Though Don Jr. became more heavily politically involved as time went on, during most of Trump's presidential tenure both his older sons continued to work in the Trump Organization.

By all reports the relationship between Donald Trump and his three oldest children – especially his two sons, Don Jr. in particular – had always been fraught. If they were enablers as adults, which they unreservedly were, part of the reason was because when they were children, he was not only distant as a father but frightening. "Fear radiated outward from Trump, but it also sent its radioactive waves inwardly, into the family," wrote Michael Cohen, who knew the family relatively well.[20] In their adulthood though, all three, for whatever reasons, stayed close. Don Jr. played a bit part in getting his father elected president. In fact, he was the one who "excitedly and naively" set up that problematic 2016 meeting in Trump Tower, supposedly to extract from a certain Russian political dirt on Hillary Clinton.[21] And by the time 2020 came around, all three of Trump's older children were "their father's most ardent cheerleaders."[22] They defended the president against perceived slights; raised money for Republicans; and began early on to rally supporters. The big surprise though was the change in Don Jr. By 2020 he had "grown arguably into his father's most valuable political weapon." Additionally, he had walked away from many of his duties in the Trump Organization, having been, as one observer put it, "electrified and transformed by his father's presidency."[23]

In May, *The Guardian* reported that Don Jr. and his partner
Kimberly Guilfoyle, as well as Eric and his wife Lara, were among
the president's "most important surrogates and strategists, constantly
pushing his cause, rallying his base, trashing his opponents, and earning a reputation as a modern political mafia."[24] Again, Don Jr. was
especially active. He held virtual fundraisers and meetings with
voters, he attended pro-hunting events (he is known as an avid hunter
and shooter), and he recorded calls and videos on behalf of Republican
candidates for the House and Senate. Hence the brothers' place in the
middle ring of the inner circle. They are their father's sons but, more to
the point, they were important to Donald Trump because of what they
did for him. In fact, their dedication can be downright unsettling. In
May 2020 Eric went so far as to claim that the coronavirus was
a scheme concocted by Democrats who wanted to rob Trump of his
greatest campaign tool, "which is being able to go into an arena and fill
it with 50,000 people every single time, right?" As soon as the election
was over, Eric Trump insisted, the virus would "magically, all of
a sudden go away and disappear."[25] Then "we'll find out that the
whole Covid pandemic was cooked up by the Democrats."[26]

In 2020 Fox News continued to dominate the media empire over
which it ruled. It boasted an average of 3.5 million prime time viewers
and a 218-month streak as the most watched cable news network. In
June and July 2020 Fox News was the highest-rated television channel
in the prime time hours of 8 to 11 p.m. "Not just on cable, Not just
among news networks. *All* of television."[27] It was in this firmament
that one star shone more brightly than the rest – Sean Hannity. His
prime time show was the most watched of all cable news shows.[28] It is
no exaggeration to say that if, during his tenure in the White House,
Donald Trump can be said to have had a single friend, it was Hannity.
The same Hannity who was among the most influential voices in
American media.[29] Though Hannity and Trump shared a hometown,
a world view, and a certain swagger, their history together was short.
They had known each other for years, but it was not until Trump ran
for president that they became close. Why? Because Hannity was an

early and strong supporter of Trump. And because Hannity was among the few movers and shakers who came reliably to Trump's defense, including at the low point of his presidential campaign, after the release of the "Access Hollywood" tape on which he bragged about grabbing women by their genitals. Though Hannity said on the air that Trump's "locker room" remarks were wrong, he put them in what he considered their proper perspective, joking at one point that, "King David had 500 concubines, for crying out loud!"[30]

In time theirs became a near perfect relationship from which both men stood to benefit. Trump got a diehard supporter, a media headliner who would reliably and regularly go publicly to bat for him. As one of Hannity's colleagues, longtime newsman Geraldo Rivera, put it, Hannity "is firm in his support of the president, and woe unto you if you don't see things the same way. He's a shield."[31] For his part, Hannity got unrivaled access to the president of the United States – for a Fox News mainstay a matchless commodity. One may think of it as a transactional interaction from which both men profited – which is true. But this underestimates the nature of the relationship, and its importance, which in Trump's case at least was unique. Precisely because Trump is a loner, Hannity's place in the president's inner circle was singular. It is not clear that during Trump's time in the White House he was as close to anyone as he was to Hannity.

The two men talked all the time, almost every day or, more accurately, almost every night, often immediately after Hannity's prime time show. They had a routine, in which Hannity would call the president who by then was alone in his quarters.[32] Hannity was content not only to be Trump's earpiece and mouthpiece, but also his foil and his shill. "Regardless of the news of the day," reported the *New York Magazine*, "the overarching narrative of [Hannity's] show is the political persecution of Trump and by extension of Hannity and Hannity's viewers, at the hands of the so-called deep state and the Democratic Party, and the corrupt mainstream media, a wholly owned subsidiary of both."[33]

By mid-2020 Hannity was viewed by most of that same mainstream media as the basest of Trump's propagandists. He was so reliable a wealthy wingman – Fox alone paid Hannity a fortune every year – that he led a Trump "town hall" that avoided entirely, in the middle of the pandemic, the subject of the pandemic. It was, as Susan Glasser put it in *The New Yorker*, an alternate reality in which Hannity provided the bunker in which Trump hid.[34]

Finally, in the middle ring of the inner circle was Mike Pence. The vice president would play one of the leading roles in managing the coronavirus crisis. Accordingly, he reappears, as does Hannity, in Part III of this book, which is focused on Trump's team. But given Pence's position in the administration he was also in the president's inner circle – notwithstanding the cavernous difference between the former realtor from New York and the former governor from Indiana. In other words, just as Hannity was in many ways like Trump, so Pence was in most ways unlike Trump. But this difference was precisely how it came to pass that Trump chose Pence as his running mate. It was a choice on which Melania Trump, atypically, weighed in. When Trump was considering who to pick for vice president, she spent time with both Mike Pence and his wife, Karen. They shared several meals and Melania spoke with the couple at relative length. When their time together was over, she urged Trump to pick Pence over the other two leading candidates for the post, Newt Gingrich and Chris Christie, on the reasonable grounds that they were alpha males.[35] Pence, in contrast, was not. Quite the opposite. She predicted that Pence would not compete with her husband and that he would defer to him. Both were predictions on which she was proved right.

For most of Trump's presidency he was king and Pence one of his subjects. Pence was an important subject but, nevertheless, a subject. Tim Alberta wrote, "From the moment last July when Trump picked Pence as his running mate ... his inconspicuousness [was] engineered to keep all eyes on the president."[36] A year later the same view was expressed, though from another angle. This time it was Trump who went "out of his way to make sure that Pence stays in his shadow."[37]

Another year later more of the same. Even when the president was impeached for soliciting Ukrainian involvement in the 2020 election, Pence bent over backward to make sure that between him and Trump there was not a sliver of daylight. He apparently believed as did nearly every other prominent Republican that even when Trump was "setting fire to his presidency," risking his wrath was politically suicidal.[38]

Pence's history of unswerving subservience paid off during the pandemic. Trump was sufficiently confident of his loyalty to allow Pence, finally, episodically, to be a little bit in the limelight. Of course, for the privilege of presiding over the White House Coronavirus Task Force Pence would have to pay a price. He would have to do so with his hands tied.

INNER RING OF THE INNER CIRCLE

During the time Donald Trump was president the inner ring of his inner circle consisted of only two people. They were the older of his two daughters, Ivanka Trump, and her husband, Jared Kushner. "Javanka," as sometimes together they were called, were in the inner ring for good reasons. First, she, Ivanka, is arguably the only person on the planet who seems important to Trump. Second, Jared is arguably the only person who seems indispensable to Trump. She will be important forever. He will be indispensable only so long as he remains married to Ivanka.

I earlier described President Trump as a loner and quoted one of his biographers who wrote that he lacks what it takes to "build deep relationships with other people." If there has been an exception to this rule, it is Ivanka. By every account if anyone has been singled out for his special attention and affection, it has been his older daughter. "You could tell by his eyes," remembered one close observer, "the way they popped and gleamed ... Only one person gets that kind of look from Donald Trump, Ivanka."[39] Oddly, sometimes Trump was somewhat inappropriate in how he related to his daughter – describing her to others, for example, as "hot," or as "very voluptuous."

However, his admiration of her went well beyond her physical appearance.[40] He extolled how she behaved and what she accomplished, and he thought her future limitless. He called Ivanka "Baby" in official meetings, described her as "unique," and said that if "she ever wanted to run for president, I think she'd be very, very hard to beat."[41]

As soon as Trump decided to run for president, Ivanka was all in. During the campaign she would introduce her father at public rallies, and "assume many of the duties of a political spouse" while Trump's wife, Melania, stayed home with their son, Barron.[42] Ivanka was tall, blonde, attractive and perfectly polished; as well, she was an experienced public speaker who knew how to handle an audience. The next step was inevitable: as soon as Donald Trump moved to Washington, so too did Ivanka Trump, along with her husband and their three children. In short order the Kushner couple was living in an upscale manse in Washington's toney Kalorama neighborhood, not far from the White House.

Though Ivanka had a professional tie to her father for years – as a regular on his television shows *The Apprentice* and *Celebrity Apprentice*, and as an executive vice president of the Trump Organization – it was not always clear she would choose to remain in his orbit. After graduating from college, she went on to enjoy some success under her own name, in fashion. But once Donald Trump the real estate developer became Donald Trump the candidate for president, Ivanka went all in; she was right behind him. She, like her father, was drawn to the limelight and like him, was drawn to the idea that fame and fortune in business could be joined to fame and fortune in government.

Her father was delighted. Especially early in the Trump administration, whenever Ivanka could reasonably, or not so reasonably, be included in the conversation, she was. "She's a great diplomat," the president would say about his daughter. Or "she would've been great at the United Nations." Or "I even thought of Ivanka for the World Bank ... She would've been great at that because she's very good with numbers."[43] But, the honeymoon, such as it was, did not last. It was not long before Ivanka, who had been appointed "Senior Advisor to the President," was attacked for some of her behaviors and mocked for some of her choices. For instance, when she and her father attended the G20 summit in Osaka in 2019, she was insulted for inserting herself into conversations with world leaders and derided for trying to "play at being secretary of state."[44] Some of the criticisms directed at Ivanka were criticisms less of her than of her father. But her constant proximity to him and her unswerving loyalty meant that as he sunk in the estimation of growing numbers of Americans, so did she. Of course, at no point was she the most popular person in the White House room. Some of Trump's aides were fine with Ivanka. But others found her "a spoiled princess who had absorbed her father's worst narcissistic, superficial, and self-promoting qualities."[45]

In one respect at least, Ivanka did not, however, hold a candle to her husband, Jared Kushner. Criticisms of him were constant, and withering, virtually from day one. For obvious reason. For perhaps never in the history of the American presidency has a chief executive turned over to anyone so demonstrably unqualified so enormous a portfolio. As mentioned, like his father-in-law, before he came to Washington Kushner was mainly in real estate, though secondarily, he was also in publishing. And, like his father-in-law, before he came to Washington Kushner had no government experience, or political experience, or military experience. Notwithstanding, from the outset, beginning when Trump was a candidate for president, he carved out for Kushner an outsized role. This continued throughout the presidential transition and into their time in the White House, when Kushner was promptly given the title of "Senior Advisor to the President." As stated in the *New York Times* around the time of the inauguration: "Trump intends to adopt the management style of a New York real estate empire, with family at the pinnacle and staff members . . . somewhere below."[46]

Within a few months the enormous scope of Kushner's responsibilities was clear, as was the degree of trust the president placed in him above all others. The president's trust in Kushner was so great he gave him that "vast portfolio that so far includes negotiating an Israeli-Palestinian peace deal, helping oversee relations with Canada, China and Mexico ... and reinventing the federal government through the new White House office of American Innovation." In short order Kushner had become – and so he remained throughout Trump's tenure as president – the "ultimate decider."[47]

It is no surprise then that during the pandemic, especially in the first half year, it was Kushner who usually was the point person. In April 2020, the *New York Times* noted that at one of the "most perilous moments in modern American history" Kushner, because of his "unique status," was at the epicenter of the virus crisis. This despite his being a "real estate developer with none of the medical expertise of a public health official nor the mobilization experience of a general."[48] What this meant obviously was that in addition to Kushner's already bulging portfolio, he now had a whole other set of responsibilities, all of the utmost consequence. In short order it became clear that Kushner was out of his league. By early July, the number of COVID-19 cases in the United States had passed three million, a number that in comparison with other developed countries was woefully high.

During Trump's time in the White House, Ivanka Trump and Jared Kushner were a special couple with a special status. Because the president trusted hardly anyone, and because his love for his daughter was "unique," and because Kushner was the husband of his daughter and, additionally, fiercely loyal, the "kids" were effectively given the run of the place.[49] They were, each in their way, indispensable to the president, the only ones privileged, so to speak, to be enablers meriting membership in the inner ring of his inner circle.

TOGETHER

Since John Kennedy was president and Jacqueline Kennedy first lady it has been widely understood that the president's spouse makes a difference. The ways in which and degrees to which first ladies have had influence and impact varied of course. But Jacqueline Kennedy, Lady Bird Johnson, Pat Nixon, Betty Ford, Rosalynn Carter, Nancy Reagan, Barbara Bush, Hillary Clinton, Laura Bush, and Michelle Obama all left their imprint on the White House and, in some cases, on the American people. Moreover, each was admired and appreciated for her contributions.

Melania Trump was not exactly an exception to this rule. She was not disliked nor was she disapproved of. (Though in 2018 her favorability rating was a rather meager 43 percent.[50]) But she was during the entirety of Trump's political life implicitly if not explicitly dismissed as irrelevant and unimportant. Much of this was her doing. With relatively few exceptions she deliberately remained out of the public eye and deliberately stayed silent. And with relatively few exceptions she also refrained from doing what her predecessors did: associate herself, regularly, visibly, with a good cause. Additionally, Melania Trump's relationship to Donald Trump remained opaque. They were, of course, seen together, but only occasionally, only fleetingly, and only awkwardly. As if holding hands was more a reflection of their public relations than their private feelings. An example of how irrelevant and unimportant Melania Trump seemed during her time in the White House was the amount of ink she got in Bob Woodward's *Fear: Trump in the White House*, which in hard copy ran to 420 pages. Essentially this is the total text Woodward devoted to the first lady: "West Wingers and those who traveled regularly with Trump noticed that he and Melania seemed to have some sincere affection for each other despite media speculation. But she operated independently. They ate dinner together at times, spent some time together, but they never really seemed to merge their lives. Melania's primary concern was their son, Barron."[51]

To say that Melania Trump was independent is not, however, to say that she was inessential. She was most certainly not inessential to the president, either before or during his time in office. Moreover, given the paucity of people to whom Trump was in any way close, and given the small size of his anyway fungible inner circle, her role in his life, his interior life and his exterior life, should not be dismissed. She was without question one of his enablers, one of the people who made his presidency possible.

For all the talk about Donald Trump and the many women in his life, the fact is that during most of his adulthood he was married. He married his first wife, Ivana, in 1977, when he was thirty years old. They remained married until 1991; two years later he married Marla Maples, from whom he was divorced in 1999. Some six years later – after being together for five years – he married Melania.

In important ways they are a good fit. Melania's biographer, *Washington Post* reporter Mary Jordan, wrote that Melania and Donald Trump share many of the same qualities: "They are both independent, ambitious, image-conscious, unsentimental, and wary of those outside their inner circle. They are both fighters and survivors and prize loyalty above all else." Additionally, both are loners. Though she never played the part of doting, dutiful wife, when Melania married Trump, she had nothing in her life that would intrude on their marriage. She had given up her modeling career, and she came into the marriage with only a small family and a very few friends. She was close to her parents, especially to her mother (in 2018 both parents became American citizens), but otherwise she had hardly any intimates. In fact, one could reasonably argue that even her husband was not an intimate, at least not in the usual sense. Jordan noted that to a degree that is "remarkable" for a couple, "Melania and Donald have always lived quite separately; they are often in the same building but rarely in the same room."[52]

Notwithstanding her unusual marriage, her independence, and her appearance as a "mysterious first lady," there should be no mistaking the facts that all along Melania Trump was a member of her husband's inner circle, such as it was; that she was in his corner, more or less; that she was influential, if only intermittently; and that throughout she played the part of proper first lady, if only reservedly.[53] Though the president and first lady virtually never worked together, and virtually never played together, they did never-theless stay together and live together.

Melania Trump was, moreover, one of Donald Trump's most crucial political supporters. She encouraged him to run for president in 2016, telling him that "if you run, you're going to win." And, she saved his political neck when that potentially devastating "Access Hollywood" tape came to light a month before the 2016 election.[54] At first the tape was thought to have dealt Trump's campaign for the presidency a fatal blow. But it was quickly decided that Melania, and only Melania, was in a position, possibly, to save the day. She agreed to try. She put out a statement that read in part, "The words my husband used are unacceptable and offensive to me. This does not represent the man I know. He has the heart and mind of a leader. I hope people will accept his apology, as I have."[55] Notwithstanding the scandal, Trump won the election.

Melania Trump during the pandemic was like Melania Trump before the pandemic. To be sure, there were signs, here and there, that she did not fully share her husband's view either of the virus crisis or of the White House response. For example, unlike her husband, even in spring, she occasionally, very occasionally, wore a mask. And, unlike her husband, she urged Americans to "take action to prevent further spread" and to "visit cdc.gov for updated health info & updates."[56] But never once did she in any significant way stray from the party line. Nor did she ever, even as her husband doubled down on wishing away the virus crisis, in any significant way deviate from his overarching mes-sage. Moreover, unlike most first ladies who preceded her, she did not in a time of trouble offer the nation a healing word or a helping hand. Instead, she did what everyone else did in Trump's inner circle – she enabled.

PART II   Virus Crisis

5 Prequel to the Pandemic

Plagues haunt. They have always haunted, hovered, burrowed their way into our collective consciousness, and they still do so now. They are calamities that seem to come out of nowhere – unimagined, unforetold, undetected – and that seem similarly to resist the usual remedies. They seem in the ether, even in the air we breathe, so we imagine them impermeable, indestructible, destined indefinitely to infest us.

Like Aesop, Jean de La Fontaine, the famed French fabulist, penned hundreds of fables in the 1700s, stories in which animals were characters that were stand-ins for people, and allegories that were instructions on lives well lived. The animals were archetypes, recognizable not only then but now – the regal lion, the sly fox, the humble donkey. One fable from 1678 was titled "The Animals Sick with the Plague." It was a cautionary tale about a plague that had descended on the animals and changed their lives, maybe forever. Redolent of the frightening first pages of Rachel Carson's *Silent Spring*, in "The Animals Sick with the Plague" no one any longer eats. No one any longer falls in love or experiences joy among the ruins. And many creatures die.

"The Animals Sick with the Plague" is about power. Animals with power are self-serving and self-aggrandizing, interested only in themselves.[1] The point is that in the literature of the early modern period plagues had a pedagogical purpose. Story tellers used them to tell cautionary tales, to warn people they could be punished for their sins by being attacked by an infectious and possibly fatal disease. "One of those dread evils, which spread terror far and wide, and which Heaven in its anger, ordains for the punishment of wickedness upon earth – a plague ... So hopeless was the case that not one of the [wolves or foxes or turtledoves] attempted to sustain their sinking lives ... Love and the joy that comes of love were both at an end."[2]

During the pandemic of 2020, Orhan Pamuk, the Turkish writer who in 2006 won the Nobel Prize for Literature, revealed that he was working on a novel set in 1901, during an outbreak of bubonic plague that began in Asia a half century earlier. In researching his book Pamuk became an expert on plague literature. He was struck not by the differences over centuries but by the similarities. Similarities in how people responded to plagues, no matter where or when.

Denial as an initial reaction is not, for example, peculiar either to this time, the third decade of the twenty-first century, or to the United States. To the contrary, according to Pamuk the first response to the outbreak of any pandemic usually has been denial. National and local governments have often "been late to respond and have distorted facts and manipulated figures to deny the existence of the outbreak." To make his case he turns to Daniel Defoe – an approximate contemporary of La Fontaine – who wrote, in addition to *Robinson Crusoe*, *A Journal of the Plague Year*. Defoe reported that in 1664, local London authorities tried to make the number of plague deaths seem lower than they really were by registering other, sometimes invented diseases as the cause of demise. Pamuk also cites the Italian writer Alessandro Manzoni, whose 1827 novel, *The Betrothed*, described the official response to the 1630 plague in Milan as insufficient and duplicitous. Manzoni wrote that because the threat was initially ignored, the plague spread, rapidly; the absence of restrictions and the requisite enforcement turned out costly.

Pamuk points to another similarity between past and present – rampant rumors and misleading information. In the past, this was exacerbated by incomplete and inaccurate information, imaginations then running rampant. But even now, when it often seems there is not too little data but too much, facts can remain elusive, contradictory, and vulnerable to preexisting biases. Finally, there is this: plagues are

everywhere perceived as invaders. As aliens worming their way in –
literally, figuratively, into our spaces, into our bodies, and into our
hearts and minds. Pamuk notes in his account of the plague in Athens
that, "Thucydides began by noting that the outbreak had started far
away, in Ethiopia and Egypt."[3]

More contemporaneously there is of course Albert Camus –
born in Algeria, though he lived most of his life in France – whose
novel, pointedly titled *The Plague*, is considered a classic. It is read not
only by the literati, but in high schools and colleges, in courses in
history and political science, in literature, theology, and philosophy,
in America and around the world. Originally published in 1947, *The
Plague* is also an historical novel. For though it is situated in the
1940s, it draws on the experience of the French Algerian city of
Oran, which in 1899 experienced an epidemic of cholera that killed
a large portion of the city's population. (Oran was also decimated in
the sixteenth and seventeenth centuries, both times by the bubonic
plague, the "Black Death."[4])

The Plague is sometimes described as an existential novel, but it
is quite realistic, raising the question of what would happen if, of
a sudden, a pandemic disrupted life as we knew it. The story is full
of omens: rats, for example, emerging from their netherworld only
quickly to die. Initially these "bewildering portents" are ignored, the
residents of Oran, like everybody else, "wrapped up in themselves,"
disbelieving in pestilences. But then, disease, followed by death, takes
over. Early attempts by the authorities to describe the plague as
merely "a special type of fever" were revealed for what they were –
badly misleading, dangerously mistaken.

Like La Fontaine's "The Animals Sick with the Plague,"
Camus's *The Plague* was an allegory. The physical contagion represented a psychological contagion – a dangerous spread of any of the
"isms" that plagued, yes, plagued, the twentieth century. "Isms" that
included Nazism, communism, and totalitarianism. Camus himself
was deeply immersed in the politics of his day. While writing *The
Plague*, he served as editor in chief of *Combat*, the underground

magazine of the French Resistance. Implicit then was the comparison between being infected physically and being infected psychologically. Contagion is contagion, whether literal or metaphorical.[5]

"Contagion" happens also to be the name of an American film made by Steven Soderbergh in 2011. It features a large and well-known cast, and a plot that centers on the spread of a virus transmitted by respiratory droplets. At the time of its release the film was successful; but thereafter it was largely forgotten, apparently irrelevant to anything with which any of us was familiar. Until 2020. Until COVID-19. Until what became posthaste a pandemic. *Contagion* is of course a work of fiction, but it was eerily prescient. Which is why between December 2019 and March 2020 the film jumped from being ranked number 270 in the Warner Brothers movie catalogue to being number 2. And why by May it ranked number 5 on the iTunes movie download chart, right behind recent blockbusters such as the latest *Star Wars*.[6]

It is small wonder plagues haunt our imagination as they inhabit our experience. They do disappear. But they return. Always, they return.

DISTANT PAST

We should never have been so arrogant as to think ourselves exempt. Exempt from an epidemic that would become a pandemic. Exempt from the kinds of contagions that for eons have caused widespread disease, mass death, and political, economic, and social upheaval.

Our first written record of a pandemic dates to the year 541, in the city of Pelusium, in Northeast Egypt. According to the historian Procopius, who was alive at the time of the events he described, the "pestilence" spread to the west and to the east, toward Alexandria in one direction and Palestine in the other. Then it kept going, almost "as if fearing lest some corner of the earth might escape it." According to science writer Elizabeth Kolbert, the earliest symptom of the pestilence was fever. But within days the symptoms worsened, then they worsened further. Victims of what we now recognize as classic symptoms of bubonic plague developed lumps in their groin or under their arms. "The suffering," Kolbert noted, "at that point was terrible; some people went into coma, others into violent delirium. Many vomited blood." Procopius wrote that those who attended the sick were similarly in agony, "in a constant state of exhaustion." So, they too were objects of pity, "no less than the sufferers." A year later the same plague struck Constantinople. Among its victims was the emperor, Justinian, who, though he survived, was weakened, as was his reign. Finally, in 750, the plague burned itself out, by which time, in large part in consequence, there was a new world order.[7]

Bubonic plague is still with us. It has struck several times in the last two thousand years, most dramatically in the late Middle Ages, in the 1300s, when, as mentioned earlier, it was known as the Black Death. The disease is caused by a strain of bacteria that lives on fleas and lice, who in turn live on rats. However, because bubonic plague, like COVID-19, can be passed from one infected person to another through respiratory droplets, killing rats did not and does not kill the virus that causes it. Moreover, though there are therapies now, there is still no vaccine for bubonic plague which is why, though incidence of the disease has dropped dramatically, it has not been eliminated.

In the fourteenth century there was no remedy or therapy for bubonic plague, not even an effective palliative. Which is how it happened that after spreading from Asia, specifically from China into Europe, the Black Death killed a third of Europe's population in the four-year period 1347 to 1351. It was an awful business, causing its victims immense suffering, and disastrously impacting economies on two continents. Barbara Tuchman described sailors who brought the disease from the Black Sea to Europe showing "strange black swellings about the size of an egg or an apple ... The swellings oozed blood and pus and were followed by spreading boils and black blotches ... The sick suffered severe pain and died within five days of the first symptoms."[8] Jared Diamond wrote that the impact of the Black Death on Central Asia was incalculable: It affected "history's largest land empire, the Mongol Empire, which stretched from China to Persia and Russia. By cutting off travel and trade, plague severed connections between the empire's parts, thereby causing Mongol control of Persia and China to collapse . . . and control of Russia slowly to wither away."[9]

Germs can and sometimes do "transform" history. Diamond found the "most lethal, permanent and far-reaching effect" of germs ever was "the European conquest," which resulted in the "extensive replacement of Native Americans, Pacific Islanders and Aboriginal Australians." Deadliest of the germs was smallpox. While over thousands of years of being exposed, Europeans had developed a level of herd immunity, native populations had no such protection. They were, therefore, "immunologically almost defenseless," succumbing to smallpox in horrific numbers. The disease may have killed more than a billion people before it was finally vanquished, in the mid-twentieth century, by a vaccine.

Like bubonic plague, smallpox goes all the way back; signs of it have been found, for example, in Egyptian mummies. The first epidemic of smallpox in the New World was in 1518, with infected individuals almost always developing first a high fever, then a rash that became ulcerated and encrusted. Countless numbers succumbed; in some places the fatality rate among young children was 90 percent. In the 1500s a Spanish priest based in the New World wrote, "In many places it happened that everyone in a house died, and, as it was impossible to bury the great number of dead, they pulled down the houses over them." Kolbert described smallpox as having "reached the Incan Empire before the Spaniards did; the infection raced from one settlement to the next faster than the conquistadores could travel." William Bradford, a leader of the Plymouth colony, chronicled smallpox in Native Americans. Broken pustules, he wrote, effectively glued a patient's skin to the mat, only to be torn off "when they turn them." Sometimes, a "whole side will flay off at once as it were, and they will be all of a gore blood, most fearful to behold."[10]

We will never know the real number of smallpox fatalities in the New World. The historical record is scant, and Europeans brought with them several other potentially lethal diseases such as measles, typhoid, and diphtheria. Suffice to say here that on account of the various contagions, the "discovery of America was followed by possibly the greatest demographic disaster in the history of the world."[11]

Americans tend not to be historians. So, in 2020, when the new coronavirus started to spread in the USA, in the hunt for an historical parallel the American people settled on just one – the influenza pandemic that occurred approximately a century ago. Known at the time as the "Spanish Flu" it was one of the worst contagions in the history of humankind. Around the world, anywhere from 50 to 100 million people died. And in the United States there were between 10 and 14 million cases, and between 500,000 and 750,000 deaths.[12] The pandemic peaked in 1918 and lasted about one year. It devastated urban populations in, for example, New York and Pittsburgh, and rural areas as well, such as in Arkansas, where public health infrastructures ranged from weak to nonexistent.[13] The consequences of having the disease could be horrific. "Infected individuals exhibited heliotrope cyanosis, a bluish discoloration of the skin resulting from suffocation as their lungs filled with blood and fluid. The end result for the host was often systemic hemorrhaging and ultimately death."[14]

While there are some similarities between what happened then, in 1918, and the pandemic in 2020, there are also significant differences. The most important of these was context: COVID-19 hit, especially in the West, during times that in most ways were good. The world was relatively at peace and prosperity was relatively high. The Spanish Flu, in contrast, was exacerbated by World War I, which, in turn, exacerbated the flu. As the war dragged on, the influenza had an especially pernicious effect on Germany and the other Central Powers, in part because there was an embargo on shipments of food. But it was the proximity of military forces, one man so close to the next, that had the most toxic effect. The pandemic was at its worst in fall 1918, when the disease attacked fighting men on both sides of the war, "overwhelming field hospitals, transports, and lazarets in the rear with fevered, debilitated, and dying young men." In fact, the ground war was a vector that allowed the virus to mutate and become the more lethal. The Spanish Flu was, then, a "product of the pernicious ecology of war, with high population densities of combatants, poor sanitation, stress, and the movement of forces collectively serving as remarkably efficient vectors of transmission around the world."[15]

In the United States, what began in army camps in spring 1918 spread by fall 1918 to the population at large. But the effects on the US military remained for the duration especially devastating. In spring, soldiers at Camp Funston in Fort Riley, Kansas began reporting acute flu-like symptoms including chills, coughing, high fever, and respiratory distress. Within a month 1,100 men had contracted the disease and 46 had died.[16] By fall it was clear that the pandemic had been responsible for a high rate of absenteeism, loss of morale, and logistical chaos. Combined with other factors typical of wartime generally, the result was an ineffective American army with low morale.[17]

Nor was the situation among the civilian population much better. What happened then rings familiar now. Hospitals lacked the capacity to deal with the sudden surge of patients: they did not have the necessary beds, or the necessary supplies, or the necessary medical personnel. The contagion had other effects as well, ranging from cuts in the deliveries of good and services to the inability promptly and effectively to bury the dead. Among all American cities, Philadelphia was one of the hardest hit. Even before the war, it was in bad shape; by the end of the war it was much worse. The city was teeming with new workers and migrants, who stretched its capacities. Moreover, Philadelphia's director of Public Health and Charities was a political appointee, not an expert in infectious disease. Like so many similarly positioned, he initially downplayed the threat, assuring the city's residents that the local authorities would "confine the disease to its present limits, and in this we are sure to be successful ... No concern whatever is felt."[18] Sound familiar?

Ideally, Philadelphia's failures, its inability to respond quickly and effectively to the public health crisis, would have been a lesson from which other cities learned. In some cases, they did. But in most they did not. As historian Joshua Zeitz wrote about America's response to the Spanish Flu, "The broader pattern that emerged was dismissal, dissemblance, and outright deception on the part of public officials who either did not perceive the severity of the threat or who would not acknowledge it, for fear of political consequences. What mayor or governor, after all, wanted to go to war with local businesses, which in every city vocally opposed forced shutdowns?"[19] Again, does this sound familiar?

The pandemic of 2020 is in many ways different from the pandemic of 1918. But, obviously, there are similarities. Now as then Americans were miserably ill-prepared to combat a pandemic. Now as then there has been a proclivity to denial by the authorities. Now as then there has been a failure of leadership.

IMMEDIATE PAST

Do Americans learn from their past, specifically from their past mistakes? The evidence suggests they, like other countries, do not. The American people seemed to have learnt little from the pandemic of 1918 or, at least, not enough to stave off what a hundred years later became a major public health crisis, and then in short order a major economic crisis. It is not that there were no warnings. There were many warnings, different warnings made by different people in different places at different times. Rather it is that in the United States the warnings were not heard or not heeded, or they were heard as if only faint in the distance or heeded only intermittently and half-heartedly.

Where to start? Perhaps with one of the "Coronavirus Cassandras," Laurie Garrett, whose 1994 best-seller, *The Coming Plague*, foretold future plagues by chronicling past ones. Or maybe with Bill Frist, who was a Senator but also a doctor and who, while he was a member of Congress, in 2005, delivered a speech at Harvard University that was prescient. His warning of course was for naught. But the fact that he stood in two camps – as a high-level elected official and as a highly trained surgeon – and thus exceedingly well-qualified to opine on matters of public health makes the ignoring of his warning the more striking. Here is part of what he said a decade and a half preceding the 2020 pandemic. "We will not be able to sleep through what is likely coming soon – a front of unchecked and virulent epidemics, the potential of which should rise above your every other concern."[20] Nor were forecasters such as Garrett and Frist alone. Along with them were others, many different scientists with many different areas of expertise, who regularly and repeatedly sounded warnings and who, in a series of papers published over a 15-year period, pointed specifically to the connections among coronaviruses, bats, and people.

In a curious way, the American experience with other recent diseases, infectious diseases akin to COVID-19, did not help. Though SARS and MERS were themselves red flags, precursors to COVID-19, because they grazed the USA only lightly, most Americans were content to ignore both. Similarly, Ebola. In 2014 Senator Lamar Alexander told a crowded hearing room on Capitol Hill that, "We must take the deadly, dangerous threat of the Ebola epidemic as seriously as we take ISIS." Still, Americans remained by and large as ignorant of the disease as they were unscathed.[21]

Bill Gates became an expert in infectious diseases through his work with the Bill & Melinda Gates Foundation, which for years had prioritized the fight against malaria. He sounded the most attention-getting of all the cautions – though even the attention he got was scant, most of it coming only years later, after the coronavirus had already spread from China to Europe to America. In 2015 Gates delivered a TED talk titled "The Next Outbreak? We're Not Ready." He warned that if "anything kills over 10 million people in the next few decades, it's likely to be a highly infectious virus rather than a war. Not missiles, but microbes." Two years later he said somewhat the same thing at an event at the World Economic Forum in Davos: "It's pretty surprising how little preparedness there is for [a pandemic]."[22]

None of this is to say that Americans paid no attention at all to the threat of a pandemic, or that they were completely unprepared for an outbreak of an infectious disease. One could argue, in fact, that compared to the administration of President Donald Trump, the administrations of both President George W. Bush and President Barack Obama took the possibility of a pandemic seriously. Bush had read a book about the 1918 flu pandemic, and so pushed his aides to develop a strategy to prepare for another perhaps similar contagion. The result was an "excellent 396-page playbook for managing such a health crisis."[23] Some years later Ebola appeared, which at home seemed a distant threat, but abroad, especially in West Africa, did not. There it was an immediate threat. As a result, the White House, under Obama, got involved in tracking and containing the disease, which killed about 50 percent of the people it infected. Moreover, though Obama had eliminated the White House Health and Security Office, after the Ebola pandemic he established an agency somewhat analogous: The Directorate for Global Health Security and Biodefense, under the aegis of the National Security Council. Like other similar directorates, it had its own staff and director, in this case Beth Cameron, who reported to the national security advisor. Cameron's task, as she later described it, was to "do everything possible within the vast powers and resources of the U.S. government to prepare for the next disease outbreak and prevent it from become an epidemic or pandemic."[24]

Cameron was succeeded in her leadership role by Rear Admiral Tim Ziemer, but he did not last long. For at the direction of John Bolton, Trump's national security advisor at the time, the directorate was disbanded. Soon thereafter Ziemer departed "abruptly," which left no senior official in the administration of President Donald Trump whose mandate was health security. According to the *Washington Post*, once Ziemer was gone, health experts worried that the United States was badly "underprepared for the increasing risks of a pandemic or bioterrorism attack."[25] While Bolton later defended his action, there is no doubt that his boss, Trump, famously a science sceptic, was determined to cut funding for all health-related initiatives, including the exceedingly important and globally prominent Centers for Disease Control and Prevention (CDC). The administration's budget for fiscal year 2019 proposed cutting funding for the CDC by 20 percent, which, had it been passed by Congress, would have brought the agency back to its lowest level of funding since 2003. Gates's response to the proposed cutbacks not only to the CDC but to virtually all federally supported health-related entities and activities, was to warn that it did not bode well for what he thought was the "necessary international collaboration in global health."[26]

Cameron later wrote that it was impossible accurately to assess the impact of the decision to disband the White House office tasked with responding to a pandemic. But she did say it was clear that eliminating the office "contributed to the federal government's sluggish domestic response."[27] Cameron was in good company. By the time it became apparent, in spring 2020, that the United States was in the throes of a pandemic, Trump's gutting of Obama's pandemic-preparedness systems became a favorite target. Administration critics were especially quick to compare Trump's anti-science biases with his predecessor's fact-based analyses. As one member of the Obama administration put it, "One of the principles that [Obama] was very clear on when it came to public health crises is you have to be guided by science and facts and speak clearly and consistently and credibly on those issues. That means, frankly, having public health and medical experts do the communicating."[28] As remarked by the nearly always politically cautious Dr. Anthony Fauci, Director of the National Institute of Allergy and Infectious Diseases, "It would be nice if the office [the directorate] was still there. I wouldn't necessarily characterize it as a mistake [to eliminate it]. I would say we worked very well with that office."[29]

FUTURE

The United States was by no means alone. In October 2019, the Global Health Security Index indicated that none of the 195 countries that were ranked on the index, including the United States, was perfectly prepared to combat a pandemic or even an epidemic. Among the many concerns, only 3 percent of countries had committed to prioritizing services for healthcare workers who became sick on the job. And fully 89 percent of countries did not have a system in place for delivering medical supplies during public health emergencies.[30]

To be sure, some countries were far better prepared than others. When the new coronavirus hit, Germany and South Korea, for example, both of which had a history of investing regularly and generously in public health, fared far better than not so prescient counterparts. On the other hand, other countries, such as Britain, were similar to the United States – "ill equipped to handle a pandemic."[31] Britain's National Health Service did not have sufficient numbers of intensive care beds; it did not have sufficient protective equipment for staff; and, initially, it did not have a sufficient number of ventilators.

What does this say about America's capacity to learn from the present health crisis to prepare for a future health crisis? And what does this say about America's capacity to prepare for other sorts of crises that might seem remote, but are not, such as threats posed by climate change including raging fires and rising waters? The signs are not good. Though some leaders in some places are smart and deliberate about investing in the present to prepare for the future, most leaders in most places are not. Once again, it is not as if Americans are not being forewarned. For example, in October 2020 the Council on Foreign Relations released findings from its independent task force, including specific recommendations on pandemic preparation. They included, for instance, developing and funding a strategy for testing and tracing; ensuring an adequate stockpile of equipment and supplies for future pandemics; and the use of incentives to diversify global supply chains.[32] But, as Fauci put it years before COVID-19 struck, "There's always a reluctance to put resources into something that isn't happening yet." Outbreaks that seem still a remote possibility, "go low on the priority list."[33] Why is that? Why do leaders not better prepare for exigencies and emergencies – and why do ordinary people not oblige them better to prepare?

Healthcare expert Ali Khan described the problem as a "lack of imagination." It is not, he pointed out, that there were no warnings about the possibility, the probability, of a pandemic. There were warnings aplenty. Rather it was that the warnings that were sent even by other, recent coronaviruses that had spread quickly and easily, such as SARS and MERS, were not heeded. The issue though is more complex than our inability simply to anticipate and then to prepare for a pandemic. Our lack of readiness for any sort of disaster, for example, for Hurricane Katrina, which devastated New Orleans in 2005, is a reminder of how pernicious is the problem of avoidance.

Experts had warned for years that a calamity like that of Katrina was highly likely. Among other individuals and institutions, the Federal Emergency Management Agency (FEMA) had cautioned that a major hurricane in the vicinity of New Orleans was one of three catastrophes most likely to hit the United States. So, the evidence of risk was clear to the experts – and it was clear even to ordinary people, especially if they lived and worked in or near New Orleans. Still, when Katrina made landfall, it was immediately apparent that whatever the investments and preparations that had been made, they were tragically inadequate. Levees were breached in more than 50 places. Shelters were overwhelmed. Destruction was massive – the damage ran to about $125 billion. And over a thousand people died. Given countless similar examples of disasters foretold but warnings not heeded, willful blindness would seem endemic to the human condition.

In 2003 Professors Max Bazerman and Michael Watkins wrote an article that appeared in the *Harvard Business Review* titled, "Predictable Surprises: The Disasters You Should Have Seen Coming." Their conclusion: "The human mind is a notoriously imperfect instrument." Because we are biased in how we process information, we tend to ignore, or at least to underestimate the likelihood of impending disasters. They described four such "cognitive biases," each of which impedes our capacity properly to prepare even for a problem that is "predictable." First, we tend to think that things are better than they really are. Second, we tend to be persuaded by evidence that supports what we anyway think – and not to be persuaded by evidence that does not. Third, we tend to live in the present, to avoid a little pain today even if it means more pain tomorrow. And fourth, we tend to find it easy to ignore problems with which we are unfamiliar – such as a pandemic.[34]

There are other ways the human mind is constrained, for example, the gap between recognizing that there is a problem and being willing (not to speak of able) to act on it. Psychologists have labeled our passivity in the face of clear and present danger "normalcy bias," or "negative panic." In other words, first we are slow to recognize the danger and then, even after recognizing the danger, we are slow to respond. Another example is our proclivity to "optimism bias" – to be unreasonably optimistic in situations that do not warrant it. A book titled *The Ostrich Paradox* presents evidence that while East coast residents were aware of the risks to them posed by Hurricane Sandy, they remained "confident that it would be other people who suffered." Finally, there is what the experts call "exponential myopia." The term refers to our tendency to find the mere concept of exponential growth – growth that is at lightning speed, such as in the case of the new coronavirus – difficult to grasp.[35]

All of these are good reasons or, at least, explanations for why we are ill-equipped to prepare for disasters such as pandemics. One could argue, of course, that this is precisely why we hire leaders. We hire leaders, specifically leaders in government, to do this sort of work for us. To protect us from harm, whether harm coming from within or without. The problem is that leaders are like the rest of us. They are prone to the same sorts of cognitive biases, and they are prone to the same sorts of other constraints on the capaciousness of the human mind. It gets worse. For leaders are prone also – especially if they perceive themselves to be powerful – to see themselves as immune from problems that beset those less powerful than they. President Donald Trump comes to mind – Trump who refused during the pandemic to wear a mask. Prime Minister Boris Johnson comes equally to mind – Johnson who boasted of shaking hands long after the experts had repeatedly warned against it. (For their misplaced bravado, both, of course, paid a steep price. Johnson and Trump both contracted COVID-19, the former falling severely ill.)

Plagues are "a feature of the human experience."[36] They are not new to our species – they are new to us as particular individuals. One could conclude then that we are stuck. But we are stuck only if our leaders are ignorant or stubborn or both – *and if they surround themselves with enablers.* With people – subordinates, family, friends, followers of all stripes – who let them get away with ignoring the evidence and distorting the truth. The fact is that though we are living in the twenty-first century not in the fourteenth, we are, as we have come to understand, vulnerable to plagues now just as we were then. *So, unless our leaders introduce into the conversation the appropriate experts – and then listen to and act on what they have to say – we will be condemned to repeat history.* We have more information in the present than we did in the past, and more medical and scientific expertise. But unless resources such as these are tapped, they are utterly, completely, useless. In which case new coronaviruses and their equivalents, literal and metaphorical, will continue to hover and haunt, and in time to hunt us down.

6   Sequence of the Pandemic

The past emerges only in the present. Only with the benefit of hindsight can we configure the chronology of what happened. Such was the case with the new coronavirus. Only after the fact did we understand that two people who lived north of Seattle, who had respiratory illnesses in December, likely had what later came to be called COVID-19. Similarly, a health official in Florida. And, similarly, in early February, a death in California. Not only did we not know then what we know now, the precise trajectory of the coronavirus will remain for the time being difficult precisely to pinpoint.[1]

What we did know early on was that the new coronavirus emerged first in December, in Wuhan, China.[2] While the source of the virus was in dispute – some insisted it was from a lab, others that it was from a marketplace – never in dispute was where the first cases were. On December 31, 2019 the government in Wuhan confirmed that local health authorities were treating dozens of cases of pneumonia of unknown origin and, within days, there was additional information that a new virus was infecting not just Chinese, but other Asians as well. China said it was monitoring the situation to preclude the outbreak from becoming more severe, but in mid-January Chinese state media reported the first death known to be caused by the virus. The man was 61 years old, and he was a regular customer at the Wuhan market suspected of being the point of origin.[3]

During January, most Americans remained oblivious to the virus, but not all Americans. An article that appeared in the *New York Times* on January 8 reported that China had identified a new virus that was causing a pneumonia-like illness. Still, in general, to Americans, even to the small number who knew about it, the virus seemed distant, remote, like others that recently had plagued places other than the United States, for instance SARS. But by early January the Centers for Disease Control and Prevention was on the alert, warning US residents about traveling to China. It was not much more than a week later that the alarm started to sound. By January 20, cases were confirmed in several countries in Asia – and in the United States. Specifically, in the state of Washington, where a man in his thirties developed symptoms after returning from a trip to Wuhan. By the end of January, the World Health Organization (WHO) declared a "public health emergency of international concern." And on the last day of January President Donald Trump suspended entry into the United States by any foreign nationals who had been in China during the 14 days preceding.

It soon became clear that whatever measures the administration had taken were insufficient. While only a handful of infected travelers entered the USA from China early in 2020, "a vast wave of infected travelers … came in February from other countries in Asia, Europe and the rest of the world, each a dangerous spark that could set off a wider outbreak."[4] Most of those sparks died out – but a few did not. A few became outbreaks. By mid-February there were 2,000 hidden infections, each spreading ominously, perniciously, through American cities. Even then, though, most Americans remained unaware of, or at least unconcerned about a possible epidemic. Nor did the federal government evince much alarm. While the president did impose that travel ban on people coming from China, for several weeks thereafter that was about it. In a call with reporters at the end of January, Dr. Robert Redfield, director of CDC, assured them that though he understood "this may be concerning," based "on what we know now, our assessment remains that the immediate risk to the American public is low."[5]

In contrast to Redfield, who was already starting to straddle the line between science and politics, there were other experts, specifically in infectious diseases, who warned early in February that the "Wuhan coronavirus spreading from China" was "likely to become a pandemic that circles the globe." Dr. Anthony Fauci, director of the National Institute of Allergy and Infectious Disease, who came a few months later famously to lock horns with President Donald Trump, predicted that the virus was "almost certainly" going to become a pandemic. He went on, however, to calm the waters, adding it was unclear the consequences would be "catastrophic."[6] In any case little mention was made of the implications for Americans of what "almost certainly" was going to become a pandemic. Was "almost certainly," in other words, going to have a major impact not only outside the United States but within? On February 11, the WHO bestowed greater gravitas on the new coronavirus by giving the disease it caused a new name – COVID-19. Of itself this made clear the virus was no longer so new. It had originated in 2019, meaning that by then it was at least a couple of months old.

The first death from COVID-19 in Europe was supposedly in France, in mid-February. Not long after, Italy announced a significant surge in cases, from only two on February 19, to 61 (the figure included 12 deaths) less than a week later. On February 29, the United States had its first death, a patient near Seattle. That was the beginning of the fear and trembling – including in the financial markets. During the last week of the month global stock markets plunged in direct response to escalating concerns over the consequences of the new coronavirus. On February 24, the Dow Jones and S&P 500 posted their sharpest daily declines since 2018. The Dow plunged by 3.5 per-cent – or more than 1,000 points. Why specifically was Wall Street spooked? There were several reasons, one a warning from Dr. Nancy Messonnier, director of the CDC's National Center for Immunization and Respiratory Diseases, who told reporters that disruptions to daily life could be "severe." (More about Messonnier later.) Another was that investors generally were starting to worry that the ballooning numbers of cases in China, and the growing numbers of cases else-where, "could mean a prolonged economic slowdown around the world."[7] COVID-19 was beginning to threaten to derail what up to then had been the longest economic expansion in US history.

On the surface at least, it appeared the dramatic drop in the stock market had finally caught the president's attention. Though by February top federal health officials had already concluded that the "virus was likely to spread widely within the United States," and there were already reports that "shortages, confusions, and poor communications were complicating coronavirus preparations," the White House did little in response until the end of the month.[8] The administration continued to reject the idea of a coronavirus czar – an expert in managing infectious disease – but it did put a person in charge of the federal government's response to the threat of spread. That someone was the ultimate presidential loyalist, the ultimate presidential follower, the ultimate presidential enabler, Vice President Mike Pence.

On February 26, Pence was named chair of the White House Coronavirus Task Force. (Formally the task force had been established a month earlier; initially it was headed by Secretary of Health and Human Services, Alex Azar.) "We're doing really well," said Trump at the time he announced Pence's appointment. Trump took credit for making "very good early decisions," and assured the American people that the risk from the virus "remains very low." Pence in turn used the occasion as he invariably did: to heap praise on the president and to remind people of "the importance of presidential leadership and administration leadership." Ironically, he went on to foreshadow the abdication of leadership at the federal level. He said that in managing the coronavirus crisis, state and local agencies would play a "vital role."[9]

Of course, thanks to the reporting of Bob Woodward, we know now what we did not know then: that President Trump had been told face to face, and warned in no uncertain terms about the new coronavirus, weeks earlier, specifically on January 28, 2020. That was the day on which the nation's chief executive was cautioned by his national security advisor Robert O'Brien, and by his deputy, China expert Matt Pottinger, that a mysterious virus outbreak in China would be "the biggest national security threat you face in your presidency."[10] We further know now that Trump immediately understood the implications, for it was not much more than a week later that he called Woodward and told him not just about the virus but about how dangerous it was. The virus "goes through the air," said the president. "You don't have to touch things . . . You just breathe the air and that's how it's passed. And so that's a very tricky one. That's a very delicate one. It's also more deadly than even your strenuous flus."[11]

It was not, in other words, what we first thought: that either the president did not fully know or that he did not fully understand the risks of a pandemic – the disease and the deaths that could be in consequence of the new coronavirus. Rather it was that he did not want to think about it, or talk about it, or do anything about it. He wanted to avoid it being discussed in public; he was afraid that doing so would hurt the markets specifically or the economy generally. He did not want it to tarnish his presidency, and, above all, did not want it to diminish his chances of being reelected president in November.

MARCH 2020

On March 10, New York Governor Andrew Cuomo announced the creation of a "containment zone." It was, in effect, a one-mile circle around a suburb of New York City, New Rochelle, that was intended to keep people who were inside the circle in, and people who were outside the circle out. It was to quarantine the people of New Rochelle, to keep them isolated from everyone else because so far as was known, New Rochelle, population 77,000, had the largest cluster of cases anywhere in the United States. It turned out the suburb was a precursor, and a harbinger, of what was to come. (During the first half of 2020 Cuomo's own record as a leader was mixed. He was good at marshaling resources, and at presenting to the public a picture of the pandemic that was clear and calming. At the same time, the governor was slow to detect the seriousness of the new coronavirus, and his incessant fighting with New York City's mayor, Bill de Blasio, did not help either the city or the state.)

Notwithstanding President Trump's continuing to play down the threat of the coronavirus – he said it would "go away" – by mid-March alarm bells were ringing nationwide or, more accurately, worldwide. Austria, for example, had already restricted access along its border with Italy, while Greece and the Czech Republic had shuttered their schools and universities. For its part, the WHO officially transitioned from announcing "a public health emergency of international concern" to declaring a pandemic. In a gesture that many experts thought was overdue, on March 11 the director general of WHO issued a statement that said: "We are deeply concerned both by the alarming levels of spread and severity [of COVID-19] and by the alarming levels of inaction. We have therefore made the assessment that COVID-19 can be characterized as a pandemic."[12]

It was in March 2020 that the worm turned – that many if not most Americans went from being complacent to being concerned, some deeply concerned. A happening that up to then had been only occasionally in the news – the advent of a new coronavirus – was now incessantly in the news. For the first time COVID-19 became the focus of national attention, frustration, and consternation. On March 11, movie star Tom Hanks and his wife, actor Rita Wilson, made it known that they had contracted the disease and were quarantining. That same day there was another announcement, this one by Adam Silver, commissioner of the National Basketball Association (NBA): the NBA was canceling the remainder of its 2019–2020 season. One of its players had tested positive, which persuaded Silver that the league could not continue safely to play. Hanks and Silver together constituted a wake-up call. As the latter put it, "It sucks. But it just may be our reality for a while."[13]

Of course, for every NBA commissioner there were many others who continued in a cavalier fashion. For example, the Princess Cruise line's top doctor, Grant Tarling, was remarkably relaxed about the coronavirus, especially considering the growing number of warning signs. Even after a case of COVID-19 was confirmed on one of the Princess's ships, company officials assumed, incorrectly, that the immediate risk was low because the ailing passenger had disembarked. So, despite health authorities' strong recommendation that the vessel undergo a "thorough environmental cleansing and disinfection," the company responded only minimally. It cleaned the ship – but not that carefully. Dr. Tarling said in an interview, "There's no point in going and start cleaning the ship when we really didn't know what, if any, risk there was onboard."[14]

In short order Tarling and many like him were overtaken by events on the ground. By the end of the month it became impossible to be so blasé. In fact, it was during March that the knives first started to come out. An issue of *New York Magazine* featured an article by David Wallace-Wells that foretold the fury to come. "In the face of an onrushing pandemic, the United States exhibited, for months, a near-total evacuation of responsibility and political leadership – a sociopathic disinterest in performing the basic function of government, which is to protect its citizens."[15]

President Trump was about to endure a long period of unrelenting pressure. Whatever people's views of Trump, which tended to be either strongly approving or strongly disapproving, up to the pandemic his presidency had been essentially free of crisis imposed by anything or anyone other than himself. I refer specifically to his 2019 impeachment. Other than this self-inflicted wound, Trump's time in office had been going well, certainly from his perspective. Above all, notwithstanding the persisting inequities, the economy was booming, continuing its long expansion. Financial markets were reaching new highs; wages were rising; and the unemployment rate had fallen to its lowest level in 50 years.[16] At the beginning of the year, then, the president had good reason for optimism, especially regarding his prospects for reelection. But, once it became clear that it was impossible for him completely to avoid responsibility for managing the nation's worst public health crisis since the pandemic of a century earlier, the nature of his tenure in the White House irrevocably changed. Like it or not – he did not, not a bit – beginning in March 2020 Trump's White House was in crisis mode.

Trump continued to resist calls for a nationwide lockdown, which by then was a step that some governors, such as New York's

Andrew Cuomo and California's Gavin Newsom, had already taken at the level of their states. Trump though insisted that New York and California were "hotbeds," while the other 48 states had nothing much to worry about. "They don't by any means have the same problem."[17] The conflict that came to characterize the government's response to the pandemic was by then beginning to surface. I am referring to the tension between the responsibilities of the federal government and the responsibilities of the states. With the virus continuing to spread, and the economy apparently in free fall, President Trump tried to have it both ways. On the one hand he took measures such as authorizing his aides to work with Congress to provide assistance to industries and individuals already starting to suffer, and invoking, albeit to only to a meager degree, the Defense Production Act. (The Act allowed him to, among other things, order the private sector to make and distribute supplies including the ventilators and masks that already by then were in short supply.) But on the other hand, he continued to insist that the federal government was not a "shipping clerk." That it was up to the individual states to procure their own supplies, to address their own needs, and, generally, to manage the pandemic with only minimal assistance and even less coordination from the Trump administration.

In the meantime, in the hardest hit states such as New York, the news became daily more alarming. New York City had to cope with so many cases of COVID-19 that they threatened to overwhelm the healthcare system. Here is an excerpt from an article in the *New York Times* dated March 25:

> Elmhurst, a 545-bed public hospital in Queens, has begun
> transferring patients not suffering from coronavirus to other
> hospitals as it moves toward becoming dedicated entirely to the
> outbreak. Doctors and nurses have struggled to make do with a few
> dozen ventilators. Calls over a loudspeaker of "Team 700," the code
> for when a patient is on the verge of death, come several times
> a shift. Some have died inside the emergency room while waiting for

a bed. A refrigerated truck has been stationed outside to hold the bodies of the dead … "It's apocalyptic," said Dr. [Ashley] Bray, a general medical resident at the hospital.[18]

Given reports as graphic as this one and given the equally dire warnings from health experts across the country about what still lay ahead, Trump, normally resistant to reversing course, concluded he had no choice. In mid-March he reluctantly issued federal guidelines for a national shutdown – "15 Days to Slow the Spread." The guidelines included precluding people from going to work, closing schools, and recommending that everyone avoid groups of more than ten, as well as closing bars and restaurants and eliminating discretionary travel. Previously the president had said he wanted to relax these guidelines by April 12, which was Easter. However, on March 29 he again, reluctantly, retreated. He announced that Americans would have to continue to lockdown – perhaps even until June. At the same time, he started lashing out at the state governors, especially if they were Democrats, insisting that they were ingrates, that they were insufficiently apprecia-tive of the assistance he was providing and, further, that they were disrespectful. "When they disrespect me," he said, "they're disrespecting our government." For her part, the Democratic governor of the state of Michigan, Gretchen Whitmer, replied, "I don't have the energy to respond to every slight."[19]

By the end of March there were the first public reports that though the White House had acted as if the threat posed by the new coronavirus was unanticipated, beginning in January America's intelligence agencies had warned the president about a pathogen that could lead to a pandemic. It was reported that President Trump had been given this information in a timely fashion, but that he had continued effectively to ignore it. In the meantime, though the "system was blinking red," and though those close to the president "just couldn't get him to do anything about it," they continued to go along.[20] His enablers continued to do as he did, which was to remain for the time being effectively silent about the virus that potentially threatened the well-being of every American.

APRIL 2020

By April, this issue – the issue of who knew what when – was front and center. It was front and center because by then the implications of what had happened, and was continuing to happen, were clear. By then the number of Americans who had already been sickened because of the virus, and the number of Americans who had already been killed by it, had escalated. Additionally, by then Trump had signed into law a critical stimulus bill. More states had issued stay-at-home directives. And the United States had led the world in confirmed cases of COVID-19. The costs of American prevarication – during the first few months of 2020 especially – were starting to become clear. By March 1, the country already had thousands of infections. But because Americans had not been told what exactly was going on, they continued to live their lives as they normally did. As just one example, during the first few weeks of March they were still traveling around the country by the millions, some carrying the virus right along with them.

Again, how exactly the new coronavirus spread during the early months of 2020 will take years fully to understand. (Apparently as far back as November 2019, American intelligence officials had warned about a contagion sweeping through the region around Wuhan.[21]) By April, though, there was growing understanding that the degree to which the Trump administration had concealed early warning signs, and minimized the threat even after the threat became clear, were key to understanding why the pandemic was particularly pernicious in the United States. And it was far more pernicious than in other somewhat analogous countries such as, for example, its neighbor to the north, Canada.

To be sure, denial and delay are, in such circumstances, not unusual. Recall Pamuk writing that governments have often been "late to respond" to a pandemic. Moreover, President Donald Trump was by no means the only national leader to push the unpleasantness into the distance. There is ample evidence, for instance, that China's

President Xi Jinping postponed informing the public about a possible pandemic for several critical weeks if not months, during December and January. Furthermore, other governments around the world "dragged their feet for weeks and even months in addressing the virus."[22]

Still, there can be no gainsaying what during April – months before Bob Woodward provided further details – already was clear. Trump had been warned repeatedly about the new coronavirus – more than a dozen times – to no avail. "It snuck up on us," Trump said, disingenuously, in March. "The virus was a very unforeseen thing." No, it was not. According to the *Washington Post*, while the president was telling Americans not to worry, to stay calm, repeating over and over again that the virus would just "go away," the many different warnings given to him, directly and indirectly, had already "taken on the aspect of a dire drumbeat."[23]

On April 11, the *New York Times* published a detailed account of how President Trump effectively willed and wished away all the early cautions about the new coronavirus. According to the *Times*, Trump "repeatedly played down the seriousness of the virus," preferring instead to turn to other issues. He was "slow to absorb the scale of the risk and to act accordingly, focusing instead on controlling the message, protecting gains in the economy, and batting away warnings from senior officials."[24] Which raises this question: *What exactly did these "senior officials" do and not do when Trump failed to hear and/ or failed to respond to their cries of alarm?*

As April ground on, the damage done by the pandemic was worsening. By the end of the first week the coronavirus had sickened more than one million people in 171 countries across six continents. It had put nearly 10 million Americans out of work – the speed and scale of job losses without precedent. Britain's Prime Minister Boris Johnson was so seriously stricken with COVID-19 that he was moved into intensive care. In Russia, the number of people in Moscow who were hospitalized with the disease doubled in one week. Trump, in the meantime, was struggling, still laboring in vain to navigate his way through a labyrinth with which he was completely unfamiliar and for which he was totally unprepared.

He tried several different tactics. One was to pass the buck, this one a favorite, especially passing the buck to governors who were among his preferred targets. For instance, in April he pinned the blame for the shortage of ventilators on the states. "The states should have been building their stockpile," he charged. "We're a backup," he said, referring to the federal government, "We're not an ordering clerk." For their part the governors, especially of hard-hit states such as Michigan and Massachusetts, were furious at being forced to compete, even with each other, to buy critical supplies such as ventilators on the open market.[25]

Another tactic was to sound optimistic even when optimism seemed not only misguided but mistaken. Typically, this optimism was based on Trump's own ostensible accomplishments. On one such occasion in April he breezed through a list of statistics about medical equipment and supplies while maintaining they had been sent around the country well before they were needed. "Tremendous progress has been made in a very short period," he claimed.[26] Similarly, on another occasion he maintained that, "everything we did was right," going on to add that "governors should have had ventilators, they chose not to have them. We chose to get them ventilators. They got the ventilators."[27] Concomitantly he was of course furious when he was challenged. Particularly by reporters who in general he despised, especially if they were purveyors of what he deemed "fake news," his preferred term, as we have seen, for news from mainstream media such as the *New York Times*, the *Washington Post*, or CNN. "You're so disgraceful," he told a reporter from CBS. "You know you're a fake, you know that."[28]

A final tactic was Trump's all-time favorite: the transformation of facts into fabrications, the telling of lies as opposed to the truth. The extent of the president's dishonesty about the national emergency was breathtaking. "Overwhelming," the *Atlantic* called it in an article titled, "All the President's Lies About the Coronavirus." In April there was this infamous example: Trump claiming that he was just being "sarcastic" when he suggested to his medical experts they should look into the use of powerful light, and the injection of disinfectants, to treat COVID-19. (He repeated the claim that he was just being sarcastic during a debate with Joe Biden in September.) The truth was that neither his manner nor his tone had so much as hinted at sarcasm even for a nanosecond. He was obviously deadly serious when he turned to one of his experts, Dr. Deborah Birx, to ask her, "Is there a way we can do something like that, by injection inside or almost a cleaning? It would be interesting to check that."[29] But, did Dr. Birx say anything, however gently, to rectify the president's idiocy? She did not. She sat there, wordless, or maybe speechless, looking stunned, her head down, silent. The episode was one of the most humiliating of Trump's presidency. The humiliation was Trump's, obviously. But one could reasonably argue, and I do, that it extended as well to one of his enablers, Birx, who sat there mute while the president proposed a remedy that could be deadly.

In retrospect in any case, April came to be seen as pivotal to the pandemic. While there were many earlier missteps – such as the failure to create a vast testing and contact tracing network and, in New York especially, the reluctance promptly to close schools and businesses – over time late April came to be seen as a turning point. The president had turned over the management of the pandemic from the federal government to the states, and he was openly encouraging the states to open up. Said one Columbia University infectious disease expert in retrospect, late April "was the opportune moment that was lost."[30]

MAY 2020

By the beginning of May, the pandemic had killed some 200,000 people and sickened more than 2.8 million worldwide. It was known that the actual figures were significantly higher, but they remained difficult to pinpoint. In France, for example, it was discovered only in May that a patient who had been treated in December for pneumonia, in fact had what later was known as COVID-19. This meant that the new coronavirus was in Europe "nearly a month earlier than previously understood and days before Chinese authorities first reported the new illness" to the WHO.[31] Similarly in May, the CDC director, Dr. Robert Redfield, confirmed the coronavirus had begun quietly to spread in the United States as early as late January, a full month before community contagion was first detected.

Given that he was head of the CDC, Redfield was all along one of the administration's leading spokespersons on COVID-19. He was, for example, an original member of the White House Coronavirus Task Force, the one chaired since February by Vice President Pence. For a period of several weeks, from about mid-March to mid-April, task force press briefings were held almost daily. The briefings were usually presided over by the president and they were, for a month or so, the administration's main forum for communicating with the American people, specifically about COVID-19. According to the president, they were a resounding success, at least as measured by the metric that to him mattered most – ratings. Trump later claimed, "We had very successful briefings. I was doing them and we had a lot of people watching. Record numbers watching. In the history of cable television, there's never been anything like it."[32]

Why then did these briefings come largely, and quickly, to an end? The reasons are indicative of the administration's mishandling of the virus crisis and include these two: (1) the president's realization that his dominance over the proceedings was a political detriment, not a political benefit; and (2) the president's realization that his many missteps and mistakes, some of which were egregious, such as his reference to the ingestion of bleach, were not only politically costly but personally embarrassing. In other words, the president's political fortunes trumped other considerations.

The other problem was that though the task force was supposed to sell the president, it was regularly undercut by what was happening on the ground. Unforced errors especially abounded. For example, the president not only touted the drug hydroxychloroquine as a remedy for COVID-19, he also insisted that he personally was taking it – preventatively. This while the nation's most highly respected medical professionals, such as those associated with the American Medical Association and the National Institutes of Health, either warned against taking the drug or simply said that it was ineffective. Additionally, constantly, there were cases of demonstrable mismanagement – the initially chaotic manufacture and distribution of masks high on the list.

If pandemics had a symbol, this one, COVID-19, would be symbolized by a mask. Not only did masks evolve, devolve, into a sign of political preference and protest – about which more later – equally they were a sign of an administration caught behind the eight ball. An administration plagued by failures brought about by simple mismanagement and in fairness, also by its predecessors. A long piece in the *Wall Street Journal* pointed out that America's shortage of masks in spring 2020 was not only on account of mistakes made by the Trump administration, but on account of mistakes made long before. There was blame enough to go around. Hospitals had long since cut their inventories of supplies. Manufacturers had long since cut their emergency capacities. The federal government had for a long time focused more on possible terrorism than on a possible pandemic. And the Trump administration added to America's lack of readiness. It had "weakened the safety net as it rejiggered the Health and Human Services Department's main-emergency-preparedness agency, prioritized other threats over pandemics, cut out groups such as one that focused on protective gear, and removed a small planned budget to buy respirator masks for the national stockpile."[33]

The Trump administration made another serious mistake. Instead of putting in charge of pandemic-related supply chains someone with experience and expertise, it appointed someone with neither, Jared Kushner. Kushner was of course the president's son-in-law, who, notwithstanding his unsettling lack of credentials, had already been given too large a portfolio. In May it was learned that the bureaucratic chaos that resulted from putting Kushner in charge of procuring masks was not only a consequence of his own unpreparedness. It was also a consequence of the unpreparedness of those he had brought on board – and a result of the cronyism and favoritism that characterized the Trump administration more generally. To help him address the mask problem, Kushner brought in "roughly a dozen young volunteers" who had "little to no experience with government procurement procedures or medical equipment." And it was they "who were put in charge of sifting through leads," and instructed to "prioritize tips from political allies and associates of President Trump, tracked on a spreadsheet called 'V.I. P. Update.'"[34]

By May, the nation's chief executive had lost interest in the virus. Trump's concern was the economy, the reopening of which was now being prioritized above all else. It became Trump's focal point because he believed, not unreasonably, that his chances of winning reelection in November depended on a measurable, demonstrable, palpable economic recovery. So, he pressed to reopen America, specifically to reopen businesses and schools as rapidly and seamlessly as possible.

As before, there were tensions between the federal government and the state governments, especially if these were led by governors who were Democrats. There was another tension as well: between the detailed guidelines for reopening that had been provided by public health officials, and the vague outline that was provided by the president. Administration officials fell roughly into two camps: on the one side were those such as Pence's influential chief of staff, Marc Short; Treasury Secretary Steven Mnuchin; National Economic Council Director Larry Kudlow; and Kushner, all of whom shared the strong belief that "the economy had been shut down for long enough." And on the other side were mostly medical and scientific experts who provided the president with facts and figures that made clear that reopening the country too quickly was risky.[35]

As May wore on, it became apparent that the efforts to reopen the economy were failing on two counts: first, they were putting the health of Americans at greater risk; second, they were not restoring the economy to anything resembling what it was previous to the virus. The most persistent and pervasive of the problems was unemployment: the flood of layoffs did not stop or even slow. (Over a two-month period, April and May, unemployment claims tallied more than 36 million.) Georgia, under the leadership of a staunch Trump loyalist, Governor Brian Kemp, was an exemplar of the dilemma. Georgia's reopening did bring some people back to work. But the number of initial jobless claims continued to climb, which indicated obviously that the economy remained weak. Moreover, within weeks the number of COVID-19 cases had skyrocketed. By July Georgia had the eighth highest number of confirmed COVID-19 cases in the United States.

Trump meanwhile was being Trump. He was refusing to wear a mask. He was flouting the advice of his own medical and scientific experts. He was conjuring conspiracies. He was portraying himself as a warrior against an unseen enemy. And he was continuing to inflate his own performance into an unmitigated and even unparalleled success. In mid-May, when by every measure the United States was underperforming, he characterized his administration's (mis)management of COVID-19 in glowing terms. "I view it as a badge of honor. Really, it's a badge of honor."[36] However delusional the American president and however disastrous the American trajectory – a public health crisis and an economic crisis – his Republican allies, especially his allies in the Senate, continued to support him. As *Politico* noted in May, though by then the coronavirus had killed more than 70,000 Americans, and tanked the once-soaring US economy, nearly all GOP[37] senators running for reelection were aligning their fortunes with Trump's. Why? Because they decided there was "little utility in breaking with the president, particularly after seeing some fellow Republicans collapse at the ballot box with such a strategy."[38]

By October, the degree of Republican fealty was even more striking, if only on account of what had happened during the previous six months. The news website Axios developed a "Trump Loyalty Index" which showed that the president's grip on his party had, counterintuitively, hardened during the last two years of his presidency. Why? Because by then his dissenters had "largely piped down, been tossed out, or currently [faced] the threat of losing reelection."[39] It was just another in a long line of signs that, notwithstanding the pandemic and its disastrous consequences, Trump retained near total control over his base and, in consequence, near total control over his party. They, in turn, continued to enable him, no matter how high the costs of his manifest mismanagement.

JUNE 2020

The end of June marked the end of the first half year of the new coronavirus. During this six-month timeframe the United States was led by a president who was unqualified to lead in a time of great peril. I write "unqualified" not because of a preexisting political bias, but because of professional preference. I prefer anyone I hire for any task to have at least modest experience and expertise – a general rule to which leadership is no exception. But, of course, President Trump was unqualified to lead during this time of crisis not only because of his lack of credentials, but also because of his lack of character. His simple, seemingly congenital inability to tell the truth, which is more grievous a problem than an unwillingness to tell the truth, is evidence enough. By July, not only had the president made more than 20,000 "false or misleading claims," the pandemic had "spawned a whole new genre of Trump's falsehoods." In just a few months' time the president had made nearly 1,000 false claims – just about the new coronavirus.[40]

It is hard to know when or what exactly is a tipping point, and similarly difficult to identify a turning point. However, if America's early experience of COVID-19 did have a tipping point and a turning point these might be said to have occurred in the month of June. First, the coronavirus continued to spread and then spread some more. It spread to places, and spiked in places, that previously had seemed impervious at least to the worst of it, as in the Sun Belt, in states such as Arizona, Florida, and Texas. Second, instead of deescalating, the numbers continued to increase: the numbers of those infected and then sick, and the numbers of those sick and then dead. Third, despite items one and two, large numbers of Americans, foremost among them the president himself, continued to seem largely oblivious or, at least, largely unconcerned.

Notwithstanding the slew of measures indicating that things were getting worse rather than better, Trump continued to ignore what by then was the most basic, and the most obvious, of all protective imperatives: wearing a mask outside the home, especially in places that were enclosed. On June 20, the president held a political rally in Tulsa, Oklahoma that can best be described as both gratuitous and idiotic. The rally was held indoors, and social distancing was not only not encouraged, but actively discouraged. Moreover, the overwhelming majority of those present for the occasion were not wearing a mask – including the president himself. (Admittedly it is impossible to say for certain this was why, two weeks after the rally in Tulsa the number of COVID-19 cases in the city and its environs surged. Onetime Republican presidential candidate Herman Cain famously died not long after attending Trump's Tulsa event.)

Notwithstanding the objective evidence, assurances from the White House that all was well or, at least, that the nation was on an upward trajectory, kept coming. Trump said in early June, "We've made every decision correctly. We may have some embers or some ashes or we may have some flames coming, but we'll put them out. We'll stomp them out."[41] To keep the administration on message, it effectively silenced its own coronavirus task force – which, I would point out, *acquiesced to being silenced* – the daily briefings having by then ground to a halt. The impression was that the administration had effectively decided to live with the virus, and to encourage in so far as it could a return to normal life, to life as it was before the virus first struck and then spread.

But the plan failed. It failed because as medical experts kept warning, viruses like this one have a mind of their own. This one chose further to rub salt into the nation's already existing wound. On July 2, Robinson Meyer wrote in *The Atlantic* that the American pandemic was "careening out of control." The day before, 52,000 new cases of COVID-19 had been reported, setting a new daily record. Nor was the outbreak any longer limited to a handful of states and cities. It was everywhere across America, with many places seeing caseloads spike, again, especially but not exclusively in the Sun Belt. California had gone from being a state with one of the best track records to one of the worst, and Ohio, which had also done well, was worrisome, with a two-week increase both in the numbers of cases and in hospitalizations.[42]

In short, what had seemed in April to be the worst of it, was not. Despite the (brief) lockdown of much of the nation's economy, the near record high levels of unemployment, the shift to online schooling and all that working from home, despite, that is, all the sacrifices that had been and in many cases were still being made, with some notable exceptions (almost all in states in the northeast – most of which had Democratic governors – where the rates of death and disease had started to go down), the progress they yielded was short lived. On June 26, Americans suffered 46,000 new infections – nearly 10,000 more than on the worst day in April.

Commentator David Frum argued that the first coronavirus spike, in April, was because of what Trump did not do. He further argued that the second spike, the one in June, was because of what Trump did do. "This is Trump's plague now," Frum wrote.[43] But if the pandemic belonged by then to Trump, it also belonged to every one of his enablers. These included among others studiously silent Republican senators, reliably obsequious Republican governors, right-wing media in Trump's hip pocket and, of course, Trump's team. Team members such as Mike Pence and Deborah Birx, Jared Kushner and Robert Redfield, all of whom, among others, were deeply involved in Trump's management/mismanagement of the pandemic. Every step of the way it was they who allowed or even encouraged the nation's chief executive to do and say what he did and said – and not to do and not to say what he did not. Trump could not have fabricated and prevaricated as he did without them. Trump could not have mismanaged and misled as he did without them. He was their unarguable leader, they his unarguable enablers.

By Election Day their handiwork was clear. The number of COVID-19 cases was climbing in virtually every state, and the death toll was continuing to rise. By the time night fell on one day numbers from the previous day were obsolete. Former commissioner of the Food and Drug Administration, Dr. Scott Gottlieb, whose track record on the pandemic was strong, was predicting that the nation was "at the beginning of what looks like an exponential growth in a lot of states. This is very worrisome as we head into winter."[44]

7   Science of the Pandemic

Even now science is open to question, a grab bag of what people believe and what not. Most people, for example, believe that the earth is round, but many people do not believe that it is being despoiled by too much carbon in the air. Similarly, while most people believe that COVID-19 is caused by a virus, many people do not believe that this virus behaves like every other virus – that it is contagious. And that, to avoid widespread contagion, before a vaccine becomes commonplace, when outside the home, certain behaviors should be adopted such as mask-wearing and social distancing.

The Age of the Enlightenment formed the ideological foundation on which Western democracies were built. The ideas and ideals that supported it were those that every American child is taught, among them liberty and democracy, individualism, and constitutionalism. But what is not so much taught is that integral to the Enlightenment, as important as its political ideals and ideas, were its scientific ideals and ideas. During the Scientific Revolution starting in the sixteenth century and continuing through the seventeenth- and eighteenth-century Enlightenment, there were developments in mathematics and physics, anatomy, chemistry, and astronomy, all of which were separate and distinct from the religious beliefs that had up to then dominated Western thought. Advances in the sciences were grounded in objective observation, not in subjective preconception; in reason, not in conviction.

Among America's Founders were several who perceived themselves, and were perceived by others, as men of science as well as of politics. Paramount among them was that polymath, Benjamin

Franklin. Franklin was exceptional in that in addition to his excellence as a statesman, he was a prodigious inventor and explorer, especially but by no means exclusively in electricity. Though his famous kite experiment did not take place as it is often depicted – to wit that famous painting by Benjamin West showing Franklin flying a kite with a dangling key into a sky dark with clouds, assisted by heavenly angels (circa 1816) – even early in American history he was a hero, admired as much for being a scientist as a statesman.[1]

Similarly, Thomas Jefferson, though less brilliant in his scientific pursuits, was nevertheless perceived "a statesman of science." Jefferson was passionate about, for example, archeology and agriculture, and he was active in promoting science on a national scale. For over two decades, including when he was president of the United States, he was president of the American Philosophical Society, at the time preeminent among scientific foundations. Further, he popularized the notion that scientific achievements were essential to American success. Among his enduring accomplishments is the founding of the University of Virginia (UVA). UVA was intended as a liberal, secular alternative to his own alma mater, the College of William and Mary. Unlike the latter, UVA was to be independent of religion, literally centered around a library not a church. "Nature," Jefferson said, "intended for me the tranquil pursuits of science, by rendering them my supreme delight."[2]

Notwithstanding the preeminence of science in the early days of the Republic, the United States has been riven by a tension between those whose policy preferences are driven by science, and those whose policy preferences are driven by something different, such as religion, or money, or ideology. Think, for example, of the divide between evolutionists and creationists. Or the divide between those who believe that the climate is changing in large part because of what humans are doing, and those who do not. Or the divide between those who during the first half year of the pandemic thought public policy should be driven by the science of the virus, and those who thought it should be driven by the dictates of the economy. In spring

2020, when the important issue of when to reopen schools, businesses, and houses of worship dominated the national discourse, those whose preferences were dictated by science almost always opted for the slower the better, while those whose interests were dictated by the economy almost always preferred the faster the better option. President Trump, as we know, was far more fixated on jump starting the economy than he was on staving off the virus.

For example, he put science in second place in May 2020, when the CDC issued school guidelines that were cautious and considered, intended first and foremost to protect the health of students, teachers, administrators, and staff. Two months later, in July 2020, in response to pressure from the president, the guidelines were changed, if not exactly reversed then aggressively modified. Trump had complained that the CDC's previous recommendations were too "tough and expensive," that they would hobble the economy. So, the CDC was pressured by the White House to change its language, which it did. The title of the revised guidelines said it all: "The Importance of Reopening America's Schools this Fall." The materials themselves said the same: though the science on this was far from settled, there were assurances that children were at low risk not only for contracting the virus, but for transmitting it.

How did it happen that the CDC, an agency previously admired worldwide for its scientific excellence and integrity, succumbed to political pressure? According to the *New York Times*, the July statement was the product of a working group that excluded CDC experts from its deliberations. The group did, however, collaborate with CDC director, Dr. Robert Redfield.[3] Which is to say that Redfield was caught between science and politics, between the virus and the president. Redfield did nevertheless make a choice. He chose to stay the course. To remain in the administration, and to remain largely compliant to the point of being mute, even though Trump was regularly undercutting the science that Redfield, as a physician and expert on infectious disease, was ostensibly in his post to defend.

SCIENCE AND SCIENTISTS

As we have seen, other countries were far better equipped than the United States to cope with the new coronavirus. Some, such as Germany, had a healthcare system that was far superior. Others, such as Taiwan, had recent experiences with other viruses, such as SARS, that prepared them for this one. And still others, such as New Zealand, were endowed with an excellent leader, and excellent followers, who collectively were quick to understand that COVID-19 required a swift, safe, and efficacious response organized at the national level. Moreover, some countries were exceptionally well endowed in this regard. Germany, for instance, not only had a first-rate healthcare system but, additionally, a smart and seasoned leader, Chancellor Angela Merkel, who, among her virtues, had an advanced education in the sciences.

The United States, in contrast, had no such luck. For a country supposedly highly developed it did not have a strong healthcare system. Further, since the so-called Spanish Flu pandemic of a hundred years earlier it had had no experience with an extremely contagious and potentially deadly virus. Finally, the country did not have a national leader known for his competence. In sum, for a country that had long been considered a great power, the United States was remarkably ill-prepared and ill-equipped to meet the various challenges of the new coronavirus.

The lack of effective signaling that a virus was threatening was the fault not only of America's policymakers, specifically those in the federal government, but also of America's scientists, specifically those inside the government, who during the first few months of 2020 did not exactly distinguish themselves. Some recognized the threat of the new coronavirus early on, but chose not to warn about the impending danger, at least not long and loud. (To this general rule were a very few exceptions, about whom more later.) Others seemed not fully to grasp the level of the threat until late in the game.

The United States was not, however, alone. Other people in other places were equally rudderless and similarly slow on the uptake. In mid-January 2020, the WHO issued a statement saying that China might have seen human to human transmission of a new coronavirus, and that this might lead to a wider outbreak. The WHO did, in other words, say something, but what it said and how it said it were not exactly calculated to get the world to take notice. To the contrary, the acting head of the WHO's emerging diseases unit said that there was no evidence so far of sustained human contagion, nor was there yet a "clear, clinical picture."[4]

Two weeks later a doctor in Germany had a patient who tested positive for a new coronavirus. How was this possible, the doctor wondered, as the patient could only have been infected by one person, by a visitor from China. This visitor had appeared, however, to be perfectly healthy. It made no sense because at the time most experts believed that only people with symptoms could spread the coronavirus – and that those who were asymptomatic could not. This single difference between the new coronavirus and other viruses that preceded it explains in part why so many in the scientific community were slow to recognize the threat. By erroneously assuming that what came to be known as COVID-19 could not be transmitted by people who were without symptoms, they failed to recognize that in order to slow the spread of the disease, unusually aggressive measures would be required. So, notwithstanding a few feeble early warnings, weeks went by during which politicians, public health officials, and academics downplayed the threat or ignored it altogether. Again, Americans were not the only ones: in Europe, initially, it was the same. "The disease was spreading unnoticed in French churches, Italian soccer stadiums and Austrian ski bars." The *Diamond Princess*, a large cruise ship, was another early though already "deadly harbinger of symptomless spreading."[5]

The following lines, from a piece in the *New York Times*, describe how what a British doctor called the "biggest science policy failure in a generation" came to pass.[6]

Interviews with doctors and public health officials in more than a dozen countries show that for two critical months ... Western health officials and political leaders played down or denied the risk of symptomless spreading. Leading health agencies ... provided contradictory and sometimes misleading advice. A crucial public health discussion devolved into a semantic debate over what to call people without clear symptoms. [The two-month delay that resulted] was the product of faulty assumptions, academic rivalries and, perhaps most important, a reluctance to accept that containing the virus would take drastic measures. The resistance to emerging evidence was one part of the world's sluggish response to the virus.[7]

The name of the British doctor was Richard Horton, editor of the prestigious medical journal *The Lancet*. As the quote suggests, Horton was one of the fiercest critics of his own government's slow response to the virus crisis. His focus was less on the ambiguity and insufficiency of the early information, than on "the resistance to the emerging evidence." He pointed out that *The Lancet* had published a paper in late January that made clear there was a new, highly contagious virus that potentially was dangerous. "Why wasn't that paper read?" Horton asked, why wasn't it read by all those committees and all those offices and all those organizations that should have been paying close attention? Horton strongly believed that had people in positions of medical and political authority paid close attention, "lives could have been saved."

When the history of this period is written – specifically the period January through June 2020 – there will be, as indicated, blame enough to go around. America's scientific community was not notably fast to grasp the nature of the new coronavirus; nor did it quickly and efficiently convey to the community at large its implications. Similarly, America's elected officials were slow to respond and to warn their constituents. Even those who came in time to be considered among the most responsive and responsible, initially were sluggish. New York's Governor Andrew Cuomo admitted in April,

"We underestimated this virus … It's more dangerous than we expected."[8]

The history of mask-wearing during the first half of 2020 is as good a case in point as any of how at the beginning of the pandemic, scientists, not just politicians, confused or even misled the American public. In mid-February, the head of the National Institute for Allergy and Infectious Diseases, an expert who came to be widely admired, Dr. Anthony Fauci, said that people now asked him all the time, "'Should I start wearing a mask?'" To which he replied, "Now, in the United States, there is absolutely no reason whatsoever to wear a mask."[9] At nearly the same moment, the same message came from another American top health official, the Surgeon General, Dr. Jerome Adams. On February 29 Adams tweeted: "Seriously people – STOP BUYING MASKS! They are NOT effective in preventing [the] general public from catching #Coronavirus."[10] Adams went on to add that masks should be reserved for healthcare providers – which later was the excuse given by just about everyone, including Fauci, for being slow to say that everyone should wear a mask, or some other sort of face covering when outside the home and unable adequately to socially distance.[11]

It soon became clear that wearing even a makeshift mask would all along have been better than wearing no mask at all. Which is to say that any way you cut it the public was misled, even by the experts. While by April the CDC was recommending wearing a mask – any mask, even "cloth face coverings fashioned from household items or made at home from common materials" – it still said that mask-wearing was "voluntary."[12] Did experts at the CDC really believe that it should be voluntary – or were they just trying to please the president? A rhetorical question – about which I will have more to say in Chapter 12.

Dr. Steven Corwin, CEO of New York Presbyterian Hospital, which in spring 2020 was at the center of America's coronavirus crisis, was forthcoming about the failure of America's healthcare system properly to prepare. The CDC, he said, had provided testing that was "faulty." The assumptions around "pandemic preparation" had been "flawed," he continued. And the supposition that America's stockpile of personal protective equipment was enough to "weather the first surge of the pandemic" turned out "completely false." According to Corwin, "Our preparation around the pandemic was insufficient, and the state and the national level was also insufficient."[13] America's miserable record on testing and tracing further confirmed Corwin's conclusions.

TRUMP AND THE SCIENTIFIC COMMUNITY

First candidate Trump and then President Trump was famous for boasting that he knew more about whatever there was to know than anyone else. For example, "I understand politicians better than anybody." And, "I know more about renewables than any human being on earth." And, "I think nobody knows more about taxes than I do, maybe in the history of the world." And, "I know more about ISIS than the generals do."[14] No surprise, then, that when the new coronavirus wormed its way into the United States, Trump thought himself expert on it as he did on everything else. "I like this stuff. I really get it," he told reporters in March, during a tour of CDC headquarters in Atlanta. "People are really surprised I understand this stuff," he went on. "Every one of these doctors said, 'How do you know so much about this?' Maybe I have a natural ability."[15]

It is not necessary to be a licensed psychologist to suggest that Trump's tireless need to trumpet his excellence and expertise, and further to declare that these surpass everyone else's, is born out of deep insecurity. One need not necessarily to be a soothsayer to have foreseen that when the new coronavirus caused a crisis, Trump would feel an overweening need to pronounce himself expert on everything related to it and, simultaneously, to diminish those who legitimately were. Not just to diminish them, but to take them on, to wrestle them to the ground, to show them and everyone else who was, and would remain king of the mountain. So it was that notwithstanding this was a pandemic, a matter of life and death, the president's need to prevail persisted. It was bottomless.

Donald Trump had a contentious relationship with the scientific community since the beginning of his administration. The problem was, in other words, a larger one; it was not just about COVID-19. To the contrary. Trump's antipathy to experts in the sciences who insisted on their independence and objectivity, especially when they ran counter to whatever his agenda, was evident from day one. Effectively immediately the Trump administration began implementing one of its most far-reaching policies: the "systematic downplaying or ignoring of science in order to weaken environmental health and climate change regulations." In the process it "marginalized key scientists, disbanded expert advisory boards, and suppressed or altered findings that made clear the dangers of pollution and global warming."[16] And, toward the end of the president's tenure he was still at it. The Trump administration chose in fall 2020 to remove the chief scientist at the National Oceanic and Atmospheric Administration, to install instead new political staff who had a track record of questioning "accepted facts about climate change," and who were willing to tolerate stricter controls on what the agency could and could not communicate.[17]

The president's approach to and management of the pandemic was in keeping with this previously existing pattern. Trump established the White House Coronavirus Task Force on January 29, 2020. Officially it was charged with monitoring and mitigating the disease that by February had been named COVID-19. The task force was also responsible, supposedly, for keeping the American people informed about what in March was declared a pandemic. But, though a few task force members, notably Drs. Anthony Fauci and Deborah Birx, became familiar faces, most others remained for the duration nearly entirely in the background. Similarly, while Vice President Mike Pence was appointed chair of the task force in February, whenever the president was present, it was he, Trump, who totally dominated the discourse.

It soon became apparent that the real purpose of the task force was not to convey objective information or to respond clearly, completely, and expertly to questions. It was to propagandize – to portray the president as a supremely competent leader. It did not take long, therefore, for the task force to be seen as farcical rather than as serious. Task force briefings especially became objects of derision and ridicule. Trump used the occasions to sideline his own experts, to make outrageous and sometimes dangerous claims about cures, to undercut key task force recommendations, and to push his own personal and political agendas. Come May, the heyday of the task force had come and gone. Its briefings were charged with having sown chaos not comfort, and with underplaying as well as understating the "human cost" of the virus crisis.[18] In the meantime, task force members, especially the physicians and scientists, were marginalized, victims of Trump's apparently congenital inability to share the spotlight. *The experts were, in other words, closer to being servile followers than independent leaders. Closer to being enablers than free agents.*

Around that time, the administration's attacks on the scientific community were becoming overtly political and frequently personal. By May the hard right was fired up, transforming Trump's personal antipathy to the experts into a larger war, a culture war. Ostensibly this was a war about a virus. But beneath the surface was a struggle for control over the American narrative. Yuval Levin wrote in the *Wall Street Journal* that so far as Trump's supporters were concerned, there was no virtue in having "specialized knowledge" contribute to public policy. The experts were just muddying the waters, deliberately misleading "an angry public." Fauci was, not incidentally, a favorite target, accused of hoarding information and being a "grandstander," a "showman."[19]

As spring 2020 turned into summer, the divide between the White House and the experts widened, and the tone of their exchanges hardened. President Trump continued to undermine, and to sideline, the scientists, and his enablers did the same. For example, Trump's trade advisor Peter Navarro, who knew better, penned an opinion piece in July in which he took on Fauci – no holds barred. Navarro charged that since the inception of the pandemic Fauci had been "wrong about everything I have interacted with him on."[20] Similarly, Trump's deputy chief of staff, Dan Scavino, shared a cartoon on social media that mocked Fauci as "Dr. Faucet," showing him drowning Uncle Sam with "extra cold" water. The White House meanwhile sent multiple news outlets a document that smacked of nothing so much as opposition research. "It carried a list of statements Fauci had made about COVID-19, purporting to show that he had contradicted himself about the outbreak and that he 'had been wrong on things.'"[21]

Finally, because the costs of the pandemic were continuing dangerously to escalate, experts with ties to the administration started, ever so slowly and carefully, to speak up and speak out. Instead of remaining completely or at least largely silent, gradually, cautiously, they made their voices heard. Fauci led the pack, not once taking on President Trump directly, but nevertheless addressing the attacks against him personally, and the administration's posturing more generally. The attacks against him, he said, were "bizarre," "nonsense," "completely wrong."[22] About the administration's posturing he said, "It's not helpful if people get signals about not wearing masks when we are trying to get people to universally wear masks." As to the president's promotion of hydroxychloroquine, in one interview Fauci at first demurred, saying it would not be "productive or helpful for me to be making [judgments] on right and wrong." But then, he went on effectively to reverse himself, to say without equivocation, "We know that every single good study ... has shown that hydroxychloroquine is not effective in the treatment of Covid-19."[23]

Fauci was in good company. As the pandemic droned on, and as the situation continued further to deteriorate, notably in the United States, more scientific and medical experts spoke out, including more with ties either to the Trump administration or to previous administrations. Four former directors of the CDC wrote an opinion piece for the *Washington Post* in which they charged that no president had ever politicized the agency as had Donald Trump. One of the authors, Thomas Frieden, took the lead in taking on the administration. "It seems that some are more intent on fighting imagined enemies," he said at one point, "than the real enemy here, which is the virus." He continued, "The virus doesn't read talking points. The virus doesn't watch news shows. The virus just waits for us to make mistakes. And when we make mistakes, as Texas and Florida and South Carolina and Arizona did, the virus wins. When we ignore science, the virus wins."[24]

TRUMP LOSES – AS DOES EVERYONE ELSE

One might reasonably ask why experts such as Drs. Fauci, Birx, and Redfield – and for that matter the Surgeon General, Dr. Jerome Adams, and the head of the Food and Drug Administration, Dr. Stephen Hahn – did not loudly and clearly speak up and speak out, did not immediately or at least early on speak truth to power when they believed that people in power were doing something seriously, even egregiously, wrong. Such as refusing to wear a mask and to socially distance. Such as refusing vigorously (not just feebly) to invoke the Defense Production Act to compel businesses to manufacture much needed equipment and supplies. Such as pushing responsibility for the health crisis from the federal government to the 50 states. For one of the most significant of the administration's many managerial mistakes was in fact creating a situation in which 50 different states were effectively compelled to cope with the virus in 50 different ways – instead of in one single way that was initiated, organized, and implemented by the federal government. This war against the virus was, after all, similar to every other war that the United States had fought: it demanded strategies and tactics that were coherent and coordinated, as opposed to their polar opposite, incoherent and uncoordinated. The government's prolonged failure to provide for efficient and effective testing and tracing was a withering example of the costs of the unnecessary confusion, and the equally unnecessary jockeying for position among 50 different competitors.

So then, why so quiet? Why did medical professionals not speak out and speak up virtually throughout? Chalk it up first to fear. Even they, with all their medical credentials, were scared. That even though they were widely known, well positioned, and highly respected, they would put themselves at risk if they contradicted the president, however obliquely. Just as fear explains in part why so many politicians followed President Trump so abjectly for so long, fear explains in part why so many scientists followed President Trump in the same way. They were afraid that if they contradicted him, not to speak of crossed or countermanded him, he would fire them. Or demote them. Or humiliate them. Or exile them. If they were afraid for their jobs – it is hard to think of anything else they were afraid of – they had good reason. For two prominent medical professionals, both administration experts in infectious diseases, met just this fate. The first was the previously mentioned Dr. Nancy Messonnier. The second was Dr. Rick Bright.

Think of Messonnier as a canary in a coal mine. As we saw, in February, well before most Americans were paying much if any attention, in her role as director of the CDC's National Center for Immunization and Respiratory Diseases, she warned, publicly, of what likely lay ahead: "We expect we will see community spread [of the new coronavirus] in this country," said Messonnier in the last week of February. "It's not so much a question of if this will happen anymore, but rather more a question of exactly when this will happen and how many people in this country will have severe illness." She continued by asking the American people to "work with" the CDC "to prepare in the expectation that this could be bad."[25] However virtuous her openness and frankness, and however accurate and important the caution she conveyed, she was judged by Trump to be a transgressor, if not a traitor. He was infuriated by what she did and said – especially as it connected to a significant dip in the stock market – and so he sought promptly to punish her. According to the *Wall Street Journal*, Messonnier got "immediate blowback." She was removed from her post and just missed being fired from her job. In marginalizing Messonnier-the-messenger early in the year, the White House sent an unambiguous signal to every scientist who worked for the federal government: "There would be a price for speaking out and speaking up."[26]

Dr. Bright was less lucky. (Though he got luckier later. Just days after the November election, president-elect Joe Biden pointedly selected him to be a member of his coronavirus task force.) Bright was dismissed from his post as director of the Biomedical Advanced Research and Development Authority, the agency that worked on coronavirus treatments. He claimed it was because he urged caution in using hydroxychloroquine, the controversial drug that Trump had tirelessly trumpeted as a treatment for COVID-19. Bright's case became big news in May 2020, when it became known that he had filed a whistleblower complaint claiming that he was forced out of his job after resisting pressure to fund "potentially dangerous drugs promoted by those with political connections and by the administration itself." Bright's charges were serious because they were not only about corruption and cronyism, and about retaliation and revenge, but also about an administration that was entirely too cavalier about COVID-19. This even as the disease was threatening the entire country and threatening to overwhelm the American healthcare system. Bright additionally provided evidence that he had sounded the alarm as early as January. As reported by the *New York Times*: "On January 23 [Bright] met with [his superiors] to press for 'urgent access to funding ... that would be necessary to develop treatments [for the new coronavirus].'" His superiors, however, turned him down. Instead they insisted that "the United States would be able to contain the virus" through travel bans. According to Bright's complaint, in partial consequence of his insistence that attention must be paid, he was "cut out of all future department meetings" relating to COVID-19.[27]

Dr. Bright's whistleblower complaint uncovered at least four inconvenient truths. The first is that there were early warnings, deep inside the government, of an impending health disaster. In May, Bright testified before the House of Representatives that in late January he had been told by an American mask manufacturer, "We're in deep shit. The world is. And we need to act." However, when Bright "pushed forward to the highest levels" of the Department of Health and Human Services to alert them to the issue, he received no response. As he described it, from that point on he knew for certain that, "we were going to have a crisis."[28]

The second inconvenient truth is that during the first six months of 2020 nearly every member of Trump's team, including men and women of science and medicine, were intent on shielding the president and, thereby, themselves. It is fair to say they knew for certain that if they did not protect Trump from political fallout – from damage to his reputation and, or, to the economy – they would put themselves at professional risk. It is also fair to say that some at least concluded that no matter their opinion of the president, they could better serve the country from within the administration than from without. Still, we should be clear-eyed about the path they took. *During the first half year of the coronavirus crisis, doctors and scientists who went along with President Trump, without contradicting him, publicly if necessary, had a choice. The choice they made was to follow a bad leader, to enable a bad leader.*

The third inconvenient truth is that at the expense of the American people there was money to be made, big money. Bright claimed that he was finally fired for refusing to funnel contracts worth millions of dollars to a company controlled by a friend of Jared Kushner. Finally, the fourth inconvenient truth: that the professional harm inflicted on Drs. Messonnier and Bright was an unmissable and unmistakable warning. A warning that confirmed the fears of every expert who was a member of Trump's team. Edward Luce, writing in mid-May for the *Financial Times*, put it perfectly, "Scientists are terrified of saying anything that contradicts Trump."[29] Which raises the question: What, exactly, were they "terrified" of? *If they did speak out, contradict the president, or detract from the president, what was the worst that could happen?*

It turned out that Trump lost every which way. Politically, professionally, personally. Most importantly, his antipathy to the truth, to facts, to science, to medicine, lost him the trust of the American people. By early July, fully 67 percent of Americans disapproved of the way he led during the first six months of the virus crisis. This similarly suggests that science lost, and scientists, especially those on Trump's team who allowed themselves to be bullied by the president. Finally, the American people lost. Whatever constituted America's health policy between January 1 and June 30, 2020, it was a failure. It was recognized as a failure not only at home, but abroad. When they were asked in June how their views of the United States had changed during the pandemic, 71 percent of Danes said it had "worsened." So did 70 percent of Portuguese, and 65 percent of Germans.[30] No wonder. By then the costs of America's healthcare crisis, and America's financial crisis, which was the result, were already dramatically in evidence. On June 28, 2020 there were 9.95 million confirmed cases of COVID-19 worldwide; 2.51 million of these, or almost 25 percent, were in the United States, which constitutes only about 4 percent of the world's population.[31] Additionally, during the second quarter of 2020 America's GDP had dropped a record 35.2 percent. In summary of this aspect of the disaster: "No event in American history [had] wrecked the U.S. economy faster than the pandemic-driven recession."[32]

By August 1, the situation had deteriorated still further. Dr. Deborah Birx was herself forced to admit that COVID-19 was now "extraordinarily widespread." Though she insisted that the situation in August was "different from March and April," at a fundamental level it was not.[33] Earlier was a pandemic and later was a pandemic. But, in large part on account of enablers like Birx, in August it was worse.

THE ENLIGHTENMENT IN ITS ELEMENT

If in twenty-first-century America the political and scientific ideas and ideals of the Enlightenment have a last bastion, it can reasonably be claimed institutions of higher education. America's colleges and universities are more dedicated now than before to having students study science, technology, engineering, and mathematics. And though in recent decades the liberal arts have been under siege, charged with being no longer so necessary in the twenty-first century, they remain nevertheless alive and, in many colleges around the country, well. How then did the nation's leading institutions of higher education address the coronavirus crisis? Specifically, how did they decide whether to stay open or to close, and how much did they draw on science, and to a lesser extent on ethics, in making what in late winter 2020 was an agonizingly difficult decision?

True to the Enlightenment spirit, most American institutions of higher education pride themselves on the rigor of their intellect and the independence of their thinking. During a pandemic they may be presumed further to pride themselves on making decisions in accordance not with the vicissitudes of politics, or even of economics, but with the verities of science. One could reasonably argue, then, that for those who value fact over fiction, objectivity over subjectivity, evidence over bias, institutions of higher education should have provided a model for how to proceed during a pandemic. Harvard University provides one such model.[34] This is not to imply that Harvard can or should be a template for other colleges and universities. Each in numberless ways is different. However, in this instance Harvard's decision-making process is not just illustrative but instructive.

In an interview with *Harvard Magazine*, University president, Lawrence Bacow, reflected on how the school decided during the first quarter of 2020 "both to disperse the students from campus and to separate professors . . . from essentially everything they need to pursue research." Not surprisingly, unlike the president of the United States the president of Harvard turned to experts for guidance, literally for leadership, on what to do. "The decisions were absolutely informed by the University's scholarly expertise," recalled Bacow. He set up a group to monitor the situation. It "drew upon University specialists in infectious diseases, epidemiology, virology and public health, giving Harvard leaders early insight into the developing pandemic." The group also included University provost Alan Garber, a physician who had studied and written about epidemics, and executive vice president

Katie Lapp, who had management experience in public safety. So, as Bacow put it, there was a lot of "subject-matter expertise on staff." Additionally, his decisions were driven by "emerging data from Massachusetts, an early hot spot, where reported cases of coronavirus infections had proliferated, from a low base, at an exponential rate." Finally, Bacow's announcement on March 10 that Harvard would be closed to residential learning was determined by exploration of implementation. Specifically, before "pivoting to remote teaching and learning, the University had to know whether it was possible." Again, Harvard's president pointed to "a lot of expertise" he leaned on, in this case experts in information technologies and online learning, who confirmed the University had "sufficient Zoom capacity, infrastructure, and faculty and staff training in place" for remote learning to begin as soon as spring recess was over.[35]

Harvard's decision-making process seems from a distance to have been careful and considered. Large amounts of information were obtained. Experts of different sorts were asked throughout to weigh in. Alternatives were considered. Costs and benefits were calculated. And questions about implementation were raised and debated. Obviously, most institutions of higher education cannot approximate Harvard's enormous resources, human, fiscal, and other. There were countless school systems around the country that in winter 2020 were obliged to make essentially the same decision – to remain open or to close – without anything approximating the expertise on which Harvard was able to draw.

Recall that during the first three months of 2020 making decisions about schooling at any level was especially difficult because the coronavirus was new. In the second week of March, Lowell Elementary School in Tacoma, Washington closed after someone at the school tested presumptive positive for the novel coronavirus. By then hundreds of schools across the country had already been shuttered, affecting some 850,000 students from kindergarten through twelfth grade. It was only the beginning of what would become a long and excruciatingly exacting balancing act pertaining to students of every age at every level: how to choose between allowing them to learn on site (and to socialize) on the one hand, and keeping them, their teachers, administrators, and staff safe from the virus on the other.[36]

To exacerbate the situation, over time passions on every side intensified. By summer 2020 it seemed everyone was weighing in. Teachers' unions, for example, were expressing alarm at the idea that teachers and students might be pressed to return to the classroom before it was safe. President Trump, in contrast, had no such qualms, no such concerns. All along he had wanted everything to remain open – a general rule to which schools were never an exception. From spring into summer, notwithstanding what was happening, he sang the same song. "We want to reopen the schools. Everybody wants it. The moms want it, the dads want it, the kids want it. It's time to do it ... We want to get them open quickly, beautifully, in the fall."[37]

Ironically, the school attended by Donald and Melania Trump's son, Barron, announced in summer 2020 that it would not reopen in the fall as originally scheduled. On what grounds did officials at St. Andrew's Episcopal School in Potomac, Maryland make their decision? The determination was made by a local health officer, Dr. Travis Gayles, who reported that his decision to keep all schools in Montgomery County closed until at least October was based on "science and data."[38] RIP Benjamin Franklin.

8   Politics of the Pandemic

THE PANDEMIC POLITICIZED – AT HOME

There have been plagues before. And there have been politics before. And there have been plagues and politics in which the one had an impact on the other. But in the United States hardly if ever has there been a plague so affected by politics or a politics so affected by a plague.[1] In this sense the pandemic that was declared in 2020 – in which millions of Americans became sick, hundreds of thousands died, and countless numbers including, disproportionately, again, African Americans and people of color, were devastated by an economy that tanked – was singular. Moreover, hardly ever in America had there been a virus that did this: set people against each other because of what they believed about the disease, COVID-19, and how they behaved as a result.

The new coronavirus entered the United States at a time when the country was already riven by division. It was divided by so many factors – income, race, gender, geography, demography, ideology, and party – and fundamentally divided by a president, Donald Trump, who habitually tried to sunder the American people rather than to bring them together. The virus, therefore, fell upon fertile soil – a context rife with conflict. In this sense the pandemic was familiar – it too was a divider. During the first half of 2020 the new coronavirus divided the American people into roughly two camps: those who were followers of President Trump who continued throughout the year to go where he led, and those who were not. On one side of the divide, then, were Trump and his followers, including enablers. They were his base, his party, his administration, his inner circle, and his team. And, on the other side of the divide was essentially everyone else.[2] The pandemic particularly was not an issue on which Americans tended to be mealy-mouthed. Either they were strongly pro-Trump, or strongly anti.

The virus was especially divisive when it came to science. On one side were those whose faith was in science, who believed that the virus would be with us until we had a vaccine and that, until then, precautions were in order. On the other side were those like President Trump, whose faith was in faith. Those who seemed to believe as Trump did, that somehow, as if by magic, the virus was a problem that would "just disappear." That would just "go away" – even without a vaccine and that, until then, it was perfectly fine to live life as usual. By mid-July, the president had 22 times reiterated, without any evidence whatsoever, that the virus would vanish, even with no medical intervention.[3] Need I add that Trump's was a view, a belief really, that had virtually no support in the scientific community? As it pertained to the pandemic his chronic anti-science bias was not just embarrassing, it was devastating.

COVID-19 was politicized from the start. By politicized I mean the virus was never confined to science, a realm in which objectivity prevails and facts always are the determinants. Rather the virus was always, also, in the realm of politics, in which subjectivity prevails and facts sometimes are the determinants. In politics sometimes the determinants are fictions or fantasies, conspiracies, opinions, or biases, or beliefs, proclivities, preferences, or ideologies – or loyalties.

President Trump weighed in on the virus almost immediately. In January 2020, he maintained, fallaciously, that it was "totally under control" and he insisted that he was unconcerned about the possibility of a pandemic. To the contrary. "It's going to be just fine," he said.[4] His groundless, disingenuous optimism had consequences. By participating in his charade from the outset, just as the new coronavirus was establishing an American beachhead, members of Trump's team became his enablers. I refer here especially to those who worked with Trump on the pandemic on a day-to-day basis; who knew that he regularly lied and extravagantly exaggerated; who knew that he had a habit of painting the rosiest of all possible pictures; who knew that his fount of knowledge on nearly everything pertaining to the pandemic was minimal; who knew that he was antipathetic to science generally; and who knew that the threat of a COVID-19, of widespread contagion, was real. These included in addition to members of Trump's team, some prominent Republicans; some members of the administration; and every member of his inner circle.

The degree to which the American people continued to adhere to and act in accordance with their preexisting preferences even as the virus spread, was palpable. While the number of US coronavirus cases was still low, Republicans across the board were satisfied just to follow the president's lead. And, even as evidence was beginning to accumulate that the virus was spreading, Trump's base remained relatively unalarmed. In a national poll taken in March, it was clear that many more Democrats were worried about contracting COVID-19 than Republicans.

We know, of course, that when people respond to pollsters they tend to "cheerlead" for their party. "To give the answer that their team is supposed to give," even if the answer does not reflect what they really believe, or how they actually behave or, for that matter, if it "contradicts indisputable reality." This would explain why regular watchers of Fox News were relatively unconcerned about the virus.[5] This would also explain why those who watched Fox News host Sean Hannity as opposed to Fox News host Tucker Carlson came down with more cases of COVID-19. Both hosts are very conservative, but the former, Hannity, was a member of Trump's inner circle. So, almost invariably, he was in lockstep with the president. Carlson, in contrast, at least on this issue, took a somewhat different tack. As early as January 28, he "spent a chunk of his show discussing the dangers of a global pandemic." He continued, moreover, "to warn of deadly consequences." The result? According to researchers at the University of Chicago, regular viewers of Hannity relative to Carlson were "associated with approximately 30% more COVID-19 cases by March 14, and 21% more COVID-19 cases by March 28."[6]

By late March there were rumblings of what in short order became a full-fledged, all-out culture war. The foot soldiers in this war were neither scientists nor politicians, they were ordinary Americans who sometimes chose sides based not on objective evidence but on subjective preference. If they were Republicans, followers of President Trump, they tended to fight on one side of the culture war; if they were not, then they fought on the other. In the March 30 issue of *The Atlantic* was an article about a country club in suburban Atlanta that had recently imposed guidelines that were proving divisive. To encourage social distancing the club had removed communal water jugs, closed the restaurant, and requested that golfers limit themselves to one person per cart. But, instead of these cautionary measures being met with widespread approval, they created a fault line: between those who gladly complied and those who deliberately resisted and made a show of shaking hands and complaining loudly about the "stupid hoax" being propagated by virus alarmists. The same dynamic was being played out in many parts of the country. The article similarly described a sales representative from Texas who remained entirely unfazed by the threat of a virus outbreak. In his view, the March wave of government-mandated lockdowns was a "product of panic-mongering in the mainstream media, and he welcomed Trump's call for businesses to reopen by Easter."[7]

Given the virus crisis was more apparent, more virulent, and more costly every which way as time went on, logic would dictate that it would bring Americans closer together by making most people, even Republicans, come to realize the importance of taking pandemic precautions. But there was no such luck. In May, polls showed that the pandemic had become more politicized, not less. Sixty percent of Democrats were "extremely concerned" about the virus; but only 12 percent of Republicans. Conversely, only 2 percent of Democrats were "not concerned at all," and 33 percent of Republicans.[8] It turned out that, like so much else in American life, what people believed about the pandemic and how they behaved in response depended in large part on their political identity. To be a Democrat generally meant contagion was of considerable concern; to be a Republican generally meant it was not. In consequence of this concern, or the lack thereof, was behavior. In other words, as the culture war intensified, certain behaviors, prominent among them mask-wearing and social distancing, became signifiers. They signified not the science of the pandemic but the politics.

As the coronavirus crisis went from being a sideshow in early 2020 to being center stage in mid-2020, it became clear that associated with the politicization of the pandemic were costs. Costs that were incurred precisely because of the partisanship that President Trump and his enablers continued to propagate. This partisanship not only tolerated but actively encouraged behaviors in deliberate opposition to those recommended by health officials. To be sure, for many months these recommendations were less than full throated and sometimes even less than fully articulated, especially if they emanated from anyone associated with the Trump administration. However, the media were replete with doctors and scientists repeatedly sending a simple message – the vital importance of preventative measures such as washing hands, wearing masks, and socially distancing. Notwithstanding the scientific consensus, researchers at Vanderbilt University conducted a study published in late June that concluded, "Rampant partisanship in the United States may be the largest obstacle to the social distancing most experts see as critical to limiting the spread of the Covid-19 pandemic."[9]

MASKS

Of all the indicators that in short order the pandemic had become politicized none was more evocative than masks. Masks have power. They send messages, sometimes concealing, sometimes revealing. In 2020 though, in the United States at least, wearing a mask was unambiguous, an unmistakable symbol. People who wore masks generally trusted doctors and scientists, so they wore a mask to protect themselves, and others, against contagion. Simple. But as it emerged that wearing a mask was not only the smart thing to do but the right thing to do, the motives of those who chose not to wear a mask became increasingly opaque. Were they genuinely unconcerned? Were they too young or too ignorant or too distracted fully to understand? Were their priorities different? Were they more persuaded by President Donald Trump than by Dr. Anthony Fauci? Or were they just making a statement, one in keeping with their political and cultural identities?

In other countries around the world to wear a mask or not was not a burning question. While different national cultures had different national practices, the act of putting a covering over the nose and across the mouth was not generally perceived as political. The United States though was different. It became different at precisely the moment when President Trump distanced himself on the issue, even from his own experts, who by then had got to the point of recommending "face coverings." I write "by then" because it took time for the government to get its act together on face coverings. As we have seen, the debate over masks went on for weeks, contributing to the impression that the administration was less than supremely competent. To his credit, in April, the Surgeon General, Dr. Jerome Adams, admitted that the government's own uncertainty over the issue of face masks had been "confusing to the American people." Trump though was not confused; he was never confused. Notwithstanding the recommendation of his own administration, he remained adamant. Masks might suit others, but they did not suit him. "I don't think I'm going to be doing it," said the president on April 3. "Wearing a face mask as I greet presidents, prime ministers, dictators, kings, queens – I just don't see it."[10]

Though by then Trump was already deviating from what had become accepted practice, he continued to insist that wearing a mask was "voluntary." That "you do not have to do it." To underscore the point, when he toured a Honeywell mask production facility in early May, his face was conspicuously uncovered. Naturally, his enablers followed suit. When Vice President Mike Pence visited the Mayo Clinic at around the same time, he mirrored the president. Despite his being in a medical facility in which everyone was required to wear a mask, Pence did not. Later, when he was questioned by reporters about being mask-less in, of all places, a hospital, he defended himself: "As vice president of the United States, I'm tested for the coronavirus on a regular basis, and everyone who is around me is tested for the coronavirus."[11] (Of course, in fall 2020, when over 30 people connected to the White House came down with COVID-19, including the president, the first lady, and their teenaged son, the system of regular testing to which Pence referred, assuming it ever existed, had broken down.)

Exactly why President Trump refused to wear a mask except on rare occasions has been a matter of speculation. Some said it was all about his hair. Some said it was all about his manliness (invincibility = masculinity). Some said it was all about his contrariness or his playing down the pandemic. Some said it was all about his playing up the economy. For weeks and even months Trump was in any case consistent. He nearly never wore a mask. Nor was he content not to wear a mask himself, he mocked those who did, such as his opponent in the November election, Joe Biden. He retweeted a post that made fun of a photo of Biden behind a mask, later adding, "I thought it was very unusual he had one on," though by then it most certainly was not.[12] The line between those wearing masks and those not, was growing stronger, masks themselves having become a political and cultural flashpoint. To Trump, masks were a visible, palpable, distraction from the message he wanted to send: that the right thing to do, the patriotic thing to do was not to focus on the pandemic but on the economy. At the Honeywell plant he said, "The people of our country should think of themselves as warriors" because "our country has to open."[13]

By early June, the numbers revealed that while the divide on masks was determined largely by political identification, other factors, such as geography and gender, also pertained. For example, a Gallup poll conducted in spring found, not surprisingly, that city and suburban residents were more likely to wear masks than those living in rural areas. Similarly, there were more mask wearers in the

West and Northeast than in the South and Midwest. And there were more women mask wearers, 67 percent, than men, 56 percent. Still, the most significant divide was by party. Of those polled, 75 percent of Democrats said they had worn a mask in public. But only 58 percent of independents did so – and less than half of Republicans.[14] But, by the end of June, there were some signs that the tide was turning. A headline in the *New York Times* read, "For Many Republicans, an Abrupt About-Face on Masks."[15] Why the change of hearts and minds? First, the situation was worsening. The coronavirus was proving a real and present danger and it was spreading to states, especially in the South and West, that had thought themselves immune, at least from the worst of it. Second, the evidence was now so overwhelming that it was no longer possible to pretend that preventative measures such as mask-wearing and social distancing were less than essential.

Moreover, after months of mixed signals, by the end of June there was a single signal. If there was any hope of containing the virus before the advent of a vaccine(s), it depended on people following the recommendations of virtually every healthcare expert – now including members of the administration. Even conservative Republicans, previously among the most reluctant and recalcitrant, fell into line. Vice President Pence "abruptly" began "regularly wearing and recommending a mask." Arizona's Republican governor, Doug Ducey, whose state faced an uncontrolled outbreak of COVID-19, now veritably pleaded with his constituents, "Arm yourself with a mask." Wyoming's Republican representative Liz Cheney tweeted a photo of her father, vice president under George W. Bush, wearing a cowboy hat and a pale blue mask. "Dick Cheney says WEAR A MASK," adding, "#realmenwearmasks." And the venerable Republican Senator from Tennessee, Lamar Alexander, appealed to the president directly – wear a mask. Though Alexander, like virtually every other Republican, had waited too long to weigh in, now he was loud and clear: "The stakes are too high for this political debate about pro-Trump, anti-Trump to continue."

The list goes on – many of the president's staunchest enablers finally turning against him, if only on this single issue. Even Senate Majority Leader Mitch McConnell, who for his own political reasons previously had allowed no daylight to come between him and the president, got to where he broke rank. "Wearing simple face coverings is not about protecting ourselves, it is about protecting everyone we encounter."[16] Finally was the president's firstborn son, Donald Trump Jr. For once he was his own man. "You know," he told Fox Business, "I don't think that it's too complicated to wear a mask or wash our hands and follow basic hygiene protocols."[17] (By no means though did he follow his own lead. Don Jr., like his father, was not usually seen wearing a mask.)

A month later, in July, President Trump caved in. He caved in because his followers were no longer following. By July, Trump had lost the trust of most of the American people on this issue particularly. When it came to COVID-19, Americans trusted Biden over Trump by a double-digit margin, 54 percent to 34 percent. No wonder McConnell had taken to wearing a mask whenever he appeared on the Senate floor, or that retail behemoths such as Walmart, CVS, Target, and McDonald's fell into line, imposing mask requirements. No wonder Trump had gone from saying the virus was "embers" to conceding that in certain states it was "big fires." And no wonder that after months of belittling Biden for wearing a mask, Trump was reduced to this: "I have no problem with masks. I view it this way: Anything that potentially can help ... is a good thing. I have no problem. I carry it. I wear it. You saw me wearing it a number of times and I'll continue."[18] (Though it turned out, famously, or infamously, he continued nearly never to wear one.)

The president's pivot notwithstanding, some of his most faithful followers chose not to pivot along with him. Trump might have blinked, but not, for instance, the Republican Governor of Georgia, Brian Kemp. In July he chose instead to sue Keisha Lance Bottoms for issuing an order mandating mask-wearing in the city of which she was mayor – Atlanta.[19] Nor did masks as a symbol, a literal symbol, of the

American political divide, abate over time. In October, the Pew Research Center published the results of a study which found that at least through the summer "no topic" continued to "divide Democrats and Republicans more than the subject of masks."[20] But, predictably, on his first day in office President Joe Biden sought to change the culture and stop the fight. He issued an order requiring the wearing of masks on all federal property and by all federal employees. And he launched a "100 days masking challenge" intended to encourage all Americans appropriately to cover their faces to prevent the pandemic from continuing to worsen.

RACE

George Floyd was killed by the Minneapolis police on May 25, 2020. From that moment on America was in the throes of three crises simultaneously. And, from that moment on, the coronavirus crisis, the economic crisis, and the racial crisis, or social justice crisis, intersected. Precisely because of chronic, endemic American racism, both COVID-19 and the bad economy were having a far more insidious effect on black Americans than on white Americans.

The hashtag #blacklivesmatter was not new. It was coined following the 2013 acquittal of George Zimmerman in the shooting death of an unarmed black teenager, Trayvon Martin. In the seven years since, Black Lives Matter had become a movement as well as a symbol, especially though not exclusively for African Americans, and especially though not exclusively to protest fatal police-related encounters.[21] Floyd's killing led almost immediately to massive public demonstrations under the banner Black Lives Matter, beginning in the city where Floyd was killed but spreading quickly across the country and then around the world. Similarly, this single act of violence against a single individual came rapidly to represent racial inequities generally which, not incidentally, the pandemic had underscored. At the time of Floyd's death African Americans accounted for at least 29 percent of known COVID-19 cases in Floyd's state of Minnesota, but only 6 percent of the state's total population.[22]

In the wake of the pandemic, Orlando Patterson pointed out that the black poverty rate in the United States is 2.5 times that of the white rate. That the enormous wealth gap between blacks and whites has expanded in recent years not contracted, and that between 1985 and 2000 a higher percentage of black children grew up in high-poverty segregated areas than between 1955 and 1970.[23] Additionally, while African Americans have always had a difficult time on the job market, COVID-19 exacerbated the problem. Given that African Americans not only earn less than white Americans, but are quicker to be furloughed or fired and slower to be hired and rehired, it was no surprise that by May 2020 when some 21 million Americans were unemployed, 12.4 percent of them were white and 16.8 percent of them were black. Federal Reserve chair, Jerome Powell, pointed out that whatever the inequities that previously existed, the pandemic had made them worse. "Everyone is suffering here," he said. "But I think those who are least able to bear it are the ones who are losing their jobs and losing their incomes and have little cushion to protect them in times like that."[24]

Again, everything is connected to everything else. In this case the coronavirus crisis triggered the economic crisis that for African Americans was aggravated by the chronic crisis of racism. Put another way, the coronavirus crisis impacted all Americans – but the impact was unequal. Black Americans were more likely than whites to catch the virus, to get seriously sick from the virus, and to die from the virus. (In New York City blacks and Latinos died of COVID-19 at twice the rate of white people.[25]) Black Americans were also more likely than whites to pay the price in other ways, such as loss of jobs and of housing. Similarly, Hispanics, who had 2.5 times increased risk of death compared with whites. And, similarly, American Indians who "represented 1 percent of the population but 2 percent of [American] deaths as of July 1, 2020."[26]

"On Black Lives Matter, the Public has Quickly Moved to the Left," read a June 11 headline in the New York Times. The evidence seemed clear. Not only had public opinion on race, criminal justice, and the Black Lives Matter movement "leapt leftward" since the death of George Floyd, it had been moving in that direction since the hashtag #blacklivesmatter was first coined. One online survey found that by a 28-point margin, American voters supported the movement, up sharply from a 17-point margin before the most recent wave of protests began. Other polls indicated the same: Monmouth University, for example, found a thumping 76 percent of Americans considered racism and discrimination "a big problem."[27] Most experts agreed that, "Never in the history of modern polling" had Americans expressed "such widespread agreement that racial discrimination plays a role in policing – and in society at large."[28]

Where in all the anger around race was the Trump administration? Trump's past record on "the other" was clear. We know, for example, that a member of President Trump's inner circle, Stephen Miller, was specifically tasked with developing policies and procedures designed to limit immigration, especially to keep out the great unwashed. We similarly know that President Trump had a long history of saying and doing things that smacked of racism. In 2019 *The Atlantic* published an oral history of Trump on race that began this way: "Trump has assembled a long record of comment on issues involving African Americans as well as Mexicans, Hispanics more broadly, Native Americans, Muslims, Jews, immigrants, women, and people with disabilities. His statements have been reflected in his behavior – from public acts ... to private preferences." Though in 2016 Trump described himself as "the least racist person that you've ever encountered," his personal, professional, and political history indicated otherwise. Beginning with his embrace of "birtherism" (the false charge that Barack Obama was not born in the United States), Trump's 2016 campaign was "fueled by nativist sentiment" including a proposal simply to bar Muslims from entering the country.[29] It is no surprise then that during the pandemic, specifically during the massive public protests following the death of George Floyd, and then again, three months later, following the police shooting seven times over of Jacob Blake, in Kenosha, Wisconsin, Trump was no different. This time, however, several of his followers were caught directly in his snare – which left them with a choice. To follow the president's lead – or not to. To speak out instead.

Given my admiration elsewhere expressed for how professionally and therefore, relatively effectively the American military educates, trains, and develops leaders, I was not surprised when, while most of President Trump's followers continued during this period to follow, and most of his enablers continued to enable, during this time of turmoil some did not.[30] Notably members of the military.

Members of the American military are taught to respect the commander in chief and virtually always they do. Most of Trump's presidency was no exception. Nearly all his military subordinates, including generals and admirals, went along with the president's singular style of leadership, and did what they were told without public objection. Now though was a step too far. Trump's threat to send active-duty troops to use against American people protesting on American soil was for some at least the breaking point. Moreover, it was exacerbated by an incident on June 1, during which US Park Police and National Guard troops used tear gas, riot batons, smoke devices, and rubber bullets to clear Washington's Lafayette Park of peaceful Black Lives Matter protesters. Why was this deemed necessary? To provide the president with a photo op. So that he and his entourage – including daughter Ivanka, son-in-law Jared Kushner, Attorney General William Barr, Defense Secretary Mark Esper, and chairman of the Joint Chiefs of Staff, General Mark Milley – could walk from the White House through Lafayette Park to St. John's Episcopal Church in front of which the president wanted to stand and hold up a Bible, and have his picture taken. Not coincidentally, this was in the immediate wake of Trump's declaring at the White House that he was the "president of law and order," and demanding that the nation's governors deploy the National Guard to "dominate the streets."[31]

Trump's highly esteemed former Secretary of Defense James Mattis led the loyal opposition. Since his December 2018 letter of resignation, which was made public, Mattis had stayed silent. Now, however, in the wake of what had happened at Lafayette Park, he spoke out. "I have watched this week's unfolding events," Mattis wrote in a statement, "angry and appalled. The words 'Equal Justice Under Law' are carved in the pediment of the United States Supreme Court. This is precisely what the protesters are demanding. It is a wholesome and unifying demand – one that all of us should be able to get behind."[32]

On one level it was easy enough for Mattis to opine – he was after all retired. It was not so easy, however, for General Milley, who had participated in the incident at Lafayette Park while on active duty – and while on the highest rung of the military ladder. How did he extract himself from playing the part of unwilling and perhaps unwitting enabler? He apologized. About a week and a half after doing something that he almost immediately regretted, General Milley took the extraordinary step of separating himself from his commander in chief by publicly expressing his misgiving for having appeared alongside him at Lafayette Park. "I should not have been there," Milley admitted. "My presence in that moment and in that environment created a perception of the military involved in domestic politics. As a commissioned uniformed officer, it was a mistake that I have learned from." Nor did Milley stop there. He went on effectively to throw his support behind the protesters, behind the Black Lives Matter movement. "The protests ... not only speak to [Floyd's] killing, but also to centuries of injustice toward African Americans." And he distanced himself from the president on race when he acknowledged that the Navy and Marine Corps had no African Americans serving above the two-star level, and that the Army had just one African American four-star. Then he added, "We all need to do better."[33]

The highly contagious coronavirus, the badly deteriorated economy, the pernicious effects of racism – all intersected, all interrelated. Again, not only did COVID-19 hit blacks far harder than whites, so did the damaged economy. The future moreover looks bleak, specifically on this issue. For African Americans will have a harder time rebounding economically from the pandemic, the poor prognosis compounded by the fact that they began 2020 far behind whites in average income, wealth, and rates of home ownership.[34] General Milley spoke to each of these when he took on the American president. When he made as loud and clear as he could without crossing the line into insubordination that he viewed Trump's leadership as deeply if not fatally flawed. Milley spoke from a position of great strength. *By explicitly admitting his mistake and implicitly implicating the president he rejected the role of enabler.*

THE PANDEMIC POLITICIZED – ABROAD

During the early months of 2020, President Donald Trump, in the interest of a trade deal with China, could hardly say enough good things about China's president, Xi Jinping. To take just a random example, on January 22, Trump said: "I have a great relationship with President Xi. We just signed probably the biggest deal ever made. It certainly has the potential to be the biggest deal ever made … I think the relationship is very, very good."[35] But half a year later, relations between the United States and China had deteriorated, badly. So badly in fact, that by August, China's foreign minister said the Sino-US relationship was at its worst since diplomatic relations were established 40 years earlier.[36] What happened?

In the drama between the two countries COVID-19 was a major player. It provided an early excuse for Trump to do what he had decided anyway to do: turn China into a bogeyman primarily because he thought it would help him to win the November election. This is not to say that in this shift China was blameless. Hardly. In recent years, China has been increasingly difficult to deal with, not only for the United States but for the global community more generally. China's ideas and institutions and its domestic and foreign policies – including its de facto takeover (in 2020) of Hong Kong – are in almost every way antithetical to those of liberal democrats generally and of Americans specifically. Xi, moreover, had evolved from what he initially was, an authoritarian leader, to what many experts now determined was a totalitarian leader. Even on the new coronavirus China was culpable. It was the "initial epicenter" of what became a pandemic. Further, China was slow to report the outbreak; China resisted transparency, especially early on; China rebuffed offers of help from global experts in epidemiology and molecular virology; and China was reluctant to share information even with the WHO.[37] Still, within just a few short months it became clear that if the coronavirus had been politicized within the USA, it was no less so abroad, outside the USA, especially as it pertained to the relationship between the United States and China. The importance of this relationship is impossible to overstate. As John Bolton put it, "America's economic and geopolitical relations with China will determine the shape of international affairs in the twenty-first century."[38]

In mid-May CNN identified at least 37 different occasions on which, since January, President Trump had praised China's handling of the coronavirus.[39] Bolton noted that despite evidence that China had "delayed, withheld, fabricated, and distorted information" about the new coronavirus, early on Trump was loath to criticize "for fear of adversely affecting the elusive definitive trade deal with China, or offending the ever-so-sensitive Xi Jinping."[40] Notwithstanding, during the first half of 2020 the administration's posture toward China shifted. Increasingly came condemnation and even ridicule – the administration's China hawks, sometimes including Trump, having taken regularly to calling COVID-19, the "Wuhan virus." Additionally, Secretary of State Mike Pompeo, America's most prominent China hawk, was now in charge of American foreign policy. Pompeo led the charge, using the coronavirus to drive a wedge or, better, to further drive a wedge between the United States and China. Again, to be clear, the virus was not the only issue, it was one among several issues that were exacerbating relations between the two countries. But for China hawks the timing was perfect. Given that there was a virus and given that the initial epicenter of the virus was China, why not seize the day and profitably politicize the pandemic abroad as well as at home.

In addition to his usual scathing remarks about the dangers posed by China, early in the year Pompeo began using the virus as a vehicle for making his case. The pandemic became, in other words, part of Pompeo's campaign to undermine the US–China relationship which for four decades had been, if not warm and fuzzy, then serviceable, civil. By early March, the Chinese were fed up. They seized on Pompeo's hostility and started giving as good as they got. A spokesman for the Chinese Foreign Ministry said, "We condemn the despicable practice of individual US politicians eagerly stigmatizing China and Wuhan by association with the novel coronavirus, disrespecting science and W.H.O ... Pompeo's attempts of slandering China's efforts in combating the epidemic are doomed to fail."[41] Of course, Pompeo was not the only Republican to take a hard line. While he often referred to the new coronavirus as the "China virus" or the "Chinese virus," so did other Republicans. For example, Representative Paul Gosar, from Arizona, announced that he was self-quarantining from the "Wuhan virus."[42] Senator Tom Cotton from Arkansas went so far as to insist that the "virus did not originate in a Wuhan animal market." Instead he floated a conspiracy theory, speculating that the virus was deliberately released from a "super-laboratory that researches human infectious diseases."[43]

America's traditional allies were not pleased either with the turn of events or with the use of incendiary language. At a meeting of G7 foreign ministers in March, they objected to Pompeo's use of the term "Wuhan virus." The French Foreign Minister said in a statement that he had "underscored the need to combat any attempt to exploit the [virus] crisis for political purposes and expressed the view that the unity of all in order to effectively combat the pandemic must now take precedence."[44] China itself put on the brakes, at least some of the time. During an online ceremony in April, occasioned by China's donation of medical supplies to New York City, China's Consul-General recalled that just a month earlier, Presidents Trump and Xi together had "called for anti-epidemic cooperation between our two nations." He went on to say that China and the United states should join to "lead the effort" to fight the coronavirus, and that in any case this was not "the time for finger pointing." Instead it was the time for "solidarity, collaboration, cooperation and mutual support."[45]

The Secretary of State was not, of course, swayed. In May Pompeo backed the idea, which the president himself recently had floated, that the coronavirus had originated not in a market in Wuhan but in a lab, this despite US intelligence agencies making clear that they had reached no such conclusion. Whatever the truth about the origins of the virus, Pompeo continued to beat the drum against China, repeatedly accusing the Chinese Communist Party, led by the Chinese president, of covering up coronavirus evidence and denying American experts and journalists access to sources that could provide information. Pompeo was not wholly wrong in his assertations. The Chinese government had, for example, recently restricted or even evicted correspondents from the New York Times, the Washington Post, and the Wall Street Journal. In any case Pompeo clearly got what he wanted: as 2020 turned from winter to spring to summer, tensions between China and the United States were ratcheted up, an escalation and intensification in which COVID-19 played a major part.

Trump's campaign to turn Americans against China in the hope that he might profit politically from their pivot worked.[46] In July 2020, 73 percent of US adults reported to Pew pollsters that they had an unfavorable view of China, up 26 points from two years earlier. Further there was "a widespread sense that China [had] mishandled the initial outbreak and subsequent spread of Covid-19." Specifically, 78 percent of those polled placed a "great deal or a fair amount of the blame for the global spread of the coronavirus on the Chinese government's initial handling of the Covid-19 outbreak in Wuhan."[47]

Americans who viewed China less favorably in June 2020 than they did a year or two earlier, had good reason. Again, by every account and every measure China had behaved dishonorably, for example – and conspicuously – on Hong Kong, and then again during the initial stages of what became a global health crisis. However, countering the China hawks are those who, precisely because they view the US–China relationship as being of paramount importance, think of it less simplistically. They acknowledge that while it is natural for big powers to compete, it is essential that, simultaneously, in areas such as public health, they cooperate. They argue that politicizing the pandemic abroad is about as smart as politicizing the pandemic at home. In other words, not very.

No matter. The point is that Pompeo was positioned to play his part to perfection. So long as he was willing to play by the only rule that had to be religiously followed – to be unswervingly loyal to Trump – his position was secure. And, so long as he was willing to play by the only rule that had to be religiously followed – again being unswervingly loyal to Trump – he was free to pursue his policy preferences. Pompeo enabled Trump by giving him an out. By whipping up American anger against China, the secretary of state provided the president with a convenient scapegoat. The pandemic was the Chinese government's fault – not America's. Between Trump and Pompeo there was a transactional relationship: Trump got what he needed, Pompeo got what he wanted: an American foreign policy focused on the idea that of America's enemies, China was much the most pernicious and much the most dangerous.

PART III **Trump's Team**

9   Vice President, Cabinet

The vice president and four members of the Cabinet were members of President Donald Trump's team – specifically as it pertained to the pandemic – during the period January through June 2020. Each was in some way directly involved in how the president managed America's worst public health crisis in over a century. Each, then, was an enabler, a follower who allowed or even encouraged Trump to engage in, and then to persist in behaviors that were destructive. Discussed in this chapter are Vice President Mike Pence; Secretary of State Mike Pompeo; Secretary of the Treasury Steven Mnuchin; Attorney General William Barr; and Secretary of Health and Human Services Alex Azar – all of whom during the coronavirus crisis prioritized the president's political interest over the national interest.

PENCE

It could be argued that during the presidency of Donald Trump no one had a more demanding and difficult job than his vice president, Mike Pence. Or at least more of a high wire balancing act: between on the one hand accepting without questioning the supremacy of President Trump, while on the other hand displaying at least a modicum of self-respect. Pence's ambition after all, was one day to run for president himself. It would be unseemly then, or so one would think, perennially to seem the lapdog, the abject underling. Still, for all practical purposes Pence had no choice. So long as he remained vice president to Trump, he could not risk disagreeing with him, distinguishing himself from him, certainly not in public, not once. Trump's demand for, need for, fealty was absolute, so, before all else, it was Pence's fulltime job to fall into line. If there was an "organizing theme to Pence's vice presidency," it was that he must never give offense to a man "whose emotional antennae quiver at any slight."[1]

It was not enough, however, for this subordinate not to offend his superior. Part of this vice president's job description was tirelessly, extravagantly, and effusively to praise the president. To some it seemed downright peculiar for any leader to require his (or her) ego to be so constantly stroked. But there it was, a Cabinet meeting, for example, at which Pence praised Trump once every twelve seconds for three minutes straight. How did Pence pull it off? Here some samples:

- "You've restored American credibility on the world stage."
- "You've unleashed American energy."
- "You've signed more bills rolling back federal red tape than any president in American history."
- "I'm deeply humbled, as your vice president, to be able to be here."
- "Because of your determination, because of your leadership, the forgotten men and women of America are forgotten no more. And we are making America great again."[2]

The pandemic descended during the fourth year of Trump's presidency. By then Pence had of course solidified his role as the president's subservient subordinate. In 2017 Pence told every member of his staff that anyone who did anything that "could be perceived as upstaging the president would not be tolerated."[3] In 2018 Pence was described by longtime conservative columnist George Will as "groveling."[4] And in early 2020, during the impeachment proceedings, Pence was persuaded that he could not "allow even a sliver of daylight to appear between himself and the president for fear of drawing Mr. Trump's wrath and, potentially, that of core Republican voters."[5] So by the time Trump put Pence in nominal charge of leading the administration's response to the pandemic, his "ostentatious displays of water-carrying" were not new.[6] The president was long accustomed to having his water carried. Pence was long accustomed to doing the carrying.

Trump pushed Secretary of Health and Human Services, Alex Azar, aside as leader of the White House Coronavirus Task Force and replaced him with Mike Pence for several reasons. First, his opinion of Azar was low. Second, he knew that Pence was under his thumb, which meant that from that point on, he, Trump, could completely control not only the task force itself but also every aspect of the virus crisis – with, of course, the single, central exception of the virus itself. And third, putting Pence in charge meant bringing the task force in-house, into the White House, close to the Oval Office, which allowed Trump personally to monitor the situation and reliably to have the last word. Pence was, in sum, the perfect front man, the titular head of the White House Coronavirus Task Force but not the leader of the White House Coronavirus Task Force. Pence moreover had a hatchet man, Marc Short, his powerful chief of staff, who could be counted on to play bad cop to Pence's good cop. (It was Short, for example, who pushed the CDC to soften its coronavirus recommendations to the meat packing industry. Short was also part of a group that pushed the CDC to modify its guidelines for reopening churches.[7])

The vice president's sole qualification for even this nominal job was his fealty – he could be counted on to collaborate and conform for the duration. Pence had no other apparent asset; in fact, his track record on healthcare was poor. As an aspiring congressman he had once claimed that "smoking doesn't kill," and as governor of Indiana he was heavily criticized for how he handled the worst HIV crisis in the state's history. No wonder then that Pence's appointment as head of the task force was widely attacked, one Yale epidemiologist charging it was like "putting an arsonist in charge of the fire department, a bank robber in charge of the US mint."[8] The critics missed the point, however. Pence was demonstrably qualified according to the only criterion that mattered, so far as this president was concerned.

Those who thought that now, finally, Trump would empower Pence, give him not only some authority but some power, turned out wrong, dead wrong. An example of those who misread the tea leaves were authors of an article in *Politico*. They predicted that with his appointment as head of the task force, Pence would gain "outsized power to run the government during the coronavirus crisis," and that while Trump would "rally" the people, it was Pence who would "govern" them.[9] No such luck. Pence did of course have a part to play, and he did have some influence. But his part was only a bit part and his influence remained modest. His leash, in fact, was short, only so long as Trump would allow. Initially, briefly, Pence was under the illusion that with his new appointment things would change. His office was set to take over coronavirus communications, and he began holding daily press briefings. Not for long. Just a few days later Trump reinserted himself into the process, put himself front and center, most visibly at those same daily task force press briefings that from then on, at least for the next several weeks, constituted by far the most prominent White House forum for messaging anything remotely related to the pandemic.

Once Trump reassumed his role as spokesperson, Pence contented himself with being no more than a prop, though only in public and only when Trump was around. In private, away from Trump's prying eyes, he played a slightly more substantial role, though never of course did he depart from the White House script. Pence tried, for instance, to coordinate what the federal government was doing with what the states were doing. To this end, in spring, summer, and into the fall, sometimes flanked by Dr. Deborah Birx and Admiral Brett Giroir (another member of the task force, also a physician), he led weekly calls, sessions with dozens of different governors during which he tried to be helpful. By all accounts, Pence handled himself well. "Without Trump in the room," observed Maryland governor Larry Hogan, "Pence was all business. Sober. Methodical." However, also by all accounts, he had no real leeway: he was not independent from the president and he had hardly any influence on him. Inevitably this resulted in what some governors at least experienced as an "exasperating gulf between Mr. Pence's private remarks and the public edicts issued by the president."[10]

Throughout the pandemic the vice president maintained his usual demeanor, never once deviating from his preternatural calm. His face was opaque, hard to read, concealing more than it revealed. Usually he was expressionless, reaction-less, poker-faced, even standing alongside his boss who likely as not was telling outright lies about the crisis that Pence ostensibly was managing. No frowning or scowling, no eyebrow raising or facial flickering, occasionally a slight smile, rarely more, that was about it. The vice president's voice remained always the same: soft, stable, steady, calming rather than alarming, never once raised, not even slightly. Above all he was gentlemanly, old fashioned in that he was unfailingly polite and unflaggingly civil – this in an administration that was well known for being neither. As it turned out, temperamentally certainly, Trump and Pence seemed straight out of central casting – a deliberate counterpoint. The first mean and mercurial, coarse, crass, and contemptuous; the second courteous and cordial, apparently well-raised and demonstrably well-mannered.

Mike Pence's decision made years earlier to lash his political fortunes to those of Donald Trump would prove costly. History is not likely to treat Pence kindly. He will be viewed as having been an enabler, an abject subordinate who, among his other failings, not once corrected or contradicted the president's numberless lies particularly as they pertained to the pandemic. Pence, moreover, perpetrated his own untruths, his own fabrications and falsifications. At the end of June, for example, he made these statements, all demonstrably false: "As we stand here today, all 50 states and territories across this country are opening up safely and responsibly." (At the time, several states were pausing or even reversing course.) And "We flattened the curve." (By then, late June, the number of COVID-19 cases was once again rising.) And "We want the American people to understand that it's almost inarguable that more testing is generating more cases." (Ramped up testing was not, however, accounting for the uptick in cases.)[11]

A week after Pence's serial dissembling, in early July, the number of Americans dead from COVID-19 was 133,000. And, by late August, when Mike Pence formally accepted his re-nomination as President Trump's running mate in the November election, the number of Americans who had died of the disease was more than 187,000. The approximate number of Americans who died in the war in Vietnam was 58,000. But, of course, by summer 2020 that war was long since over while the war against what Trump called the "invisible enemy" was not. This was a war in which the number of dead was still climbing to what just a few months earlier were unimaginable numbers. By the end of the calendar year the number of Americans dead exceeded 340,00.

Ironically, for all of Vice President Pence's four-year fealty, before it was all over President Trump dissed and ditched him. In the frenzy that accompanied the January 6, 2021 attack on the US Capitol – a frenzy that was the result of Trump trying desperately to overturn at the last minute the results of the 2020 presidential election – he tweeted abuse against the man who had served him so faithfully. "Mike Pence didn't have the courage to do what should have been done to protect our Country and our Constitution," tweeted Trump just before Twitter threw him off.[12] Notwithstanding this final insult, Pence clearly concluded that he did not want war. And so days before Trump's term was over, the president and his vice president met one final time, to make peace or, at least, a truce. Yet on the day of Joe Biden's inauguration Pence chose not to bid his boss a final farewell but instead to attend the swearing in of his successor.

POMPEO AND MNUCHIN

Mike Pompeo was named to the highest position in President Trump's Cabinet, secretary of state, in April 2018 – after Rex Tillerson, who was Trump's first secretary of state, was summarily dismissed. Like most other Republicans, Pompeo was not at the start a Trump supporter. Only after he had the delegates necessary to secure the 2016 presidential nomination, did Pompeo, reluctantly, endorse him. But once Trump won the White House and Pompeo was offered the job of director of the Central Intelligence Agency, he accepted with alacrity, as he accepted with alacrity the post the president offered just over a year later, secretary of state. Pompeo was, moreover, a quick learner. (He graduated first in his class at West Point.) He learned fast faithfully to follow the rules, rule number one being, as invariably it was, to be unswervingly loyal to the man behind the Resolute Desk in the Oval Office. "A Secretary of State has to know what the President wants," Pompeo said, early in his tenure. "To the extent you get out of synch with that leader, then you're just shooting the breeze." In fact, Pompeo soon developed a reputation within the administration of being among Trump's most servile subordinates. Said one former senior White House official, "There will never be any daylight publicly between him and Trump. [Pompeo] is among the most sycophantic and obsequious people around Trump."[13]

From the start Pompeo excelled at managing up. There was some tension between the president and the secretary during the impeachment hearings – career foreign service officers were prominent among those who testified against Trump – but they got past it. Thus, during the two years preceding the pandemic it was left largely to Pompeo to take "Trump's shifting foreign-policy instincts" and weave them "into something legible, defensible and sometimes even coherent."[14] When the new coronavirus led to a crisis, therefore, it was Pompeo who framed the administration's foreign policy response which was, first and foremost, to pit America against China.

Pompeo's reaction to the virus crisis was initially viewed as sluggish – he was said, for example, to have paid inadequate attention to the thousands of Americans who were stuck overseas. But once he got in harness he did not let up. In late March, Pompeo sent his subordinates at the State Department a message boasting of the number of Americans that US diplomats had by then arranged to get home and praising his people: "I couldn't be prouder of what you've accomplished during this global pandemic."[15] And, by late April he was regularly accusing China of duplicity and bad faith. "The Chinese

Communist Party now has a responsibility to tell the world how this pandemic got out of China and all across the world, causing such global economic devastation," he told Fox News. "America needs to hold them accountable." Pompeo was by then singing straight from what recently had become the administration's hymnal. After making nice to China early in the year, Trump was now accusing the WHO of acting as "a pipe organ for China," while Jared Kushner was insisting that Trump would take whatever actions were necessary "to make sure the people who caused the problems are held accountable for it."[16]

There is, however, another way of framing the administration's foreign policy response to the new coronavirus: that it was not Pompeo singing from Trump's hymnal, but Trump singing from Pompeo's. For at least the past year Pompeo had positioned himself as a China hawk, repeatedly saying things such as, in 2019, "In China, we face a new kind of challenge. It's an authoritarian regime that's integrated economically into the West in a way that the Soviet Union never was."[17] What the virus crisis did, then, was to seal the deal. It gave China hawks – who included as we saw, in addition to Pompeo, national security advisor Robert O'Brien and his deputy, Matthew Pottinger – more running room. It additionally gave China hawks more ammunition – for example they charged China was concealing the coronavirus's real point of origin, a research laboratory in Wuhan. Finally, it gave China hawks the upper hand in an administration that was divided on China. (Mnuchin, for instance, was perceived a "panda hugger.") So, as spring 2020 led into summer 2020, China became not only Pompeo's bogeyman but Trump's. For various reasons, including presidential politics, Trump was converted, at least for the moment, from being neutral on China or even somewhat favorably disposed – both to it and to its president, Xi Jinping – to blaming China for whatever ailed America, obviously though not only COVID-19.

Pompeo, in sum, got what he wanted. A China hawk in the White House. Trump, in turn, got what he needed which was, as we earlier saw, a scapegoat. Someplace else and someone else to blame for the pandemic. In theory at least, if not so much in practice, Pompeo provided the president with a vehicle for deflecting responsibility for the virus crisis – away from Washington and toward Beijing.

In the American political system, the second highest-ranking Cabinet member is the Secretary of the Treasury. Steven Mnuchin assumed the post a month after President Trump was inaugurated – which meant that by summer 2020 the secretary was a survivor. He was one of the few Cabinet members to have made it through nearly the entirety of Trump's presidency. How did he do it? Predictably, by being unflinchingly loyal or, if you prefer, unscrupulously sycophantic.[18] (Former Secretary of the Treasury, Lawrence Summers, called Mnuchin perhaps the "greatest sycophant in cabinet history."[19]) In any case, as Sheelah Kolhatkar wrote in *The New Yorker*, Mnuchin's fealty provided him with a "kind of job insurance." He was closer to the president than any other Cabinet member – admittedly a low bar – and he was willing at every turn to do the president's bidding. Not that there were never any disagreements between them, there were some. Rather it is to point out that whatever they were, they were behind closed doors. Never once in public did Mnuchin stray from the president's position. Moreover, more than anyone else it was Mnuchin, himself a multimillionaire businessman – one known, pointedly if unflatteringly, as the "Foreclosure King" – who was credited with easing through Congress (in 2017) Trump's single signature piece of legislation, a $1.5 trillion package of tax cuts.

Given congressional Democrats' intense dislike of Trump, they saw Mnuchin as a welcome departure from, almost a relief from, the administration norm. The Treasury secretary was more technocrat than ideologue, more moderate than immoderate, more competent than incompetent, and more eager to strike a deal than to prove a point. As the *Wall Street Journal* described him in spring 2020, Mnuchin was, in so far as he was allowed, "Washington's indispensable crisis manager."[20] He was opaque, hard to read, monochromatic in his expressions and in the timbre of his voice, but still he came across as someone with whom it was possible to do business, and Congress did. Before spring was over, Senate Minority Leader Charles Schumer and House Speaker Nancy Pelosi reached an agreement with the administration, which allowed Congress remarkably swiftly and smoothly to pass the CARES Act, initially, at least, seen as an example of how in a crisis the executive and legislative branches could still work together.

It was not long, however, before cracks appeared. As a result, there were problems with the CARES Act; problems subsequent to the CARES Act; and problems in what only recently had been a good working relationship between the White House, specifically Mnuchin, and the Congress, specifically Schumer and Pelosi. Problems with the CARES Act included how and to whom the monies intended for small businesses were to be distributed. After the CARES Act the problems included passing additional legislation that many deemed critical, a financial lifeline to those who most needed it. And there were the difficulties that beset the relationship between the Secretary of the Treasury and congressional leaders including the blame game – who was responsible, the White House or the Congress, for the failure of the federal government to continue to provide for those on Main Street as well as Wall Street, and, more specifically, for those most in need.

Problems notwithstanding, and despite the ups and downs in their relationship, Mnuchin continued unfailingly to protect Trump, to support Trump, and to agree, at least in public, with Trump's every word. When he was asked in July if the skyrocketing number of COVID-19 cases gave him pause – made him question the administration's decision to push the states to reopen their economies – Mnuchin replied in a heartbeat, "No, absolutely not."[21]

Secretary Mnuchin was widely recognized as one of the most important policymakers in the world who, if left to his own devices, would be a pragmatist. But because he was yet another Trump underling eager to remain in the president's good graces, to remain, in other words, Treasury secretary, Mnuchin continued to do what he had done since day one: prop up the president. This despite the growing evidence that as the pandemic ground on, and as the provisions in the CARES Act expired, Americans were suffering in increasing numbers. A Brookings study published in spring confirmed the impact of COVID: "Rates of food insecurity observed in April 2020 are ... meaningfully higher than at any point for which there is comparable data." Of those mothers with children aged 12 and under, 17.4 percent were reporting that "the children in my household [are] not eating enough because we just [can't] afford enough food."[22] (This in comparison with 3.1 percent just two years earlier.) By June it was clear that the impact of the pandemic was grossly uneven: that "Black and Hispanic children [were] experiencing food insecurity" at ever higher and more alarming rates.[23] And, by September, the situation had deteriorated still further. Data from several sources showed a "dramatic increase in the number of households struggling to put enough food on the table."[24] In other words, with every passing season, the pandemic was extracting a higher toll on precisely those who could least afford to pay.

The two highest ranking Cabinet members played pivotal parts in the pandemic. Whatever Pompeo and Mnuchin's private thoughts – about the president particularly – their public performances were impeccable. Moreover, so far as President Trump was concerned, that each was perceived as a "sycophant," that each *was* a sycophant, was not a deficit but a positive attribute.

BARR AND AZAR

William Barr was attorney general during the last two years of the Trump administration. His primary task was to run the Department of Justice, not to serve as attendant to the president. Moreover, Barr was not in any way in charge of the administration's response to the pandemic. Nor was he involved in its day-to-day management. However, his importance as enabler to the president was so wide-reaching that it affected every aspect of Trump's tenure in the White

House – including the pandemic – beginning when Barr succeeded his ostentatiously ousted predecessor, Jeffrey Sessions.

Democrats saw Barr as a Trump toady early on, closer to a henchman than a leader of an independent agency exercising independent judgment.[25] To be sure, Barr did what he apparently genuinely believed he should: he protected and defended the president above all, even before protecting and defending the Constitution, the laws of the land, or the American people. While Barr's opinions generally aligned with Trump's, Barr's beliefs were more to the point. He believed in an exceedingly strong executive – strong enough, certainly hypothetically, to reduce the legislative and judicial branches from being equal to being lesser than.

Barr's implicit application for the job of Trump's attorney general was contained in a letter he sent to two high-ranking members of the administration several months before Sessions was fired. Barr wrote that Robert Mueller's investigation of Russian interference in the 2016 presidential election – an investigation that Trump naturally resented and detested beyond measure – "would have grave consequences far beyond the immediate confines of this case and would do lasting damage to the Presidency and to the administration of law within the Executive branch."[26]

Just six months later Trump nominated Barr for attorney general and, soon after that, Barr returned the favor. He reduced the extended, nuanced, and complex findings of the Mueller report to what for all practical purposes was an exoneration. "While still making the report public, Barr managed to mislead the public and the congress, spinning Mueller's findings in a way that hobbled their impact and protected the president."[27] Barr's distorted dismissal was critical. Instead of following up on Mueller's findings and trying to spare the country from more foreign intrusions into its elections, wrote legal expert Jeffrey Toobin, "Barr launched an investigation of the origins of the Russia investigation itself." It was, Toobin concluded, "a shameful departure from the honorable traditions of the Justice Department."[28] It was also a major factor, arguably the major factor, in the continuing enablement of President Donald Trump. As much as anyone else, it was Barr who enabled Trump to survive the impeachment proceedings – and then to preside, immediately subsequently, over the virus crisis. (Ironically, in addition to the Mueller report was another, similar, one, issued some 18 months later by the Republican controlled Senate Intelligence Committee. It made clearer than its analogous predecessor the nature of the ties between Trump's presidential campaign and Kremlin officials. The bottom line: Barr's earlier obfuscations notwithstanding, the Senate report found the "Russian government disrupted an American election to help Mr. Trump become president."[29])

By the time the furor over the Mueller report had died down, Barr had become an irredeemably divisive figure. From then on, so far as the president's supporters were concerned, he, Barr, could do no wrong; and, so far as the president's detractors were concerned, he, Barr, could do no right. The former chose to believe Barr when he insisted that he would never allow himself to be "bullied or influenced by anybody," including the American president.[30] The latter claimed the evidence indicated otherwise, that Barr was serving "Donald Trump and not the Constitution or the United States, flouting his oath of office and corrupting the mission of the Justice Department."[31] This much in any case was clear: as long as Barr was attorney general Trump could count on the Justice Department to have his back. Barr enabled Trump to get what he wanted, including leniency or more for several of his longtime associates, such as his former national security advisor, Michael Flynn, who had admitted lying to the FBI; and his old pal and evident partner in crime, Roger Stone, who had been convicted on seven counts including obstruction of justice and witness tampering.

Though the pandemic was neither in his purview nor under his jurisdiction, Barr made it a point to intervene. About two weeks after COVID-19 was declared not an epidemic but a pandemic, Barr weighed in, on Trump's side, of course. It is not easy to imagine how one can take sides in a virus crisis but, as we have seen, many if not most Americans did. From the beginning of the pandemic Barr protected Trump along two flanks. First, robot-like he aligned himself with the president no matter what he said or did. Second, in an interesting twist on the usual Republican position, which is to support states' rights, Barr sought to protect the federal government at the expense of the states.

Again, whenever Barr did weigh in on anything pandemic related, he sided with Trump. In early April, for example, in an interview with Fox News, the attorney general praised the president, crediting him with good management and aligning with him in attacking the media. Barr claimed that Trump had been at the receiving end of "snarky, gotcha questions from the White House media pool," and took special aim at the widespread skepticism about hydroxychloroquine, which, as mentioned, was for a time Trump's remedy of choice for COVID-19. "As soon as he said something positive about it," said Barr, "the media's been on a jihad to discredit the drug."[32]

The second flank along which Barr sought to protect the president was more significant. This pertained to the debate – a debate that goes back to the beginning of the Republic – over how much authority (and over what) the federal government had versus how much authority (and over what) the states had. It was tricky territory for, among other reasons, Trump was disinclined to lead on COVID-19, a pernicious disease he liked to think would magically vanish, and from which he preferred, when he could, to distance himself. The president had, in other words, been quick to say it was the states who were responsible for managing the pandemic – not the federal government. But, when the states took the bull by the horns, some states anyway, Trump immediately worried about the restrictions they imposed, that is, that they would hurt the economy, hence him politically. Barr of course adopted the president's concern as his own. In early April, the attorney general insisted that Americans would suffer "if we go into a deep depression," which would happen if "the economy was shut down for too long." As Barr put it, again parroting the president, "measured in lives the cure cannot be worse than the disease."[33]

In late April, the attorney general made the point again, this time much more forcefully. This time he threatened legal action if any of the states imposed COVID-19 restrictions the Justice Department decided violated the prerogatives of the federal government. In a two-page memo sent to US attorneys across the country he directed them to "be on the lookout" for state and local restrictions in violation of the Constitution and, if necessary, to pursue court action. He acknowledged – again, toeing the White House line – that up to then measures had been "necessary in order to stop the spread of a deadly disease." But as the weeks went on and Trump became even less concerned about the impact of the coronavirus on public health, and even more concerned about the impact of virus-related restrictions on the nation's economy, Barr continued to follow Trump's lead. His Justice Department memo went on to say, "Now, I am directing each of our United Sates Attorneys to be also on the lookout for state and local directives that could be violating the constitutional rights and civil liberties of individual citizens." He concluded by issuing a threat: "If a state or local ordinance crosses the line from an appropriate exercise of authority to stop the spread of COVID-19 into an overbearing infringement of constitutional and statutory protections, the Department of Justice may have an obligation to address that overreach in federal court."[34] It was an issue on which Barr never let up. In September he drew fire for calling coronavirus lockdown orders "the greatest intrusion on civil liberties since slavery."[35]

Barr's enablement of the president emboldened him more generally to act in ways that he might not have otherwise. For example, Barr supported Trump's highly controversial decision on June 1 to use force to clear Lafayette Square of protesters so that he and his entourage could avail themselves of a photo op. Barr similarly supported the administration's decision to send troops to Portland, Oregon to stop Black Lives Matter demonstrations. But everything relating to COVID-19, a disease that was continuing to kill tens of thousands of

Americans, was, of course, especially sensitive. When Trump bragged that he had "total" authority over the states he presumed for good reason that Barr would back him. A reporter for the *New York Times* asked Barr whether he agreed with the president's assessment, to which the attorney general replied: "I think the federal government *does* have the power to step in where a state is impairing interstate commerce, where they're intruding on civil liberties, or where Congress ... has given the president ... emergency authorities that essentially pre-empt the states in a particular area." Added the reporter in his own voice, "Construed broadly enough, Barr's interpretation could sanitize and legalize Trump's claim to 'total' authority."[36]

Like Barr, and like Pompeo, Secretary of Health and Human Services Alex Azar succeeded someone in his post – in this case Tom Price – who had been pushed out by the president. (In Price's case the precipitating reason was exorbitant travel at taxpayers' expense.) Because of the domain over which he presided, Health and Human Services, Azar was at or close to the center of the virus crisis during the six-month period on which this book is focused. (Azar was initially briefed about the new coronavirus on January 3, by Dr. Robert Redfield.) Though Azar's position in the administration was never secure – so far as Trump was concerned, among Azar's deficits he was a "Bushie," having worked in the administration of George W. Bush – as it turned out he stayed on. He remained in Trump's barely good graces because for the duration of the administration he was both an unflaggingly good soldier and, when the occasion arose, a convenient scapegoat.

Azar had contentious relationships with several members of Trump's team, but at least in January and early February he was one of the few people who tried, albeit not hard, to alert the president to the looming threat posed by the new coronavirus. Of course, Azar's message came effectively immediately to coincide with, to collide with, Trump's message, which was to play down the danger of which Azar was trying to warn.

Azar told Trump about the virus directly, on the phone, on January 18. But Trump, who was at his home in Florida, Mar-a-Lago, had no interest in hearing what Azar had to say. So, the president cut the secretary off – Trump launching instead into a familiar rant about e-cigarettes. Azar, for his part, retreated. Obviously Azar did not do enough, did not do everything that he could and should have, either on this occasion or on any other, to get the president to pay attention.[37] He did try one more time, two weeks later, on January 30, to speak to the president directly about the new coronavirus specifically. Once again this was not in person but on the phone. And, once again, though he had already instituted the China travel ban, the president responded in a way that seemed unserious, accusing Azar of being an alarmist.

In February Azar testified before the Senate. He said the government was establishing a "surveillance network" in five American cities to "begin testing" for the "Chinese coronavirus." However, according to the *Washington Post*, there were two problems: "The cities weren't ready, and the tests didn't work."[38] Azar's bungled announcement signaled not only that the administration was flailing, but that the member of Trump's Cabinet responsible most directly for managing what was becoming a virus crisis was, at the least, unimpressive. "Trump thought Azar was a disaster," said one administration insider.[39]

It was not long after that Dr. Nancy Messonnier went public – that she told reporters that she had sat her children down and said to them, "as a family, we need to be preparing for significant disruption in our lives." Trump, as we saw, went ballistic.[40] He took it out in large part on Azar, who for the month preceding had been chairing the White House Coronavirus Task Force. Enter Mike Pence, who was handed the job instead. In other words, Azar was out, Pence was in, the authority of the former significantly reduced, the authority of the latter, if not his power or influence, significantly enhanced.[41]

Nor was Azar's time of tribulation over. In late April CNN reported that "White House officials" were discussing plans "to replace HHS Secretary Azar."[42] But one month later Azar was still in place. In fact, he remained a member of the administration who agreed implicitly, and even explicitly, to go along to get along. In May he penned a piece for the *Washington Post* in which he parroted the White House, word for word. The title of the article? "We have to reopen – for our health."[43]

Pence, Pompeo, Mnuchin, Barr, and Azar each had their own reasons for enabling the president. Pence perceived Trump's political interests as precisely coincident with his own. Pompeo and Barr, in contrast, had ideas – respectively, about America's role in the world, and about the president's role in the American political system – which their alignment with the president helped them to implement. Mnuchin and Azar were more traditional bureaucrats, functionaries who did what their superior told them to do because they wanted to stay in the administration, not be kicked out. It is amazing what people will do, will put up with, to stay in power, to stay proximate to power, to stay in a high place.

10 Senior Advisors

Eight senior advisors were members of President Donald Trump's team – specifically as it pertained to the pandemic – during the period January through June 2020. Each was in some way directly, and heavily, involved in how the president managed America's worst public health crisis in over a century. Each, then, was an enabler, a follower who allowed or even encouraged Trump to engage in, and then to persist in behaviors that were destructive. Discussed in this chapter are senior advisor Jared Kushner; chiefs of staff Mick Mulvaney (acting) and Mark Meadows; assistant to the president Peter Navarro; national security advisor Robert O'Brien and his deputy Matthew Pottinger; and counselors to the president, Kellyanne Conway and Hope Hicks – all of whom during the coronavirus crisis prioritized the president's political interest over the national interest.

KUSHNER

Jared Kushner was as we have seen a member of President Donald Trump's inner circle. When he wed Trump's cherished daughter Ivanka, Kushner became Trump family royalty. As a high-ranking member of the family, he was important to Trump partly because family members, some family members anyway, were the only ones who seemed in the least to matter. Kushner was, moreover, in important ways familiar, recognizable to a man with Trump's personal and professional history. Not only had Jared been selected by Ivanka to be her husband, he was also, like Trump, a New York City metropolitan area real estate developer. Also like Trump, he was scion of a family that had made its money, an enormous amount of money, in real estate. Additionally, there was something unsavory about Kushner's family – as there was about Trump's. Trump's father,

Fred, had been accused of wrongdoing including, twice over, profiteering. Kushner's father, Charles, had served 14 months in a federal prison after pleading guilty to tax evasion, witness tampering, and making illegal campaign contributions.

Trump in any case took to Kushner, which is why when Trump entered political life, by his side was not only Ivanka, but Jared. In fact, it was Jared who from its inception played a critical role in Trump's first political campaign, his 2016 run for the White House. It didn't matter that Kushner had been up to then a lifelong Democrat or that he had up to then no political or government experience. Kushner was family, he was Ivanka's husband, and he clearly was game. So, in no time at all Kushner was playing a pivotal role in Trump's campaign for the White House, managing the candidate's digital, online, and social media outreach efforts. Before the campaign was over Kushner was promoted, serving as Trump's de facto campaign manager. Notwithstanding it was a campaign whose integrity has since been questioned, when Trump won the election Kushner was immediately rewarded for doing what many thought a splendid job: he was put in charge of the transition.[1] (Former CEO of Google, Eric Schmidt, said admiringly of Kushner that "he actually ran the campaign and did it with essentially no resources."[2])

When Donald Trump moved from New York to Washington, so did Ivanka Trump and Jared Kushner, the latter meanwhile having been named Senior Advisor to the President of the United States. The fact that Kushner's title was amorphous, with no clear definition or delineation, was appropriate, for he was immediately given an enormous portfolio, notwithstanding the fact that for any White House job he was, certainly on paper, entirely unqualified.

Kushner's lack of the usual requisites for high-level public service, and for overseeing a large, various, and complex government portfolio, was a theme throughout the entirety of Trump's presidency.[3] Small wonder then that Kushner's management of much if not most of the coronavirus crisis was incessantly under scrutiny. An April 2, 2020 an article in the *New York Times* described the situation: "At one of the most perilous moments in modern American history, Mr. Kushner is trying in a disjointed White House to marshal the forces of government for the war his father-in-law says he is waging. A real estate developer with none of the medical expertise of a public health official nor the mobilization experience of a general, Mr. Kushner has nonetheless become a key player in the response to the pandemic."[4] In truth, Kushner was not "a" key player, he was the major player, as the article itself made clear. "Because of his unique status, [Kushner] has made himself the point of contact for many agency officials who know that he can force action and issue decisions without going to the president."

Officially of course it was the White House Coronavirus Task Force, under the leadership of Mike Pence, that was charged with managing the pandemic. As we have seen, its formal mandate was to "coordinate and oversee the administration's efforts to monitor, prevent, contain and mitigate the spread" of COVID-19.[5] But as it turned out, for a range of reasons, foremost among them Kushner's special relationship with the president, it was Kushner who took charge, who ran operation COVID-19 out of the White House by effectively setting up a "shadow task force."[6] As it turned out, this shadow task force, more than the official one, was responsible for managing the pandemic on a day-to-day basis. To this end, Kushner formed several teams and assigned each to, above all, address the problem of shortages, shortages of almost everything that was needed to fight COVID-19.

Kushner's operation was all-encompassing and all-powerful. Being all-encompassing meant that it had, among others, the following responsibilities: weighing requests from state governors for aid; coordinating with private companies to ramp up production of badly needed medical supplies and equipment; delivering said medical supplies and equipment to where they were most needed, including airlifting of gloves, masks, gowns and ventilators; breaking down barriers to enable White House teams effectively to carry out their various tasks; and expanding access to testing. Being all-powerful meant that whatever the slings and arrows directed at Kushner from the outside, on the inside he was effectively untouchable. His protector was the president, an arrangement that, so long as Jared and Ivanka remained married, was likely never to be breached. Hence the reference to Kushner's "unique status." He was also described as "one of the most powerful players in Mr. Trump's West Wing"; "perhaps the most pivotal figure in the national fight against the fast-growing pandemic"; as having the "full confidence of President Donald Trump, with whom he confers multiple times a day"; and as having "vast responsibilities." As an advisor he was said to wield "the most influence over what Trump says and does."[7]

Given that the White House's response to the pandemic was assessed by many as "chaotic," given that Kushner's shadow task force usurped to a large extent Pence's official task force, given that charges of nepotism were as reliable as inevitable and, especially, given that during the first six months of 2020 the pandemic got much worse not much better, Kushner became, predictably, a favorite target. The charge in a nutshell: he was out of his league. Way, way, out of his league. As in, he is a "feckless nepotist who presumes to criticize governors striving to fill the void left by this previously unimaginable federal failure." He is "incurious, not inclined to defer to experts, and surrounds himself with yes men, so he is unaccustomed to being told that his decision-making is bad." And "Kushner's princely arrogance" has been a "fixture in the West Wing since Trump's inauguration."[8] Kushner spoke infrequently in public, so he rarely responded to the charges against either him or the president which, in addition to mismanagement, included favoritism and cronyism.[9] On those few occasions when Kushner did open his mouth he inclined, unsurprisingly, to parrot his father-in-law: "We've done things that government has never done before, quicker than they've ever done it before."[10]

Ultimate responsibility for what went wrong during the first six months of 2020 lies naturally at the doorstep of President Trump. Nevertheless, Kushner's role and record as an enabler could hardly be clearer. Included on the list of what clearly were transgressions was his reluctance if not refusal ever in any meaningful way to risk his place in Trump's pantheon by playing the part of devil's advocate. To the contrary, instead of challenging Trump and correcting for his weaknesses, he catered to Trump and played to his weaknesses.

There is no evidence, for instance, that Kushner encouraged the president more forcefully to invoke the Defense Production Act, which would have allowed the federal government to mandate the corporate sector quickly and efficiently to provide whatever supplies were needed – from low tech masks to high tech ventilators. Nor is there any evidence that Kushner tried to dissuade the president from conducting business as usual, which was to rely on his personal connections and longtime cronies rather than on the independent judgment of experts, especially doctors and scientists. Nor for that matter are there indications that when the president pushed, Kushner had the fortitude to stand up to him. In summer 2020 *Vanity Fair* reported that Kushner and his team had developed a secret plan that, had it been implemented, would have massively ramped up testing for COVID-19. But because it conflicted with the president's political ambitions the plan was shelved, with Kushner himself delivering the coup de grâce.[11] Above all, there is no evidence that Kushner encouraged the president to coordinate a national, federal response, as opposed to pushing responsibility for managing the pandemic onto the 50 states. Much of this devolution of power was, moreover, politicized. Michigan's Democratic Governor Gretchen Whitmer said she was told by vendors in March and April that they had been instructed "not to send stuff to Michigan."[12]

But of the countless ways in which Kushner enabled Trump, to miserable effect, during the crucial, critical, first six months of the coronavirus crisis, one stands out. Kushner encouraged and contributed not only to the president's magical thinking, his fantasies and fabrications, and his self-aggrandizement, but also to Trump's entirely unwarranted, dangerously misguided, optimism. Kushner, in other words, like virtually everyone else around Trump, had a fatal flaw. He was unwilling or unable to speak truth to power. What he lacked during his time in the White House, at least as it pertained to the pandemic, was less importantly about competence and more importantly about straightforwardness. Because he was, for whatever reason, unable absolutcly to separate himself from his father-in-law, his elder, in some ways his mentor, he "seemed to have adopted Trump's delusions as his own."[13]

In March, early in the outbreak, Kushner told the president what he most wanted to hear, that the media were exaggerating the dangers of the coronavirus. In April, Kushner told the president that New York's Governor Andrew Cuomo was being alarmist when he asked the federal government for tens of thousands of emergency ventilators. "I'm doing my own projections," Kushner was quoted as telling Trump, "and I've gotten a lot smarter about this. New York doesn't need all the ventilators." In the interest of getting the president reelected, Kushner continued as well to urge the president to overrule the experts. To overrule the doctors and scientists in order to declare that America would be "open for business" by Easter with, in Trump's words, "packed churches all over our country."[14] Kushner veritably boasted of his position when he spoke to chronicler Bob Woodward in April. Woodward has Kushner on tape freely revealing that the president was deliberately excluding the experts from the decision-making process. "You know," Kushner told Woodward, "it was almost like Trump was getting the country back from the doctors. Right? In the sense that what he now did was, you know, he's going to own the open-up." And again: "We've now put out the rules to get back to work. Trump's now back in charge. It's not the doctors."[15]

Of course, Kushner and his allies – such as Treasury Secretary Steven Mnuchin – had a reason for doing what they did. Along with the president they were hellbent on sounding positive, on being optimistic – notwithstanding the science, notwithstanding the facts and figures – for the purpose of jumpstarting the economy. Which in turn was intended to maximize the probability that Trump would be reelected in November. As one Republican put it, "Jared kept [worrying] the stock market would go down, and Trump wouldn't get reelected."[16] As April turned into May, Kushner told anyone willing to listen that the administration had done its job. "We're on the other side of the medical aspect of this, and I think that we've achieved all the different milestones that are needed," Kushner said to Fox News. "The federal government rose to the challenge, and this is a great success story. And I think that that's really, you know, what needs to be told." Kushner made his comments on the same day that the Commerce Department reported that the economy had suffered its largest decline since the recession of a decade earlier. And, just as Kushner was claiming "a great success story," the death toll from the virus in the United States topped 60,000, which amounted, as Peter Baker noted, to "more killed in eight weeks than the 58,000 American troops killed in eight years of major combat in Vietnam."[17]

MULVANEY AND MEADOWS

Mick Mulvaney and Mark Meadows served the president in the same capacity. At different times in 2020 they both served as chief of staff.[18] Mulvaney served from January 2019 to March 2020; Meadows from when Mulvaney, like his two predecessors in the post, was dismissed to the end of Trump's time in the White House. The White House denied the high rate of turnover had a negative impact on its response to the coronavirus crisis. It insisted "the chief of staff intentionally left virtually no gaps in . . . between transitions out and transitions in so that balls weren't dropped and things were smooth." But, as earlier noted, high rates of turnover are nearly never to the advantage of an organization, a general rule to which the White House is, to understate it, no exception.[19]

At no point in his brief tenure as (acting) chief of staff was Mulvaney in a strong position. At the time of the president's impeachment in late 2019, he was described as "isolated, marginalized and growing more irrelevant to the West Wing staff he's meant to lead."[20] So, in late February 2020, when concern over the new coronavirus was becoming palpable, all Mulvaney could do was try to protect Trump by playing down the importance of what was about to be declared a pandemic. On February 28, Mulvaney charged the media were paying attention to the coronavirus only because "they think this is going to be what brings down" the president. "That's what this is all about," Mulvaney insisted, going on to suggest that the best way to calm the nation's nerves, including the jittery markets, was to "tell people to turn their televisions off for 24 hours."[21]

A few months later it was revealed that just when Trump was publicly trumpeting the "fantastic economy," and just when Mulvaney was minimizing the threat of the virus, he sold a large amount of stock. On March 4, while he was still (acting) chief of staff, Mulvaney sold between $215,000 and $550,000 in mutual fund holdings. The sale may not have been illegal, but for him it was atypical, and it was in any case questionable. It certainly suggested that Mulvaney was aware of an impending crisis – specifically in public health.[22]

Mulvaney was in the event a failed chief of staff. Among other reasons, he, again like virtually everyone else in Trump's orbit, could not get himself to do what should have been done, speak truth to power. Obviously, Trump made it hard, extremely hard, for any underling to level with him. Still, it was hard only if the underling was hellbent on remaining in the president's good graces. Chris Whipple, who wrote a book about White House chiefs of staff, remarked at the time that "one of the principal reasons we are in this mess is because Trump has never had a chief of staff who will tell him hard truths, and under Mulvaney, Trump essentially defined the White House chief-of-staff job out of existence." Whipple went on to add, "now, we're in a crisis that requires a strong federal response and we're getting none of it. So, good luck, Meadows."[23]

The reference was to Mulvaney's successor, Mark Meadows, who at the time of his White House appointment had served in Congress for seven years, as representative from North Carolina. Meadows was not just a Republican, he was a leading Republican, an extremely conservative Republican, and a founding member of the right-wing House Freedom Caucus. Meadows was, moreover, a "fierce

Trump defender," already an enabler who was known to have "a strong personal relationship with the president."[24]

As chief of staff Meadows began immediately to implement the arrangement the president wanted – to divest himself so far as he could of day-to-day responsibility for managing the pandemic. To this end, every day at 8 a.m., beginning in April, Meadows "convened a small group of aides to steer the administration through what had become a public health, economic, and political disaster." Members of the group included among others Joe Grogan, a domestic policy advisor; Marc Short, the vice president's chief of staff; Hope Hicks, one of the members of the president's inner circle; and Jared Kushner, there not only as the president's son-in-law and senior advisor, but also in his capacity as a presumed expert on procurement.

It was this group that devised the strategy that became the single most significant hallmark of Trump's management of the pandemic – "shifting responsibility." This involved shifting responsibility for management of the pandemic from the federal government to the state governments, and from the president to the governors. Meadows's group referred to this strategy as "state authority handoff." Though he cast the decision to shift responsibility away from the White House in ideological terms – "Only in Washington, D.C. do they think that they have the answer for all of America" – the implications of the administration's "state authority handoff" were purely practical.[25] By dividing the task of controlling the coronavirus among 50 different state executives, Trump and Meadows virtually ensured the lack of coordination that turned out as counterproductive as it was unprecedented. Never in American history had a president – a self-described "wartime president," no less – shunted so large and daunting a task from the nation's capital to the 50 state capitals.[26]

During the period on which this book is primarily focused, January 1 to June 30, 2020, April was (to paraphrase T. S. Eliot) the cruelest month. It was in April that critical decisions at the national level were made – decisions badly reached and equally badly implemented. Meadows's working group included the infectious disease expert and prominent member of the White House Coronavirus Task Force, Dr. Deborah Birx. In spring she was an inveterate optimist, assuring her colleagues that outbreaks of the virus were easing. Though her interpretation of the situation was at odds with that of most of the nation's leading health experts, Meadows's working group chose to put its faith in Birx's optimism. Experts more likely to say what the administration did not want to hear were ignored. Which left the president free to start egging on the 50 governors, criticizing those who in his view were slow to "liberate" their states. Slow, that is, to reopen their states so that, as the president purported to see it, the nation's economy could recover as quickly and painlessly as possible.

The White House Coronavirus Task Force was the public face of the president's pandemic policymaking apparatus. But, again, it was those in the administration's inner sanctum who were responsible for what was decided and how it was implemented. It was people like Kushner and Meadows who, acting on behalf of the president, pulled the levers of power. Like Kushner, Meadows felt he was up to the task. He had years of experience in Washington; he had the president's ear; and he thought of himself as a data-driven decision maker well equipped to make policy based on objective evidence. Indeed, his group was able to implement its original decision, to sustain a month-long lockdown. However, in part because of its own flawed decision-making, and in part because of the president's growing impatience, Meadows's group did not carry out what should have been its second mandate, to sustain the lockdown long enough more effectively to contain COVID-19. Likely the group was doomed from the start, destined to fail to reach what should have been its overarching goal, putting the brakes on the pandemic. It reported to an impossibly difficult superior. It was vulnerable to groupthink because it consisted only of like-minded members. And it silenced those who dared in the least to disagree. It did not, for example, take long for Meadows to muzzle Dr. Anthony Fauci, who was forbidden from making more than a limited number of appearances on television, which had of course afforded him by far his largest audiences.

By early June it was clear that the White House had gotten it wrong. With the benefit of hindsight, Dr. Robert Redfield, head of the CDC, acknowledged as much. He said that "administration officials – himself included – severely underestimated infections in April and May."[27] It was a failure for which Meadows was in good part responsible. For reasons of political identity and tribal fealty, he effectively conspired with the president to downplay the virus crisis in favor of carrying out his political agenda.

Nor did Meadows have it in him to make a course correction. In August, the *Washington Post* reported: "As White House chief of staff, Mark Meadows is responsible for coordinating the vast executive branch, including the coronavirus response. But in closed-door meetings, he has revealed his skepticism of the two physicians guiding the anti-pandemic effort" – Birx and Fauci. (By then Birx was distinctly less rosy in her outlook than she had been a few months earlier.) Additionally, though by summer Meadows was no longer holding those 8 a.m. meetings, he did get together on a regular basis with an even smaller and more insular group, all of whom were "politically oriented." No surprise then that when the subject of the virus came up, the group focused more "on how to convince the public that President Trump has the virus under control" than it did on "methodically planning ways to contain it."[28]

NAVARRO, O'BRIEN, AND POTTINGER

During the period under discussion, the first half of 2020, Peter Navarro was an assistant to the president; his formal title was Director of the Office of Trade and Manufacturing Policy. He was also policy coordinator of the Defense Production Act. Navarro was by training an economist, which would suggest, certainly on the surface, he was an unlikely member of the team responsible for management of the pandemic. However, for various reasons, not least he was a longtime China hawk who, additionally, enjoyed being at or near the center of the action, Navarro inserted himself into this story from the start. Though he helped to manage the pandemic throughout the six-month period, his most intriguing contributions to the conversation were early in the year. The first was a memo dated January 29. Originally sent to the National Security Council (subsequently it was more widely distributed), it stated clearly and unequivocally that the new coronavirus posed a major threat to the American people. At a time when the administration was still badly dragging its feet, Navarro's January memo was the "highest-level alert known to have circulated in the West Wing."[29] He did not, moreover, mince words, writing in part: "The lack of immune protection or an existing cure or vaccine would leave Americans defenseless in the case of a full-blown coronavirus outbreak on U.S. soil. This lack of protection elevates the risk of the coronavirus evolving into a full-blown pandemic, imperiling the lives of millions of Americans."[30]

One month later Navarro wrote a somewhat similar memorandum, this one directed to the White House Coronavirus Task Force. This second alert was more dire even than the first, warning of the "increasing probability of a full-blown COVID-19 pandemic that could infect as many as 100 million Americans, with a loss of life of as many as 1–2 million souls."[31] Precisely because he was saying what the president did not want to hear, it soon became clear that Navarro, unlike Azar, knew how to manage up. For he not only survived in Trump's White House, he thrived. He along with a colleague, Matthew Pottinger, persuaded the president beginning February 2 to impose restrictions (later to have been found far too porous) on flights coming to the USA from China. He was given a lead role in coordinating the pandemic-related supply chain. And he somehow wangled his way into opining on medical issues, having the temerity to insist that because he was a social scientist – "I have a Ph.D. And I understand how to read statistical studies, whether it's in medicine, the law, economics or whatever" – he was qualified to engage with and even to take on Dr. Anthony Fauci.[32] Navarro actually had several run-ins with Fauci, the economist regularly siding with the president against the medical experts. In April Navarro said how "disappointing" it was that "so many medical experts and pundits pontificating in the press appear tone deaf to the very significant losses of life and blows to American families that may result from an extended economic shutdown."[33] And in July he wrote an opinion piece for *USA Today* titled, "Anthony Fauci has been wrong about everything I interacted with him on."[34] Mark Meadows was reputedly furious at Navarro for penning the inflammatory piece, but Navarro correctly believed that what he did, what he said, and what he wrote was for an audience of only one. His willingness to do what it took to stay in Trump's good graces also explains why Navarro shot an arrow at whistleblower Rick Bright's heart. Bright had once considered Navarro an ally. But when Bright did what he did, disclosed information about the administration that was highly embarrassing, Navarro called him a "deserter" – a "deserter in the war on the China virus."[35] (Predictably, Bright was not stopped. He continued his attacks on the Trump administration, his dissent becoming louder and more frequent in the weeks running up to the November election.)

In late summer it came out that Navarro likely engaged in deals that were shady, and that he had, in any case, alienated "numerous colleagues, corporate executives and prominent Republicans" with his "harsh manner and disregard for protocol." No matter – at least to the president. Navarro's "ability to stay in the president's ear" – a man with whom he had much in common – continued to protect Navarro well past his sell-by date.[36] Again, this was a man who knew how to play Trump's game. During the controversy in which he had gotten himself embroiled, he went on television and described himself as a "soldier for the greatest president in history – President Donald Trump."[37]

Robert O'Brien was the last in the line of Trump's national security advisors. In September 2019 he succeeded in that post the arrogant and opinionated, but also experienced and expert, John Bolton. O'Brien was both advantaged and disadvantaged by being Bolton's opposite. Where Bolton was somewhat disheveled, famously sporting a bushy, unruly mustache, O'Brien was polished and perfected, straight out of central casting, just as the president preferred.

Where Bolton was in-your-face with strongly held views, O'Brien was circumspect to the point of reticence. He was more ingratiator than irritant and, unlike Bolton, he did not seem to crave or relish the spotlight. Even to those in the know, O'Brien's name was hardly known – for Trump, the perfect underling. Finally, O'Brien was, in comparison with Bolton, and even with another of his predecessors, H. R. McMaster, a relative novice. O'Brien had some experience in government, specifically in foreign affairs, but not that much. He was, therefore, malleable, willing to go along to get along, whether with his immediate superior the president, or with his longtime associate, Secretary of State Mike Pompeo.

When the history of this period is written, O'Brien will be most remembered for the moment when, on January 28, 2020, during a discussion in the Oval Office about the "mysterious pneumonia-like virus outbreak in China," he turned to the president and told him, "This will be the biggest national security threat you face in your presidency." O'Brien continued, as if to underscore, "This is going to be the roughest thing you face." According to the account provided by Bob Woodward in his book, *Rage*, O'Brien's deputy, Matthew Pottinger, sitting on a couch toward the back, then weighed in strongly to support what O'Brien had just said. "I agree with that conclusion," Pottinger seconded.[38] Theirs was a shot across Trump's bow, a warning delivered in clear, stark terms of what lay ahead unless action was taken – action as dramatic as immediate.

Pottinger's formal title was Senior Director of the National Security Council's Asia division.[39] He is important to this story because the president knew he was perfectly positioned to make his assessment. It was Pottinger, not his boss, O'Brien, who was an expert on China. Pottinger had lived in China for seven years, was a student of China, and fluent in Mandarin. Further, he knew something about infectious diseases, having worked in Hong Kong as correspondent for the *Wall Street Journal* during the SARS epidemic (in the early 2000s). His job at the *Journal* was to document "the death spread by that highly contagious virus," an experience that reportedly left him "scarred."[40] So, when it became apparent that a new coronavirus was threatening America, and that the virus was coming from China, to Pottinger it seemed a perfect storm. He was anyway, as was O'Brien, a China hawk, deeply suspicious of the Chinese authorities. Moreover, in early January, pursuant to speaking with experts in China, and to an epidemiologist in Hong Kong, and to others who were knowledgeable as well, his suspicions only grew. The Hong Kong doctor was a longtime friend. He told Pottinger that there was a "ferocious new outbreak" in China that resembled the SARS epidemic, and that was already more widespread than the Chinese government was willing publicly to concede. He said the new coronavirus was highly contagious and predicted that it would rapidly spread not only within China but without.[41]

Navarro, O'Brien, and Pottinger were all China hawks, but the first was a showboat. O'Brien and Pottinger were the opposite, with Pottinger especially being retiring, relying on his expertise on China to continue to stand him in good stead. After talking with the epidemiologist from Hong Kong, Pottinger read John Barry's *The Great Influenza*, a meticulous account of the 1918 flu pandemic. The book, along with the continuing news from Asia, was said to have persuaded Pottinger even early in the year to take his own steps toward mitigation and containment. For example, he took pains to ensure continuity in the National Security Council in the event a member got sick. He also began to social distance before social distancing became any sort of norm. And he started to wear a mask, and to urge mask-wearing and hand hygiene on everyone else well before any other member of the president's team did the same. While acting chief of staff Mulvaney was still telling staffers in the White House not to wear a face covering, Pottinger already had been wearing one for weeks. He even wore a mask in front of President Trump, who was reported to have found it "wryly amusing."[42]

But, though both O'Brien and Pottinger were among the administration's fiercest China hawks, and though both of them were among the few who fully understood the threat posed by the new coronavirus, neither of them was aggressive or even assertive when it came to the American president. On the occasion in early January when O'Brien warned the president about the "roughest" thing he would face, he was as direct with Trump as he knew how; Pottinger the same. But while they remained for the duration part of the decision-making process, such as it was, there is no record of the national security advisor or of his deputy ever having pushed the president past his comfort zone, carefully to consider the gravity of the situation. Woodward reports, for example, that O'Brien was "worried there was a hole in the original travel restrictions from China."[43] But Woodward does not report that O'Brien's worry on this or on anything else led to his pressing the president in any way that was other than extremely if not excessively genteel.

Pottinger in turn was a Marine. He had joined the US Marine Corps after (interestingly, not before) his successful career in journalism. Perhaps this explains why, though he was not shy about expressing his views, he never tried especially hard to persuade anyone of their virtues, least of all the commander in chief. Instead Pottinger had a "military-style respect for the chain of command" and "an extraordinary sense of caution." He remained for the duration of his time in the White House unwilling to "push something unless the president [had] clearly approved it."[44] This diffidence goes a long way toward explaining why whatever the level of his private concern, in public, in his capacity as a professional, Pottinger was an enabler. It explains why, though he knew about the new coronavirus before almost anyone else, and though he understood better than almost anyone else the level of the threat, he nevertheless played by the rules. Rules that in his case included not continuing to push information on a superior who did not even once want to hear. (Pottinger did ultimately resign his post, but only after Trump's supporters stormed the US Capitol and some 14 days before Trump was anyway to be replaced by president-elect Joe Biden.)

HICKS AND CONWAY

Hope Hicks and Kellyanne Conway were earlier described as being in the outer ring of President Donald Trump's inner circle. In keeping with their status as among the small number of people who could be described as close to a man to whom it was impossible to be close, they continued during the pandemic to play their parts to perfection, enablers both, rather as they had during the three years preceding. To be sure, they were bit parts: neither Hicks nor Conway had a major role or even much of a substantive role in managing the pandemic. Still, they mattered. On some occasions they mattered because of what they did. And on all occasions they mattered during the first six months of 2020 because of who they were: undying and unflagging supporters of President Trump on a professional level and, for different reasons, on a personal level as well.

Hicks was as we have seen absent from the White House for an extended time during Trump's tenure – during which she worked, not incidentally, as communications director for Fox News. But in winter 2020 she returned, again to take her place in the president's firmament, this time in an ostensibly new post, as "counselor to the president." Formally she was to report to Jared Kushner. Informally everyone who knew anything about the president knew that he liked, very much liked, having Hicks around and so her place in the White House hierarchy was not exactly rigidly defined. During the 2016 presidential campaign she reportedly became "indispensable to Mr. Trump," and once he was president, he brought her into the West Wing. Without elaboration the *New York Times* reported, dryly, that though some "newer and more senior aides tried to block Ms. Hicks's access to the president . . . her relationship with him outlasted most of their tenures."[45] In October, after Hicks and Trump tested positive for COVID-19 at essentially the same time, the *Washington Post* described their relationship this way: "Whatever [Hicks's] title . . . she has managed his moods and counseled him on nearly everything, from the most substantive to the trivial." She has "spent more time with him than almost anyone else outside the family."[46]

When it was first announced, in February 2020, that Hicks would return to the White House it was assumed she would work mainly on the president's campaign for reelection in November. However, events intervened. By the time she arrived back in Washington, in early March, to take up her new post, things had changed. It was the pandemic that was at the top of the president's agenda.

One of the ways Hicks ingratiated herself with Trump was tried and true: flattery. Hicks had always assured her boss that no one could convey his message better than he. Moreover, coming from her, whose relative area of expertise was, after all, communications, the suggestion that he was his own best spokesman carried weight. So, when the new coronavirus became a crisis, and she urged Trump personally to communicate whatever message the White House wanted to send, he listened. Instead of delegating this responsibility either to the head of the White House Coronavirus Task Force, Mike Pence, or to experts, in this case in public health, the president took it on himself to play the lead role at those daily administration press briefings. This was a role in which Hicks as much as anyone else had cast him. It was she who believed that his content should not be outsourced, and it was she who believed that he was "at his strongest when he [was] communicating directly with the public."[47]

Trump's decision to speak at almost every task force briefing – not only to speak but to elbow aside everyone else – had the desired effect, initially. Initially it led to a bump in his approval ratings and the feeling among his base, his party, and members of his administration that the White House was now, finally, in control of messaging the pandemic – and managing the pandemic. But as we saw, these feelings of relief were brief. In short order these self-same briefings became a fiasco, an embarrassment to the White House and, more importantly, to the president himself.

Notwithstanding the idea that turned sour, the idea for which Hicks was as responsible as anyone else, she remained among his senior advisors, in some ways a first among equals. Above all, she retained her prominent, apparently unassailable position as a member of the president's inner circle. Hicks was easy to get along with; she remained close to the president's family, especially Ivanka, who years earlier had been her employer; and she was included in the small working group assembled by Mark Meadows. Her substantive role in the working group remained unclear, but she was seen by the president's chief of staff as by everyone else: protector in chief of the chief executive. As Sarah Huckabee Sanders, erstwhile White House press secretary, once said of Hicks, "She is not driving her own agenda or any specific policy ... To have a staffer like that, who is a purist, is important."[48] In this case, of course, being a purist was being an enabler – an enabler pure and simple.

On March 6, 2020, Kellyanne Conway assured Americans that the new coronavirus was being "contained." That it was already contained and that it would continue to be contained. In truth, no one was able to spin Trump-truth like Conway. It was the secret behind why she remained for as long as she did in the outer ring of the president's inner circle, senior counselor to the president. Conway had arrived, of course, early to the party. She had played a significant role in Trump's presidential campaign – as formally his campaign manager, albeit his third campaign manager – and she was in her own right a successful professional, a woman of substance. But once she got to the White House her main task was to sell. To sell the American president. Famous forever for her phrase "alternative facts," Conway's job was to spin the truth in defense of her difficult and demanding boss – notwithstanding that under his leadership the American people were coping with three crises simultaneously.[49]

Occasionally she got into trouble, as she did early in Trump's term after coining the Orwellian term, "alternative facts," and as she did again in April 2020, when she went on Fox News and got tangled in the question of how "COVID-19" came to be named. (She thought the number "19" meant it was nineteenth in a string of similar viruses; in fact, it signifies the year, 2019, the virus was identified.) Still, Conway managed to skitter over the morass, remaining until she resigned in summer 2020 secure in the knowledge that so long as she hewed to the White House line, deviating from it not even a smidgeon, she would keep her job. So, throughout the first half of 2020 she did her thing, defending the president at every turn and taking on everyone who had the temerity to challenge him. In April, for example, she attacked the governor of Michigan by siding with protesters objecting to the state's COVID-19 lockdown orders. "I look at these people and I see the forgotten men and forgotten women, economically," she said. "In Michigan you can basic-ally smoke your grass but not cut your grass. This makes no sense to many people."[50] (In 2018 the state of Michigan legalized the use of recreational marijuana; during the virus crisis the state did not label landscaping an essential service.) And in August, even as she had one foot out the White House door, Conway stayed on message. Hard on the heels of the Democratic convention she laid into Joe Biden, calling his remarks on the pandemic a "confounding display of the intersection of arrogance and ignorance."[51] Trump attack dog to the last.

In fall 2020, within days of the first presidential debate, Donald Trump, Hope Hicks, and Kellyanne Conway all contracted COVID-19. Hicks had accompanied Trump (to Ohio) for the occasion. Conway, notwithstanding her formal departure from the White House, had prepped Trump for the occasion. The fact that all three contracted the disease at essentially the same critical moment in the campaign, was fitting confirmation, if any were needed, of how tight they were and remained for the duration. Though Hicks and Conway had not much in common with each other, and nearly nothing in common with the other senior advisors who hung on and hung in to the end, or nearly so, of Trump's term – Kushner, Meadows, Navarro, O'Brien, and Pottinger – they did all share this: their enablement of the president made each a critical cog in the White House machine.

11 Senators, Governors, Media

Two senators, two governors, and four members of the media were part of President's Donald Trump's team – specifically as it pertained to the pandemic – during the period January through June 2020. Each in an important way regularly and, to all appearances, enthusiastically supported the president's management of America's worst public health crisis in over a century. Each, then, was an enabler, a follower who allowed or even encouraged Trump to engage in, and then to persist in behaviors that were destructive. Discussed in this chapter are Senate Majority Leader Mitch McConnell, Senator Lindsey Graham, Governors Mike DeSantis and Brian Kemp, and Fox News heavyweights Rupert Murdoch, Tucker Carlson, Laura Ingraham, and Sean Hannity – all of whom during the coronavirus crisis prioritized the president's political interest over the national interest.

MCCONNELL AND GRAHAM

For the entirety of Donald Trump's presidency, the Senate was led by Kentucky Republican Mitch McConnell. In his capacity as Senate Majority Leader, McConnell necessarily played a pivotal part during the pandemic. Specifically, he was essential to getting the executive and legislative branches to work together at least well enough to pass several coronavirus bailout bills intended to forestall the economy from collapse. But this explains only in part his importance as an enabler, which was not so much about what happened during the pandemic as what happened preceding it. It is impossible, in short, to discuss the enablement of President Trump at any point in his term without including McConnell in the discussion. Not for nothing was Jane Mayer's April 2020 *New Yorker* profile of McConnell titled, "Enabler in Chief."[1]

At the Republican convention in summer 2020, Trump's single living Republican presidential predecessor, George W. Bush, made not even a brief, symbolic appearance. Nor for that matter did Bush's vice president, diehard lifetime Republican, Dick Cheney. Their absence from the occasion spoke volumes. But, notwithstanding the contempt for Trump among those who were part of the Republican establishment, and notwithstanding his own long history as a member of what once was called "the world's greatest deliberative body," McConnell hung in. His support for Trump during virtually his entire time in the White House remained single-minded and single-tracked. McConnell made it his mission to sustain his presidency, to enable his presidency, no matter what.

Theirs was a transactional relationship. There was no love lost on either side, partly because they were opposites, even in style. Trump was a vulgar showman, McConnell a taciturn gentleman. But though Trump stood obviously to benefit from McConnell's support, what was in it for McConnell? Why was this proud man with a decades-long history as one of the nation's leading legislators willing to enable a man who in many ways was so wanting? There were the usual reasons: ideological affinity and political expediency. But given that Trump was such a departure from the Republican norm – at one point McConnell said of him with palpable disdain, "Our new president has of course not been in this line of work before, and I think had excessive expectations about how quickly things happen in the democratic process" – what was it about McConnell that made him so willing to bend to a man from a planet other than his own?[2]

McConnell was married to a member of President Trump's Cabinet, Secretary of Transportation, Elaine Chao. It was a useful connection that McConnell was unapologetic about leveraging to his political advantage. More to the point, however, was sheer self-interest. As McConnell perceived it, his interest coincided nearly exactly with Trump's in important ways: political and ideological. McConnell can fairly be said to have long had a single goal above all: to remake the federal judiciary. In this Trump was his willing partner, supportive in every way, allowing McConnell to achieve what to him was most important. By June 2020, McConnell, who had vowed to "leave no vacancy behind," was able to claim that for the first time in 40 years there was not "a single Circuit Court vacancy anywhere in the nation."[3]

Initially, especially given he was new to Washington, Trump relied heavily on the Majority Leader to pursue a legislative agenda that was broadly consistent with that of the Republican Party: rolling back Obama-era regulations, ramming through a giant tax cut, rebuilding the military, and slashing regulations. Trump further depended on McConnell to continue to play "wingman to the White House" on judicial nominations, even those he questioned, like Brett Kavanaugh, to the Supreme Court.[4] In other words, Trump's ignorance of the ways of Washington, as well as his own malleability on public policy – "I am very pro-choice," he had said in 1999 – gave McConnell considerable latitude. It left the leader relatively free to exercise power as he saw fit – an arrangement that suited both men. Two years into Trump's term, he still considered McConnell, and McConnell still considered himself, one of the president's most important advisors. They spoke almost every day, and almost every day McConnell willingly did the president's bidding, which usually coincided neatly with what he anyway wanted to accomplish.

On a personal level it was power that most interested McConnell – not ideology. He was far hungrier for personal power than for ideological purity. He had been a legislative force to be reckoned with for decades and, at age 78 he wanted badly to stay just where he was, Senate Majority Leader, for one more six-year Senate term. This would require that he regain his Senate seat in November 2020. And it would equally require that in November 2020 the Republican Party hold on to its Senate majority. In order for these things to happen, McConnell had no choice, or so he thought, but to throw in his lot with the president, to back him at every turn, no matter his personal distaste for a man he reportedly could not stand and whom at least once he called "nuts."[5] Why? Again, because of the base. Because Trump's support among self-identified Republicans remained rock solid, and because Kentucky remained a deep red state that was taken with the nation's chief executive. A poll taken in August 2020 showed that while only a slim majority of Kentuckians supported Trump's management of the pandemic, had the election been held then he still would have beaten Joe Biden by double digits.[6]

If McConnell's enablement of Trump was in evidence throughout almost the entirety of his presidency – though as time went on his enablement was more grudging – there was a moment at which the senator's support for the president was pivotal. McConnell personally and politically protected Trump during the first impeachment trial, which made it possible for the president to finish his term without the proceedings upending or even significantly impairing him. More than anyone else, it was the Senate Majority Leader who shielded Trump from political harm, and who, by precluding even a single witness from testifying at the trial, effectively ensured that the chief executive could serve out his term unimpeded. "In the days leading up to the vote, McConnell asserted – in public, at least – that he wasn't sure if he had the votes to stop witnesses from being called ... The day before the vote, McConnell got the lifeline he needed from his old friend Lamar Alexander of Tennessee, who said he would oppose witnesses."[7] The outcome of the trial was never really in doubt. But had witnesses been called, Trump would have suffered a bad, perhaps even a crippling, blow.

Mayer's article, "Enabler in Chief," is persuasive. She points out that McConnell "stayed largely silent about the President's lies and inflammatory public remarks," and that he "propped up the Administration with legislative and judicial victories." But, with specific regard to the COVID-19 "disaster," she approvingly quotes long-time Republican consultant Stuart Stevens, who had a jaundiced view of McConnell's legacy: "Mitch is kidding himself if he thinks he'll be remembered for anything other than Trump. He will be remembered as the Trump facilitator."[8] While McConnell did not play a major role in managing the pandemic per se, his support of Trump during his presidency, including through the multiple crises that plagued the American people in 2020, was crucial. The Senate Majority Leader propped up the president before the pandemic, and during the pandemic, which made him throughout an enabler, a follower who allowed and even encouraged his leader, Trump, to engage in, and then to persist in, behaviors that were destructive. By the time McConnell's façade finally cracked – by the time he let even a sliver of daylight come between him and the White House – it was too late. By October 2020 – when the Majority Leader finally admitted he disapproved of the way the White House mishandled masking and social distancing even within its own walls – the damage was done. But it took the attack on the Capitol (in January 2021) to trigger the final break between McConnell and the man he had enabled for so long. One day before the inauguration of the next president, he said of the present president that he had "provoked" the mob guilty of the mayhem.

I already pointed to Republican senators as among the most culpable of all the president's enablers. Their studied silence throughout the early weeks of the pandemic, and then during the months subsequent, was stunning, deeply offensive even to the idea of the three branches of government as equal. No matter how egregious the president's mismanagement of the virus crisis, no matter how outrageous his falsehoods and fantasies, virtually every Republican senator chose to be a bystander, silent, effectively mute in the face of their perception of the president's power.

For various reasons, Lindsey Graham sometimes seemed in a class by himself. Among them he was the most fawning. He was hellbent on becoming a Trump crony – and a Trump crony he became. Senator from South Carolina since 2003, Graham had long been known for two reasons: first, for being relatively, if only very occasionally, bipartisan in an increasingly partisan senate; second, for his special friendship with Arizona's venerated senator (and onetime Republican nominee for president), John McCain. For years Graham and McCain were to all appearances the best of friends, so well known for being close that they, along with Connecticut's Senator Joe Lieberman, were tagged the "Three Amigos." As Graham told ABC News after McCain died, "We've traveled the world together. I've seen these guys in action ... The three of us couldn't be more different ... Yet there we were in the U.S. Senate together, and we became just the fastest of friends."[9]

Not only was Graham personally and professionally close to McCain, who pointedly loathed Trump and whom Trump loathed in return, not long before Graham himself had repeatedly denigrated Trump, calling the man who handily beat him in the 2016 primaries a "kook," "crazy," and "unfit for public office."[10] So the bond between the two men, Graham and McCain, held during the first eighteen months of Trump's presidency. But, when McCain became gravely ill and then finally died, Graham did an about-face. It was a pivot so jarringly out of keeping with his long friendship with McCain that journalist Mark Leibovich described Graham as seeming to "occupy his own distinct category of Trump-era contortionist."

As we saw, there were several reasons for the countless conversions from mainstream Republicanism to Trumpism. It is fair to say, though, that no single conversion was as baffling to pundits as Graham's, precisely because he had been so close to John McCain and was now trying with every fiber of his political being to get at least a little bit close to Donald Trump. In this effort Graham succeeded. He became as tied to Trump as he could reasonably have hoped, which was not a lot, but it was a little. In his zeal to, above all, be reelected in November 2020, Graham managed to ingratiate himself with the president to whose fortunes from that point on he would inextricably be tied. Leibovich interviewed Graham and asked him point-blank, what had happened, what explained his about-face from staunch ally of McCain to staunch ally of Trump. "From my point of view, if you know anything about me," Graham replied, "it'd be odd not to do this. To try to be relevant." As he saw it, or at least as he explained it for public consumption, he played up to Trump not out of self-interest but in the public interest. "I've got an opportunity up here working with the president to get some really good outcomes for the country."[11]

His protestations notwithstanding, Graham as much as acknowledged that many had come to see him as, simply, a Trump toady. But he insisted that catering to the president was worth it. For Graham, in any case, it paid off, at least in the short term. To his credit he achieved what he wanted to achieve – he got into Trump's orbit. He got himself invited to Mar-a-Lago. (He was present, for example, at a lavish 50th birthday party for Don Jr.'s girlfriend, Kimberly Guilfoyle.) He got to be a regular Trump golf partner. (They played a round just before the president's first impeachment trial.) And by 2019 he was able, accurately, to describe himself as a member of Trump's "smaller orbit." Who else was in that smaller orbit, he was asked. According to Graham it was Melania, Ivanka, Jared, and a few "New York types" that "still have a say." But Graham went on, "the circle is small."[12] In other words, in consequence of his efforts he had successfully entered what Trump's nemesis, Hillary Clinton, would have called Trump's "zone of privacy."

Senator Graham's relationship with President Trump was not without its ups and downs. First, Graham was never in total lockstep with Trump, for example on Dr. Anthony Fauci. For failing to fall reliably into line Trump came to distrust Fauci, while Graham made clear throughout 2020 that he did trust the good doctor, certainly over and above the political pundits. Second, the senator did not entirely abandon his previously held positions, for example on immigration, on which his position was more liberal than the president's. Because of their political differences there were, then, times during which Graham and Trump's crony-type relationship "hit the skids."[13] Still, it was in their shared interest to smooth over whatever disagreements they had, and to maintain what had evolved into a perfectly pleasant and politically profitable relationship. During the all-important first impeachment trial, Graham, who conveniently was head of the Senate Judiciary Committee, was, along with Majority Leader Mitch McConnell, Trump's most significant defender. He derided the inquiry as a "lynching." And he continued to insist, notwithstanding damning testimony from White House officials that Trump did try to get Ukrainian officials to find dirt on Joe Biden's son, Hunter, that the president had done nothing wrong.

As the coronavirus went from public health concern to public health crisis, Graham did what he had tried to do since the start of Trump's presidency: have it both ways. On the one hand he retained a modicum of independence, for example in spring when Trump was touting the nation's testing as "the best of any country in the world," Graham held his ground. Though he specifically absolved the president of responsibility for what went wrong – "I can't really blame the president" – the senator did nevertheless implicitly contradict him by admitting the nation was "struggling with testing on a large scale."[14] Graham continued to do the same on immigration, making clear that a stringent new visa order, signed by the president in June, would, in his view, have a "chilling effect on our economic recovery."[15] Still, by and large the senator stood staunchly in the president's corner, holding whoever was the other, for example China, responsible for what went wrong. Graham sided with Secretary of State Mike Pompeo in recommending that sanctions be imposed on China for refusing to cooperate on investigating the origins of the new coronavirus. Similarly, domestically. As the number of deaths from COVID-19 continued to climb, Graham kept moving the goalposts. In defending what came slowly but certainly widely to be seen as Trump's "botched response," Graham kept raising the number of deaths he said would be acceptable.[16] It was an inconsistency for which he would pay a political price: it was used against him by his opponent in the 2020 Senate race, Jaime Harrison, which turned out to be a tough campaign.

In early March, Graham, like Trump, kept it simple. He downplayed the danger of the new coronavirus by comparing it, inaccurately obviously, to an ordinary flu. In mid-March, on Fox News, Graham, again like Trump, effectively blamed the media, saying the media was exaggerating the threat and covering the pandemic "like a series of plane crashes." In early April, again on

Fox News, Graham testified that if the number of COVID-19 deaths remained below 50,000, he would be satisfied, he would "say we've acted decisively." But, just a few days later, as the number of deaths continued relentlessly to climb, Graham upped his numbers. Now his metric of success was anywhere from 50,000 to 100,000. By May, the number of deaths that seemed to him acceptable had risen again, to between 100,000 and 130,000. Graham did not at any point blame Trump for anything. "We don't blame Trump, we blame China," he said in April. And in May he wrote, "I'm convinced that if we had not engaged in aggressive mitigation practices the number [of deaths] would be much greater."

Though Graham repeatedly as typically praised the president's golf game – for example, in July, after a round together at Trump's National Golf Club in Virginia, the senator said "I've never seen him play this well . . . He beat me like a drum!" – he would deny ever playing the part of Trump sycophant. It is fair enough to say that Graham did occasionally deviate from the party line. However, it is also fair to say that to the degree that he is remembered 50 years from now, it will be as a quintessential political opportunist. Graham did what he could to become Trump's crony and Trump's crony he became and remained – effectively to the bitter end. But though Graham assumed it was a relationship from which he would benefit, for his pivot he paid a price. In some circles it made him a marked man. Steve Schmidt, who ran McCain's failed 2008 presidential campaign, effectively called him a Judas. "With regard to the cruelty and abuse that was directed at John McCain by Trump, I think Lindsey's flaccidity in defending him says a lot about his character . . . When someone walks up and punches your best friend in the face, you've got to do something. Lindsey has demonstrated he's the guy who runs out the door."[17]

DESANTIS AND KEMP

Think of Florida Governor Ron DeSantis, Georgia Governor Brian Kemp, and other state leaders who were similar, such as Texas

Governor Greg Abbott, as generals leading their troops in the field. While the president and members of his administration remained in Washington, first and foremost on the front lines were Trump's generals, Republican governors, especially those who so closely followed his lead that they took their orders effectively from him. These governors enabled the president by regularly and reliably taking their cues from the White House, even though the White House was frequently misguided or even dangerously mistaken. By repeating the administration's admonitions over and again, governors like DeSantis and Kemp sent a message. They as much as said to their constituents, to the residents of Florida and Georgia respectively, that they too should be drinking the White House Kool-Aid.

To be clear, not every Republican governor continued for months on end to follow so faithfully the party line. As we saw earlier, a few, such as Ohio's Mike DeWine, broke quietly with the administration relatively early on. Others, such as Arkansas Governor Asa Hutchinson, took longer to leave the fold but eventually did, to at least a degree. (In July Hutchinson mandated mask-wearing, including at every Trump rally held in his state.) But some held firm; on the pandemic some Republican governors never strayed from the president's side, having decided, apparently, that their political futures and personal fortunes would sink or swim with him.

Of course, in so deciding for themselves, they were deciding as well for those in their states. This is not to say that every resident of Florida, for example, swore by DeSantis's every word or followed his every lead. Instead it is to point out that even though the governor was an abject follower of the president, he was at the same time the leader of the state of Florida. What he did and did not do, therefore, was bound to have at least some impact on every Floridian. Moreover, because Trump was president during the early months of the pandemic, governors were given special powers. As we saw earlier, Trump was quick to shift responsibility for managing the pandemic from the federal government to the state governments. Thus, the 50 governors of the 50 different states were as empowered as encumbered. As the authors of an article in *The Atlantic* put it, Trump might have created an unanticipated legacy. "By ceding some control to the states, he [allowed] the nation's governors to reacquire executive muscle that [had] withered in the age of the imperial presidency." He effectively compelled them to "confront a worldwide crisis they wouldn't have imagined would be theirs to solve."[18]

Which returns us to DeSantis. After having served in relative obscurity as a congressman, he was elected governor of Florida in 2018, to a considerable extent on the strength of Trump's endorsement. So, the governor owed the president, from whose political beneficence he had profited. But by early 2020 relations between the two men had somewhat soured, DeSantis perceived by the president as being a secret centrist, who was not nearly loyal enough, not nearly fierce enough a "verbal knife fighter."[19] But once the pandemic descended, DeSantis apparently decided that the last thing he wanted was to be hung out to dry by Trump. Quite the opposite – he clearly concluded it was in his interest nearly blindly to follow the president's lead.

So, DeSantis went ahead in March and closed Florida's schools, though he was not then willing to close the crowded beaches. Moreover, he did not impose a statewide stay-at-home order until April 1, after every other major state in the union. Just as Trump did, he blamed New Yorkers for bringing the virus to Florida. Just like Trump he refused to model proper pandemic behavior: regularly to wear a mask and to socially distance. For his loyalty to the president DeSantis was rewarded: he became – for a time – a Trump favorite. When the governor faced growing criticism not only at home but around the country for refusing to shut down Florida entirely, Trump made sure to describe him at a press briefing as a "great governor," who "knows exactly what he's doing." In turn, when the governor did finally issue a statewide stay-at-home order, one that applied across the board, he made clear he did so only after talking to Trump and securing his approval.[20]

Of course, all this self-congratulatory gladhanding was easy enough to do in spring. For example, in April, when DeSantis traveled to Washington to meet with Trump at the White House the governor was able to boast, "Everyone in the media was saying Florida was going to be like New York or Italy and that has not happened ... We had a tailored and measured approach that not only helped our numbers be way below what anybody predicted, but also did less damage to our state going forward."[21] As long as the number of Florida's COVID-19 cases remained low it was also easy enough more broadly to accentuate the positive and eliminate the negative. Which explains why DeSantis continued to sound just like Trump, ever the cheerleader; and why DeSantis continued to act just like Trump, or, at least, to do what the president wanted him to do. Which was of course – despite the endlessly repeated warnings sounded by nearly every top health official – to reopen the economy as rapidly and expansively as possible. This included Florida's bars, beaches, restaurants, movie theaters, and entertainment venues.

In consequence of reopening too much too fast, by summer the situation in Florida deteriorated. On July 12, the *New York Times* reported the state had "the highest single-day total of new coronavirus cases by any state since the start of the pandemic, with more than 15,000 new infections, eclipsing the previous high of 12,274 recorded in New York on April 4 amid the worst of its outbreak."[22] Did DeSantis bend to the prevailing wind? Did he shift at least a little bit? Not a whit. The man who was sometimes called Florida's "mini Trump" did what the maxi Trump would have done. He doubled down. Despite his unfavorable ratings having risen between June and July from approximately 30 percent to 40 percent, he stayed on Trump's track.[23] He found fault with some of the science. He barred a reporter from a press briefing after she requested social distancing. He kept insisting that whatever the rising numbers were, there was no cause for alarm. And, of course, for shelter he turned to Fox News, to the hearth that was *The Sean Hannity Show*. In July *Politico* reported the following: "Staggering from a string of messaging gaffes, dire coronavirus numbers, a tough encounter with the Miami press and more mainstream media piling on, Florida Gov. Ron DeSantis is retreating to his safe space: 'The Sean Hannity Show.'"[24]

By summer 2020 nearly one third of counties in Florida were requiring mask-wearing. But not the state – not DeSantis. He refused to make masks mandatory and he himself wore one on some occasions but not on others. Given what had happened in Florida during the half year preceding, it seemed reasonable to presume that the governor would put some daylight between him and the president. But he did no such thing. Remaining steadfast, he along with other of the nation's governors still were where they had been from the start – enablers. Leaders of states who enabled the leader of the country by following him in lockstep. DeSantis even went so far as to cozy up to Dr. Scott Atlas. Though by summer, Atlas was Trump's high profile and preferred coronavirus advisor, he was a radiologist with no expertise whatsoever in infectious disease who was, moreover, widely derided as dangerous by the medical establishment.

On March 14, 2020 Georgia Governor Brian Kemp declared a statewide public health emergency. He made clear even in the wording of his announcement that he was in total alignment with the American president. "Based on President Trump's emergency declaration, I will declare a public health emergency for the State of Georgia tomorrow morning."[25]

We now know that within weeks if not days after having imposed a lockdown, Trump grew restless, impatient with the instruction that he himself had given. In short order then he and his vice president began urging states to reopen, which is what they repeatedly told Kemp to do – to reopen. In private conversations they assured the governor of Georgia that they approved of his aggressive timetable for allowing businesses especially – including restaurants, bars, and spas – to open again statewide. But, after being warned off the original plan by some of his own health experts, Trump reversed course, leaving Kemp high and dry. Notwithstanding he had just recently bestowed his blessing in private, in public Trump chastised his loyal ally for having moved too far too fast. "I told the governor of Georgia Brian Kemp that I disagree strongly with his decision to open certain facilities," said the president in late April.[26]

Kemp though was not deterred. Notwithstanding the president's public scolding, he remained at the forefront of Republican governors who were among Trump's most enthusiastic enablers. Their unwavering support of Trump at the level of the state was a critical part of what undergirded Trump's tenure in the White House. To be sure, before the pandemic even hit, Kemp already had a reputation for being a would-be strongman, in the mold of Donald Trump. Kemp was especially aggressive on the issue of voter registration, having purged more than a million voters from the state's rolls, disproportionately people of color. So, when the pandemic became a fact of everyday life, no one was surprised to see Kemp militant in his response, even, as we saw, going so far as to sue Atlanta Mayor Keisha Lance Bottoms for imposing a citywide mask mandate. (The governor later relented; in summer he began, reluctantly, himself to encourage mask-wearing, though he continued to strongly oppose any sort of mask rule.)

Kemp was in fact another mini-Trump. He was not only prepared to sacrifice himself at the president's altar – the president who had not hesitated to rebuke him – he was eager to do so. Concluded Amanda Mull writing in August for *The Atlantic*, Kemp "demonstrated a willingness to defer to the president instead of his own constituents." Millions of Georgians "suffered as a result, with no end in sight."[27] She was not wrong. Like the country under Trump's leadership, the state under Kemp's leadership fared poorly. Among the last states to institute a shelter-in-place order and among the first to reopen, in August Georgia had more deaths on any single day than since the start of the pandemic. Of the fifty states, it had the fifth most COVID-19 cases overall (the seventh most per capita), and the fourth most hospitalizations.[28]

So much for following where Trump led – especially since the old adage, "no good deed goes unpunished," ended applying to Kemp.

Though the relationship between the president and the governor had been all along somewhat erratic, they held it together out of perceived self-interest. But, when Kemp refused to go along with Trump's baseless claim that he had won the 2020 presidential election, including winning the state of Georgia, Trump let loose. He attacked and berated Kemp every which way, describing him in at least one instance as "horrible."[29] This was the price that Kemp paid for pandering.

MURDOCH, CARLSON, INGRAHAM, AND HANNITY

If Americans had trouble coping with the new coronavirus, responsibility lay not only with its leaders, but with its intermediaries, with the media, most obviously Fox News. We have already seen how central Fox News was to the Republican media machine – how effectively it, along with Rush Limbaugh, *was* the Republican media machine. Moreover, since 2016, Fox was *Trump's* media machine – his personal and political vehicle for propaganda. This changed not in the least in 2020, even as the disease caused by the virus was coined "COVID-19"; even as the pandemic was formally declared; or even as the virus spread to every corner of the country. To the contrary, like President Trump, Fox initially insisted on dismissing what others, including public health experts, were saying was a major menace at home as well as abroad. Brian Stelter, CNN media correspondent and author of a book about Fox News, concluded that while there are several reasons why the United States lagged behind other countries in coping with the pandemic, one of them was the "Trump-Fox feedback loop." During the early months of 2020, while the virus was silently spreading, "some of Fox's biggest stars denied and downplayed the threat posed by the virus." In turn, and in response, Trump did the same. In other words, Trump echoed Fox and Fox echoed Trump.

To be clear, Fox News was not the only culprit. The remarkably longtime and popular radio host Rush Limbaugh was, for example, another, providing false information and misleading assurances early in the year such as, in his case, "the coronavirus is the common cold, folks."[30] But in this particular drama Fox News was the leading actor. Its ratings continued throughout the pandemic to be sky high: in June and July Fox News was the highest rated television channel in the prime time hours of 8 to 11 p.m. not just on cable, and not just among news networks, but on all of television.[31] It mattered then that Fox repeatedly told its viewers that the coronavirus was not much more than a political ploy. When, for example, Fox Business anchor, Trish Regan, told her audience in early March that the worry over the new coronavirus was "yet another attempt to impeach the president."[32] (Regan was benched for her remark, and later fired.)

We now know, moreover, that lines like these were rank hypocrisy. For while in public Fox continued – with one exception, about which more below – to insist that the virus was nothing to worry about, in private it belied its rhetoric. In private Fox was deep cleaning its offices, developing a plan for working from home, and (on March 2) canceling an annual event scheduled for the end of the month. In other words, people at the network knew before they let on, as did members of the administration, that the new coronavirus was best treated with utmost seriousness.

The relationship between Donald Trump and Fox News was as it always had been – symbiotic. Or reciprocal, or transactional, take your pick. The point is that well before Trump became president and throughout his presidency it was perceived by both sides as it proved for both sides: mutually beneficial. But Fox News is not, obviously, an abstraction. It is an organization peopled by various players, at least four of whom were in varying ways and to varying degrees Trump's cronies. First, Rupert Murdoch, the patriarch of Fox News and its parent company, Fox Corporation, the media mogul who had created a worldwide empire. Second, the first of those who constitute Fox's prime time lineup, Tucker Carlson. His show, *Tucker Carlson Tonight*, is on every weekday night at 8 p.m. Third, Laura Ingraham, whose prime time talk show, *The Ingraham Angle*, is on every weekday night at 10 p.m. and who, since the departure from Fox of its one-time rock-star, Megyn Kelly, is the most powerful on-air woman at the network. And, of course, last but by no means least Sean Hannity, the 9 p.m. ratings-beater who additionally was a member of Trump's inner circle.

The relationship between Rupert Murdoch and Donald Trump went back to the 1970s, when they were both part of New York City's tabloid culture, the first as owner of the *New York Post*, the second as grist for the mill of the *New York Post*. It was said of Murdoch that all his life he had wanted to be close to a US president, just as it was said of Trump that all his life he wanted to be close to a media mogul. Voilà – the perfect match. *New York Times* reporter Amy Chozick wrote that at least during his first year in the White House Trump spoke "regularly" to Murdoch, and that Murdoch was so well positioned he would bypass the chief of staff (then John Kelly) who normally screened Trump's calls.[33] Trump and Murdoch had a relationship of convenience, but a relationship it was. Murdoch profited handsomely from his tie to Trump, as did Trump from his tie to Murdoch. Murdoch provided Trump with unfettered access to Fox News – not to speak of anchors who performed, tirelessly, as cheerleaders.

To be clear, this was not only about political sympathy and synchronicity, about seeing the same things in the same way. This was also, as the words symbiotic, reciprocal, and transactional suggest, about exchanging goods and services. President Trump stood to gain politically from his access to Fox News. Fox News stood to gain financially from its access to President Trump. Trump was in some part responsible for Fox's remarkably and relentlessly high ratings, ergo, for Fox's becoming a cash machine. Before the pandemic struck, Rupert Murdoch made $29 million annually just from Fox, while his son Lachlan, now head of Fox News (among other related entities), made $23 million. Not incidentally, some of Trump's on-air allies made even more. For example, Hannity pulled in a cool $30 million from Fox alone, and Ingraham $10 million.[34] In other words, their financial incentive to keep doing what they were doing was huge.

In the Fox firmament, especially among Trump's enablers, was a single coronavirus outlier: Tucker Carlson. He alone among his prime time peers took the new coronavirus seriously, on air, from the start. While his colleagues were pooh-poohing it as inconsequential, he was not. In fact, Carlson covered the virus earlier than did almost anyone else on American television. Why this was so is not entirely clear, though speculation was that it fit neatly into his view of China. Carlson was a militant China hawk who seemed almost to enjoy bashing everything from Chinese culture to American dependence on Chinese supply lines. In any case, Carlson's bona fides on the new coronavirus, and his bona fides as a prominent member of the Fox family, and as someone firmly ensconced in Trump's camp, explain why, during the first week of March, he was summoned to Mar-a-Lago. He was asked by an aide to come to Trump's Florida residence to try to talk sense to him. To try to get the president to take COVID-19 seriously, if only to save his own political neck.[35]

Notwithstanding his prescience, it did not take long for Carlson to fall into line. To toe Trump's line which meant shifting gears and raging against everything the experts were recommending, such as, for example, social distancing, He also began mimicking his colleagues by attacking experts including, again, that favorite of administration punching bags, Dr. Anthony Fauci. In mid-May Carlson called him the "chief buffoon of the professional class," and warned darkly that "we should never let someone like that run this country." Carlson got to the point of saying whatever the president was saying, most importantly that the nation should get back to business as usual as rapidly as possible. After all, Carlson said, the "short-term crisis may have passed."[36] By spring 2020 Carlson had reverted fully to Fox form. Virtually without exception and apparently without reservation he once again was among the most visible, and audible, of Trump's enablers.

Carlson's prime time colleague Laura Ingraham was consistent from day one, never deviating a smidgeon from the administration. As far back as February she labeled the Democrats the "panDEMic party," thereby politicizing the new coronavirus from the get-go, and she never let up. Throughout the first half of the year she did what she could to push the White House narrative, including providing an enormous amount of misinformation on a policy issue that should have been driven by science, not preference. According to one study, of the 253 times Fox News delivered new coronavirus misinformation during a single week in early summer, a quarter came from *The Ingraham Angle.* Moreover, of the 63 pieces of misinformation, 36 were delivered personally by none other than Laura Ingraham. These included "21 instances of undermining and mispresenting the science on the coronavirus and 13 instances of politicizing the response to the pandemic."[37]

It was also Ingraham who perhaps more than anyone else fed Trump the thin gruel that was hydroxychloroquine. Hydroxychloroquine was, of course, the drug that the president, to what should have been his everlasting embarrassment, famously touted at one of his White House briefings. On April 3, Ingraham, who had referred to hydroxychloroquine as a "game changer," visited Trump in the Oval Office for the sole purpose of talking up the drug, bringing with her two physicians charged with describing its various virtues. The *Washington Post* reported "Some senior Republicans who heard about the meeting cringed about a television host's special access to offer medical advice to the president." But those senior officials never spoke out, which explains why the door to the Oval Office remained open to Ingraham, who returned to the White House just two weeks later to make another pitch. As the weeks went by, the drug fell from whatever favor it might briefly have enjoyed – but Ingraham did not give up. Nor for that matter did Fox: by the end of March hydroxychloroquine had been mentioned on its airwaves more than 500 times. Ingraham in any case continued to "highlight anecdotal success stories," and she urged the Food and Drug Administration not to require the controversial drug to carry a warning label.[38]

Notwithstanding the fiasco that was hydroxychloroquine, Laura Ingraham was and remained one of Trump's most ardent and

consistent supporters and protectors. In early September she conducted an interview with the president during which it was widely
agreed he was not in good shape. No matter. Ingraham, who had been
an ardent and outspoken supporter of Trump's since 2016, continued
to make it her business to make the man look good or, at least, as good
as he could. As the *Washington Post* wrote about the interview,
Ingraham, a "spin artist for the president," tried her best to "stop his
self-immolation."[39]

Sean Hannity was, of course, in a category all his own. He was
a superstar at Fox News – and he was a member of Trump's inner
circle. Hannity too boarded the Trump train early on. In summer 2015
he was already doing what he reasonably could for the newly declared
candidate for president, though at the time Trump still had stiff
competition. Illustrious others wanted to be the Republican nominee,
so Hannity waited to back Trump wholly and enthusiastically until
after he knocked his competitors out of the box.[40] But, once that
happened, Hannity never let up. No matter Trump's ups and downs,
from 2016 on, in private he could count on Hannity as confidant,
counselor, and *consigliere*. And, in public, he could count on
Hannity as promoter, supporter, and public defender.

The effect of Hannity's enablement was a chain reaction: wherever Trump led he followed, wherever Hannity led followed most of
Fox's enormous audience. To be explicit: one of the main reasons
Trump's base held solid even during the exceptionally difficult first
six months of 2020 was Hannity's unflagging support. During the
early months of 2020, while Trump was still saying in public the
new coronavirus was nothing whatsoever to worry about, Hannity
said the same. In February and early March, Hannity along with others
at Fox News continued to downplay the threat to public health,
instead accusing the mainstream media of conspiring against
Trump, charging they were whipping up "mass hysteria," and calling
them "panic pushers." But, when Trump pivoted, so did Hannity.
When, finally, on March 13, the president declared the virus constituted a national emergency, Hannity immediately followed suit,

lavishly praising the president's handling of what he too was now calling a "crisis."

This then was not just an ordinary Hannity about-face, it was an extraordinary Hannity about-face, one that mirrored, or, better, mimicked the president's precisely. Just a week earlier, Hannity, like Trump, was still downplaying the dangers of the virus. Hannity said on air, one day before the president declared a national emergency, "So far, in the United States, there's been around 30 deaths, most of which came from one nursing home in the state of Washington. Healthy people, generally, 99 percent recover very fast, even if they contract it." But just a few days after that, in the wake of the president's emergency declaration, Hannity went on air and reversed himself. "Tonight, we are witnessing what will be a massive paradigm shift in the future of disease control and prevention. A bold, new precedent is being set, the world will once again benefit greatly from America's leadership."[41] This was, it should be added, not Fox's only pivot – any more than it was Trump's only pivot. As soon as the president lost patience with the shutdown, now telling the country that he was anticipating its reopening by Easter, Fox News followed suit. From one day to the next Hannity and other Fox hosts "tumbled over one another to demand more reopenings, faster, bigger – and to pooh-pooh any continuing danger from the coronavirus." As Carlson put it in late April, "The virus just isn't nearly as deadly as we thought it was."[42]

Like other cable news networks, Fox News contributed significantly to the politicization of the pandemic. But, unlike other cable news networks, Fox News also contributed significantly to the alienation and anger, cynicism and skepticism that came to be associated with the pandemic. When someone like Hannity displayed what seemed a congenital distrust of science, and an apparent congenital proclivity to praise the president, there was nowhere for his true believers to go other than into Trump's waiting arms. Moreover, some of what Hannity said flew in the face of the truth. What to do with an exaggeration as extreme as this one? Trump's decision to restrict travel from China and Europe would "go down as the single most consequential decision in history." And, what to do with what seemed on television at least to be Hannity's unbridled rage? On February 27 he opened his show by saying this: "The apocalypse is imminent and you're all going to die, all of you in the next 48 hours. And it's all Trump's fault. Or, at least, that's what the media mob and the Democratic extreme radical socialist party would like you to think."[43]

Hannity further provided the president with a platform, a place for him to sell his wares. Trump and Hannity did not just, as we saw earlier, speak privately on a regular basis. They also spoke regularly in public. Trump would often call in while Hannity was on the air, knowing that he would get an immediate hearing, one that was entirely sympathetic and uncritical, and that would allow him to send whatever his message was to Hannity's more than five million viewers. On March 4, for example, the president called in to talk about the "corona flu" – in the past tense. He praised himself for stopping "tremendous numbers of people coming in from China" even though the virus was, of course, still spreading, and even though, as we now know, the so-called China travel ban was highly porous.[44] Obviously that 40-minute call presented yet another opportunity for Trump to be more forthright, to prepare the American people for what likely lay ahead. But he chose not to reveal what he knew – nor did Hannity, ever the enabler, prompt or prod him to do so.

The pattern continued. Several months later, in June, Hannity conducted a face-to-face interview with the president, billed by Fox News as a "town hall." This time there was no discussion of the new coronavirus at all. Not a single mention, for example, of the fact that as the two men talked there was a "terrifying spike" of new COVID-19 cases, especially in the Sun Belt. Moreover, as noted by Susan Glasser writing in *The New Yorker*, during the entire broadcast, which ran just under 45 minutes, "no one so much as alluded to the hundred and twenty-five thousand or so Americans who [had] already died from the disease."[45] Once again Hannity provided the president with what he most needed – part fervent supporter, part protective bunker.

It is difficult if not impossible to exaggerate the influence of Fox News – indeed of the media more generally – on the American body politic. In fact, the media gave Trump to America: delivered Trump-the-media-magnet free of charge to the American people on their own national doorstep.[46] Specifically, during Trump's tenure in the White House, Fox was to a considerable extent responsible for numberless "unvetted White House hires," "unhinged policy decisions," and "unglued tweets." It is similarly difficult to exaggerate the importance of Sean Hannity specifically to Donald Trump. To be sure, we saw that Trump was also a gift to Hannity. Initially as candidate, then as president, Trump was a "shortcut" to Hannity's "renewed relevance." But, to the point of this book, Hannity was a gift to Trump. Hannity enabled Trump to send the messages he wanted to send – including that with the notable exception of Fox News, most American media were "fake" – especially if they were mainstream.[47]

As we saw earlier, several studies conducted during the first half of 2020 concluded there were more cases of COVID-19 among viewers of Hannity who had "downplayed the pandemic," than among viewers of Carlson who had not.[48] Notwithstanding the growing evidence that Fox News was providing information that was misleading and mis-taken, and that it was actually discouraging its audiences from taking steps to protect themselves, the love affair between the network and its audience, including many if not most of Trump's base, continued. In April Pew pollsters found that Republicans, especially if they were older and white, trusted Fox News more than any other news outlet.[49] In August, a significant proportion of those who watched the Republican National Convention live did so on Fox News. In fact, the first day of the convention turned out to be one of the biggest days in the network's history. It was not, of course, unusual for Fox's audience to be large during a Republican convention. But Fox's dom-inance during the Trump-centric spectacle was as daunting as it was striking.[50] Clearly nothing that had happened during 2020, including the virus crisis and the economic crisis that ensued, was a deterrent. As Trump continued for the duration to enhance Fox, so Fox continued for the duration to enable Trump. To his benefit, if not to their own, Republicans still trusted Fox News far more than any other news outlet.

While these two senators, these two governors, and these four people in the media were not, of course, members of Trump's administration, their enablement of his administration generally, and of him specifically, was essential. He could never have done what he did without their following his lead at every turn; without their strong, unwavering, and very public support; and without their being willing and even eager to serve as his intermediaries, as a conduit between him and some 40 percent of the American people. Each of them had their own reasons for following and, in most cases, even fawning. McConnell used Trump to his, McConnell's, political advantage. Graham seemed genuinely to like hanging around the president, genuinely to enjoy being on the edge of his inner circle, and genuinely to crave, for his own personal and political reasons, proximity to power. DeSantis and Kemp, in turn, were died-in-the-wool Republicans whose personal and political ambitions aligned perfectly with the president's, at least most of the time, and who thought it to their advantage to stay in his good graces.

For Murdoch, Trump was yet another jewel, a precious one at that, in his media crown. And for Carlson, Trump was a gift, again personal, professional, and political, that kept on giving. Ingraham, in turn, survived and ultimately thrived in an environment – Fox News specifically and right-wing media generally – that has been notoriously hostile to female stars. Her perch at Fox News has allowed her to espouse her values. And, in no small part because of her tie to Trump, to enjoy the fruits of having her own prime time news show with a multimillion-dollar salary to match, testimony to her status as a media star.[51]

Hannity benefited from his tie to Trump professionally – and, notably, financially. Hannity ended up not only with easy access to the White House, but also enormously wealthy. By 2020 Hannity was earning approximately 25 percent more than four years earlier – and was the highest paid of all American news anchors.[52] As *Forbes* put it in 2018, Hannity's "rise is inextricably tied to his close friendship with and access to President Donald Trump."[53] Interestingly, Hannity was not, apparently, oblivious to the president's deficits. In fact, two of his Fox colleagues reported he thought "Trump a batshit crazy person."[54] But nothing the president did or did not do, even as it pertained to America's worst public health crisis in over a century, deterred Hannity from his appointed rounds. He remained for the duration the president's most prominent and powerful supporter in American media.

The bottom line is that each of the enablers singled out in this chapter enabled President Trump for reasons not difficult to discern. Whether prominent elected officials, or an eminent media mogul, or on-air media stars, the siren songs of power and money since time immemorial have proven difficult to resist.

12 Medical Experts

Along with the White House Coronavirus Task Force, five physicians were members of President Donald Trump's team – specifically as it pertained to the pandemic – during the period January through June 2020. Each of these five physicians was directly, and most also heavily involved in how the president managed America's worst public health crisis in over a century. Each, then, was an enabler, a follower who allowed or even encouraged Trump to engage in, and then to persist in, behaviors that were destructive. Discussed in this chapter are Surgeon General Dr. Jerome Adams; Assistant Secretary of Health and Human Services Dr. Robert Kadlec; Coronavirus Response Coordinator Dr. Deborah Birx; Director of the Centers for Disease Control and Prevention Dr. Robert Redfield; and Director of the National Institute of Allergy and Infectious Disease Dr. Anthony Fauci – all of whom during the coronavirus crisis prioritized the president's political interest over the national interest.

WHITE HOUSE CORONAVIRUS TASK FORCE

On January 29, 2020, the White House press secretary released a statement announcing the formation of the President's Coronavirus Task Force. It was initially led as earlier noted by Secretary of Health and Human Services Alex Azar. The announcement included the purpose of the task force, which was to "monitor, contain, and mitigate the spread of the virus" while also ensuring that the American people had "the most accurate and up-to-date health information." The announcement further named members of the task force, some of whom soon became familiar, such as Drs. Deborah Birx, Anthony Fauci, and Robert Redfield; and others of whom remained entirely unfamiliar, such as Joel Szabat, Acting Under Secretary for

Policy in the Department of Transportation and Derek Kan, Executive Associate Director of the Office of Management and Budget. Finally, the announcement provided reassurance, promising the American people that the president's "top priority" was their "health and welfare."[1]

In short order, however, the following happened:

- The leadership of the task force changed. One month later Vice President Mike Pence was in and Azar was out.
- The membership of the task force changed. In May for instance five new members were added to the roster.
- The structure of the task force changed. Members with medical degrees split off and started to meet regularly on their own, some in the "doctors' group" reportedly distressed by what one official called the "voodoo" discussed in the larger group.[2]
- The frequency of task force meetings changed. According to Fauci, initially they were daily, even on weekends; then they dropped to four times a week; then they dropped to less or even none at all.[3]
- The mandate of the task force changed. It was Trump, not members of the task force who provided the American people with what purportedly was the "most accurate and up-to-date health information."
- The image of the task force changed. It quickly became clear that it was a shell, a largely empty shell. If it was in charge of anything it was not clear what that was.

Ostensibly the daily televised White House briefings held in March and April were spearheaded by the task force. But soon it was obvious that the task force was powerless or, at least, much less powerful than it was cracked up to be. Its nominal leader, Pence, came across as Trump's lackey, reduced in public to hanging back and saying little while his boss said a lot. And its medical and scientific experts, such as Drs. Birx, Fauci, and Redfield were sidelined, literally, while Trump claimed center stage, an immovable object unless and until he decided himself to move. To all appearances the White House Coronavirus Task Force never had a website. The task force appears never to have met regularly over any reasonable length of time – not even during the most crucial period (late) January through June. And it seems that the task force did not on its own, without the president's approval, make any substantial decisions or convey any objective information. The task force was real. But Trump starved it of power, authority, and influence.

In early May the president declared that by late May the task force would be disbanded, its tasks, he claimed, successfully completed. But, one day later he reversed himself. Why? Because it was "popular." "I had no idea," Trump said, "how popular the task force is" – so he decided to keep it going. Which begged the question, did it matter one way or the other? Did the task force have any significant impact? Ordinarily, such an entity would. Ordinarily when a president establishes a task force it is with the intent of using it, of drawing on its collective expertise to help the administration navigate an unanticipated crisis. Trump's task force though was different. "In Mr. Trump's world, advisory committees and lawyers are usually there to provide a way for him to put his instincts into operation. So it appears with the coronavirus task force."[4]

For two months beginning in late April the task force was mute, at least in public. When it finally reemerged to hold a televised press conference, things were different. Trump was absent and, instead of being held at the White House, the briefing was at the Department of Health and Human Services. Why the changes? It is not clear – though the fact that it was the worst week on record for cases of COVID-19 in the country, "with daily cases well surpassing the previous peak in April and erasing all intermittent progress in flattening the curve," might have had something to do with it.[5]

The White House Coronavirus Task Force was one among several government entities ostensibly charged with managing the virus crisis. Ironically, though it was the most visible, it likely was the least impactful. It did serve in spring to reassure some of the American people and to provide some information. But whatever its initial capacity to reassure the majority, it quickly evaporated, and whatever its initial proclivity to be objective had disappeared. Almost immediately the task force became largely a presidential mouthpiece, yet another one of Trump's mediums for putting across his message in the way he wanted, and at a time when it suited him to do so. In fact, one could reasonably argue that during his four years serving as Trump's toady it was Pence in his role as head of the task force that was the low point. As independent senator from Maine, Angus King, put it, Pence "was complicit in the real abdication of the federal role in confronting" the pandemic.[6]

The White House Coronavirus Task Force is, then, included in this discussion not because it was important, but precisely because it was not. Its primary purpose was to prioritize the president's political interest over the national interest. Which raises this question: Why were members of the task force, especially ones who were experts, eminent ones at that, such as Redfield and Fauci, willing, month after month after month, to conform to the president's wishes? Did they believe the task force a worthy effort? Did they think they could better serve the country on it than off it? Did they enjoy being proximate to power? Did they find it inherently interesting? Did they consider it professionally advantageous? Did they say yes because when someone in authority wanted them to say yes, they did so? There is evidence that some stayed on the task force in name only – their real work was accomplished elsewhere. Still, they did stay: they did not quietly quit or publicly resign.

This passive pattern persisted past summer and into fall. In fact, in fall the already grim situation deteriorated still further. For by then the White House and the task force had been joined by Dr. Scott Atlas, a neuroradiologist whose commentary on Fox News led him to find favor with the president. Favor on which Atlas was able quickly to capitalize, despite his lack of expertise on precisely the matter at hand, a highly infectious new coronavirus. In consequence of Atlas's having joined Trump's team, "discord on the coronavirus task force worsened." Among the problems was that Dr. Atlas routinely challenged the analyses of Dr. Birx (and others), to the point where she went to Vice President Pence, who remained titular head of the task force, to ask that Atlas be removed. Predictably, Pence chose to do nothing. He "did not take sides between Atlas and Birx, but rather told them to bring data bolstering their positions to the task force and to work out their disagreements themselves."[7] So much for the task force as an effective decision-making body.

ADAMS

We have seen that the two members of the Trump administration who did not toe the president's line on the pandemic ran into trouble. When she said something of which the president disapproved, Dr. Nancy Messonnier, a top official at the CDC, was removed from overseeing the agency's coronavirus response. And, when Dr. Rick Bright pushed too hard on, among other things, the use of hydroxychloroquine, he was dismissed as director of the Biomedical Advanced Research and Development Laboratory. According to him, he was dismissed because the administration put "politics and cronyism ahead of science."[8] Bright did not, however, go quietly. As we saw, he filed a formal whistleblower complaint with the Office of Special Counsel, alleging that removing him from his post, and transferring him to a less prominent one was punishment for, again among other things, his outspokenness on pandemic preparation going back to January and February. Bright stood out because he dared to speak truth to power. Because he dared during testimony before the House of Representatives to say out loud that which others only whispered about, which was that certainly as it pertained to the pandemic, the Trump administration did not act as swiftly or efficaciously as it could have and should have. "I believe that there were critical steps we did not take in time," testified Bright. As a result, "lives were endangered and, I believe, lives were lost."[9] (Bright finally resigned from government service in October.)

Messonnier and Bright both cried danger – and both were punished for doing so. Maybe then, given the nature of the human condition, we should not be shocked that during the entirety of 2020 Messonnier and Bright stood essentially alone. Not a single other administration official, not even another medical expert, joined their minuscule chorus by saying in public that which they surely thought in private – that, as Bright said, there were "critical steps" the federal government did not take at all, or at least not in time. Those named here, then, are physicians who came on Trump's team and remained on Trump's team. Each of these men and one woman cooperated and collaborated with the president, as opposed to deviating in any significant way from what he determined was the party line. Each decided that whatever the price they had to pay it was better to stay in Trump's tent than to be pushed out.

To be clear, there were significant differences among them. As we will see, Dr. Fauci was the furthest out: during the second half of the year especially he was much the boldest in making apparent his disagreement with the president. But during most of the first half of the year Fauci too went along to get along, and even later in the year he was careful never to take Trump on directly, personally. Moreover, the content of what he said was largely harmless, as in obvious. Mainly Fauci regularly repeated the familiar mantras of mask-wearing and social distancing, and mainly he regularly reiterated the familiar warnings about how bad the pandemic would get unless Americans, more Americans, changed their errant ways. All true, of course, and well-intentioned. But as the months passed, what Fauci did and said were not rigorous or vigorous enough to get the nation to pay much attention. He had become too comfortable a figure, rather like a granddad who was wise but whose words of wisdom became over time conventional.

From January to June 2020 (and beyond) one of the members of the task force was the previously mentioned Surgeon General, Dr. Jerome Adams. He was an African American working for a president "routinely accused of racism," and a scientist working in an administration "that has shown contempt for science."[10] This was not, as Adams would have known before taking the job, an easy balancing act. In February and March Adams demonstrated his loyalty to the president whenever there was an opportunity. He said that

Trump slept less than he did and was in better health. He echoed Trump's argument that most Americans should be more worried about the seasonal flu than about the new virus. And he defended Trump's claim that the Democrats were politicizing the virus because they were hellbent on propagating yet another "hoax."[11] Moreover, Adams was adamant on the matter of masks. Recall that on February 29 he tweeted, "Seriously people, 'STOP BUYING MASKS!' They are NOT effective in preventing [the] general public from catching #Coronavirus." Even months later, when masks were widely available and mask-wearing was widely accepted, Adams remained reluctant to cross the president. "It is not my place to say what image the president of the United States should be projecting," he ventured in summer, though by then he had pleaded even with viewers of Fox News to put on a mask. "Please understand that we are not trying to take away your freedoms when we say wear a face covering."

To his credit, Adams made clear why he made the decision to collaborate, why he thought it important for him to remain in Trump's favor. Moreover, unlike virtually every other collaborator, his reason for doing so was persuasive: "If people feel that the president needs to have a different perspective on the African American community, the one thing I would say is, he's not going to get it if there aren't any African Americans in the administration." Still, he did collaborate. He did not speak truth to power or shout from the rooftops that the pandemic was terrible for Americans generally – and markedly worse for African Americans specifically.

KADLEC

From January to June 2020 (and beyond) Dr. Robert Kadlec was Assistant Secretary of Health and Human Services. He was among those who understood in early 2020 that the new coronavirus might present a major threat not just abroad but at home. Recall that even by late December, despite a cover-up by the Chinese authorities, there was evidence that something was seriously amiss. And by early

January, though the number of those infected (nearly all of whom were in China) was still under a thousand, there were warnings in the President's Daily Brief of a possible outbreak of a dangerous virus. Of course, as everyone who was anyone understood by then, knowing there was information in a briefing book was different from knowing Trump had seen it, not to speak of read and absorbed it.[12]

Kadlec did in any case appreciate the situation better than most. When he convened the White House Coronavirus Task Force on February 21 his agenda was urgent. "There were deep cracks in the administration's strategy for keeping the virus out of the United Sates. They were going to have to lock down the country to prevent it from spreading. The question was: When?"[13] According to reporting by the *New York Times*, the plan was for Kadlec and others virtually immediately, or at least as soon as possible, to present the president with a plan for containment that was serious but not drastic. (It did not recommend an immediate national shutdown.) But, for reasons ranging from internal turf fights to presidential blowups it never happened. Kadlec's group never got to meet with the president. Instead, it was the president who continued to call the shots, who continued throughout this critical period to insist that White House messaging focus on predictions of success, not on recommendations for mitigation. The *Times* concluded: "These final days of February, perhaps more than any other moment during his tenure in the White House, illustrated Mr. Trump's inability or unwillingness to absorb warnings coming at him." *I, of course, would add they also illustrated the "inability or unwillingness" of Trump's enablers effectively to force him to face reality – or, if necessary, to quit and go rogue, to quit and go public.*

In early March Kadlec was tapped to coordinate the Department of Health and Human Services' response to the coronavirus, a post from which he reported directly to his boss, Secretary Alex Azar. By that point two things about Kadlec had become clear. The first is that he, an expert, fully understood early on the threat to the American people posed by what shortly was declared a pandemic. Though this remains little known, there was a chain of so-called "Red Dawn" emails that circulated among a small, elite group of public health and national security officials, both in the federal government and without, of whom Kadlec was one. As early as January and February, these emails confirmed the escalating levels of alarm.[14] In fact, they were described later as reading like "a chilling foreshadowing of the unfolding deadly pandemic." It was admitted later, by several of their recipients, including a public health officer in the Seattle area, Dr. Jeffrey Duchin, that they failed to do what they should have done: to get the group to "act quickly enough" to forestall the impending disaster.[15]

The second thing to become clear about Kadlec is that despite what he knew and fully understood, for the duration he kept his head down. For the duration he remained unwilling to risk his standing with the president. No surprise then that Kadlec clashed repeatedly with the man who on this issue was the lone administration outlier, Dr. Rick Bright. To all appearances their relationship was contentious. Kadlec cautious and collaborative, a team player; Bright a loner, ready to speak out, to shout out, about the impending threat. According to Bright at least, he always put science before politics but Kadlec did not.[16] The available evidence supports Bright, not Kadlec.

BIRX

Dr. Deborah Birx was the lone woman among the group of medical experts who collaborated with the president on managing the pandemic. Moreover, she played a major role in shaping the administration's policies on the pandemic not only, as her professional credentials would suggest, from the perspective of a physician, but also, given her experience in government service, from the perspective of a politician. Birx then stood out. She was also, of course, highly accomplished. A physician of long experience both at home and abroad, she was in addition a high ranking and skilled administrator who knew how to play politics. She was appointed by President Trump to be the White House Coronavirus Response Coordinator – previously she was

President Barack Obama's Ambassador at Large and US Global AIDS Coordinator. Last but decidedly not least, Birx had had a career in the US Army, reaching the rank of Colonel.

Initially Birx seemed on the side of the angels. She and Dr. Fauci made regular appearances during regular press conferences featuring, along with the president, key members of the White House Coronavirus Task Force. Birx stood at the podium with charts containing facts and figures, a medical expert with an excellent resumé, who had been charged by the president with presenting information that the American people could, presumably, count on to be accurate.

It was soon evident, however, that Birx was in a difficult position. On the one hand she was professionally obliged to do no harm. This meant telling the truth, sometimes even telling truth to power, and correcting the record when the record was wrong. It further required that she remain neutral, and professional, even in situations rife with personal and political divisions. On the other hand, Birx was saddled with a superior who was far more interested in his own welfare than in the public welfare, which became a serious issue every time they were other than on precisely the same page. For example, while President Trump was extolling the government's response to the need for testing, she knew full well that many of the labs supposedly processing tests were operating at only 10 percent capacity.[17] As early as late March, then, there were concerns that she was "squandering" her "credibility." Her apparent willingness to forgive her boss his numberless lies, and her evident willingness to heap on her boss the flattery he craved, did not help. "He has been so attentive to the details and the data, and his ability to analyze and integrate the data has been a real benefit," she gushed at one point.[18]

Hard questions about Birx's independence and, therefore, her performance, were impossible to ignore after the most excruciating moment of all the White House Coronavirus Task Force briefings. While she was sitting nearby, just off to Trump's right, he made some extremely peculiar and potentially dangerous remarks. "So, supposing we hit the body with a tremendous ... a very powerful light ...

Supposing you brought the light inside the body, which you can do either through the skin or in some other way, and I think you said you were going to test that too," said Trump, looking directly at Birx. He went on, "And then I see the disinfectant, where it knocks it out in a minute. And is there a way we can do something like that, by injection inside or almost a cleaning? ... It would be interesting to check that."[19] At the time Birx said nothing, did not publicly object or even modify the president's remarks. Instead she quietly dropped her head, her expressions of bafflement and discomfort so obvious, and Trump's remarks so outrageous, that the scene between them went viral. But not only did Birx not say anything at the time, not respond in any way to what Trump said, a few days later she went so far as to defend him. "I think he just saw the information at the time immediately before the press conference and he was still digesting that information," Birx said, choosing to excuse or perhaps to explain the president's recklessness.[20] Companies that manufactured disinfectants were not afforded the same luxury – the luxury of saying nothing. To avoid misunderstanding, not to speak of legal liability, Clorox quickly issued this statement: "Bleach and other disinfectants are not suitable for consumption or injection under any circumstances."[21]

To be fair and perfectly clear – if it is not so already – Birx was not the only administration expert who remained essentially mute on the harm done by the president's reckless rhetoric. The trouble was that many Americans believed what Donald Trump had to say. "One large and representative national survey conducted at the end of April 2020 found that 40 percent of respondents indicated that they obtained information from his briefings in the preceding twenty-four hours."[22] This was more than from traditional media outlets such as CNN and even Fox News.

As 2020 ground on, information about Birx as a presidential collaborator began to leak out. Again, she was caught between a rock and a hard place, a scientist in an administration that was demonstrably anti-science. Still, during the period under discussion she manifestly made a choice: she would continue to be one of Trump's most prominent, and visible, enablers. Birx was a member of Meadows's working group and, as the group's expert on infectious diseases, was a "constant source of upbeat news." In other words, she told the group what it wanted to hear: that the outbreaks of COVID-19 were gradually easing, and that the United States was likely to resemble Italy, "where virus cases declined steadily from frightening heights." It was during this time that, notwithstanding their joint, collegial public appearances, Drs. Fauci and Birx began substantially to disagree. Fauci was cautious, tending toward the pessimistic, warning repeatedly that the virus was not "going to disappear from the planet." Birx, in contrast, remained optimistic. She said not only what Meadows's group wanted to hear but what everyone in the White House wanted to hear, including obviously the president. "Dr. Birx was more central than publicly known to the judgment inside the West Wing that the virus was on a downward path. Colleagues describe her as dedicated to public health and working herself to exhaustion . . . But her model-based assessment nonetheless failed to account for a vital variable: how Mr. Trump's rush to urge a return to normal would help undercut the social distancing and other measures that were holding down the numbers."[23]

Birx hung in even after her image changed – from highly admired professional to sometime public punching bag. Described by late spring and early summer as a "woman without a country," she remained stuck in a no-win situation. She was lambasted by old allies and public health experts who expressed "disgust at her accommodations" to the president, and who were dismayed by her failure effectively to manage "the most devastating public health crisis in a century." But, predictably, as soon as Birx said a syllable that Trump perceived to be disloyal he called her out, he referred to her, in public, as "pathetic." Most of her medical colleagues struck a balance between attacking and defending her. Dr. Ashish Jha, for instance, at the time director of the Harvard Health Institute, who had known Birx for decades but was a prominent critic of the administration's response to the pandemic, described her initially as a "genuinely smart and caring person." But then he added that as it pertained to the coronavirus, "she has to ask herself whether she's being effective in protecting the American people, and I would argue at this point that it is not clear that she is."[24] It was Fauci actually who put it perfectly. Like Jha, he had known Birx for many years. But when asked, he did not exactly sing her praises. Instead he said she was much more political than he was. Birx, he went on, was "a different species."[25] What he did not say, but did imply, is that she was much more willing than he to be subservient to a superior who day in, day out flew in the face of science.

By summer 2020 Birx had changed her tune. By then she had joined the chorus of those sounding the alarm, saying that the United States had entered a "new phase" of the pandemic and that COVID-19 was now "extraordinarily widespread." Interestingly, she told CNN that "what we're seeing today" (in late July and early August) was "different from March and April."[26] However, to close observers it might well have seemed that she was protecting her flank, trying to salvage her professional reputation. Of course, the numbers were higher later in 2020 than they were earlier in the year. But neither Fauci nor Jha would say that the situation in summer was substantially different from what it was in spring. What they would say is that what transpired in August was the inevitable consequence of the misplaced optimism that the administration had peddled for months running. In other words, it was not the situation that had changed, it was Birx. A half year into the virus crisis she was no longer so willing to risk staining her good name by playing Pollyanna for the president's benefit.

REDFIELD

On September 16, 2020, Dr. Robert Redfield, director of the CDC, testified before the US Senate. He made two significant statements. First, that masks were so critical to combating COVID-19 that they could be more important even than a vaccine. Second, that a vaccine against COVID-19 was unlikely to be widely available until mid-2021, which effectively said to the American people they should not expect a return to life as usual for at least another year. Within hours of delivering his testimony, Redfield was slapped down, in public, by none other than the president himself. "I think he just made a mistake," said Trump. "I believe he was confused," Trump went on.[27] The president, then, not only corrected Redfield, he scorned him, as much as accusing the director of the CDC of losing his faculties. Redfield responded by tweeting, clarifying what he had said about vaccines. He did not, however, retract his timeline. Redfield did not fully accommodate the president by telling Americans that by Election Day there would be a vaccine. But, nor did he fully stand his ground.

Redfield is a virologist who in 2018 was appointed by Trump to lead the CDC. Despite warnings that Redfield was not the best person for the job, Trump went ahead anyway which, given who he was, could be considered smart: what the president got in Redfield was a cautious conformist.[28]

The CDC is the agency responsible for protecting Americans' health. Additionally, it has long been considered one of the preeminent medical and scientific establishments in the world. When Redfield learned at the end of December 2019 that China had a pneumonia of "unknown etiology," he was, then, singularly well positioned to tap into his global network to obtain what at the time he most needed: more information. He conferred regularly with Fauci and with the earlier mentioned Matthew Pottinger, who spoke Mandarin and had his own extensive contacts in China. In Bob Woodward's book, *Rage*, Redfield is described as concerned about the virus from the start. Though the Chinese were not notably forthcoming, by mid-January he had already concluded – in good part based on information that Pottinger provided – that the virus spread human-to-human and that a person could be a carrier even if they were asymptomatic. In response, Redfield assigned thousands of his staff to work on the problem of, the threat posed by, the new coronavirus. According to Woodward, it was around this time that Redfield started to worry that the virus might lead to the "greatest health crisis since 1918."[29]

Redfield continued "urgently" to monitor whatever the available virus-related data, later recalling that for him mid-February was a "tipping point." Because of a case in California of what came to be called COVID-19, he realized that Americans were vulnerable to community spread – that the virus could spread with no easily traceable source of infection. "We're going to be in a fight," Redfield reportedly told his people at the time. Nevertheless, in late February when Dr. Nancy Messonnier issued that public warning – the one stating in no uncertain terms that it was not so much a question of *if* the virus would spread but *when*, and of "how many people in this country will have severe illness" – Redfield remained silent. Trump was furious with Messonnier, as predictably were conservatives such as Rush Limbaugh. But though Redfield was later described as having "a lot of respect" for Messonnier – the center she led was within the CDC – he did not defend her.[30] In part at least because he stood silent, a bystander to what happened, she was sidelined and effectively demoted.

By mid-March, the media had picked up on the possibility, the probability, that the director of the CDC was ineffectual. Ineffectual at precisely the point when the nation faced its greatest public health challenge in over one hundred years. It was one thing for the CDC to face lacerating early criticism for botching testing for the new coronavirus, it was quite another for its leader to seem hapless.[31] (This was the first of two major embarrassments concerning testing; the second was in summer when Redfield struggled mightily though not successfully to clarify when testing was required and when not, a fiasco that required the CDC ultimately to reverse itself.) In March, the *New York Times* described him this way: "Dr. Redfield is not the most outspoken or magnetic of the Trump administration medical experts responding to the coronavirus pandemic ... At times he [comes] across as a deer in the headlights."[32]

By mid-April it was clear. The nation's premier health agency was being directed by a man who was incompetent. Normally, obviously, the CDC would have taken the lead: it would have held regular press briefings, on its own, and served as the public face of the government's response to the public health crisis. But given how weak its leader was, the agency was marginalized, aggressively, by the administration just when it should have been at the forefront. Things got to the point where Redfield was obliged to deny reports that he and the CDC were being muzzled by the White House, that at the direction of the White House, which by then was chomping at the bit to reopen the country, the CDC had been forced to revise, as in to make less stringent, its original guidelines for reopening. *Politico* put it well, describing the CDC as a "shrinking public presence," and as "largely sidelined as a messenger."[33]

As spring became summer Redfield seemed slightly to transition – from being willing to have both himself and the CDC diminished and demoralized by Trump at every turn, to being perhaps a bit less willing. As his testimony in September suggested, along with the slight subsequent retraction, with every passing month he became a tad less servile. In contrast to the president, in June he openly acknowledged "the anguish our nation is experiencing and I am deeply saddened by the many lives lost to COVID-19."[34] And, in June he admitted that the number of coronavirus cases could be ten times higher than previously reported – though even then his comments "oscillated between downplaying the latest news bulletins and declaring that the rising numbers are indeed worrisome."[35] In July the same thing happened. On the one hand the CDC issued carefully considered guidelines on how safely to open schools. But, on the other hand as soon as Trump attacked the agency for doing its job – the president called its guidelines "impractical" and "expensive" – Redfield pulled back. He hastened to assure the administration that the CDC had no intention of providing a "rationale to keep schools closed," and that the guidelines it had issued were not meant to be "prescriptive."[36] What, then, were they meant to be?

White House attempts to bend the CDC to its will continued. In late summer emails were revealed that detailed systematic efforts by Trump's political operatives to muzzle the CDC's scientists. For example, a new advisor at the Department of Health and Human Services, Dr. Paul Alexander, and, especially, a department spokesman, Michael Caputo, collaborated on an effort to "browbeat career officials at the C.D.C. at the height of the pandemic, challenging the science behind their public statements and trying to silence agency staff."[37] In October the *Wall Street Journal* published a detailed article describing what almost sounds like harassment; it included, among other details, mention of "furious" phone calls to Redfield both by Caputo and by Azar.[38]

Meddling such as this clearly concerned Redfield, who would sometimes push back, for example, when Caputo and his aides added caveats and commentaries to the CDC's regular weekly reports.[39] It is not, then, as if Redfield did nothing to stave off interference from the White House. But he did not have it in him forcefully to resist. As a result, he was unable to forestall damage to the CDC's previously stellar reputation, abroad as well as at home. Nor was he able to stop demoralization within the agency itself. Finally, he proved unable properly to protect even the men and women who worked with him. Those familiar with Redfield's responses to being pushed around by Trump's toadies reported that he would call his senior aides, "sounding resigned to the orders and asking them to navigate [their] demands." Sometimes he would try to "delay or ignore [them] until the tension subsided."[40] In short, between January and June 2020 and beyond Redfield brought a knife to a gunfight. In a series of interviews he gave only after the November election, Kyle McGowan, former chief of staff at the CDC, said political control of the agency was not sudden, it was gradual, more "like a hand grasping something, and it slowly closes, closes, closes, closes, until you realize that, middle of the summer, it has a complete grasp of everything at the C.D.C."[41]

Notwithstanding the slight stiffening of his spine over time, essentially the die was cast. Trump and Redfield, the White House and the CDC, were on a collision course in which the former invariably beat out, beat up, the latter. Redfield was no match for Trump. Which is why every time Redfield deviated even slightly from the administration's line he was immediately slapped down. His willingness to conform, to bend to Trump's will as it pertained to the pandemic, explains why the CDC, which had "led the way in every recent domestic disease outbreak," and was "the inspiration and template for public health agencies around the world," fell so far so fast.[42] Polls confirmed that between April and September Americans' faith in the CDC declined significantly. And an opinion piece published in August in the *New York Times*, written by two of the nation's preeminent medical and scientific experts, was titled, depressingly, sadly, "It Has Come to This: Ignore the C.D.C."[43]

Trump has been charged with corrupting American institutions, the CDC among them. But it takes two to tango, in this case one leader and one follower. One who corrupts, the other who permits himself to be corrupted.

FAUCI

Is Dr. Anthony Fauci an enabler? Does the man who was named by Trump's successor, Joe Biden, to be his chief medical advisor properly belong in a book titled *The Enablers*? I pose these questions for a reason, of course. The reason is that in 2020 Fauci became something of a hero, especially obviously to those who did not think the Trump administration had managed the pandemic either wisely or well. Millions of Americans believed that Fauci had done and was continuing to do everything that he reasonably could, from within the Trump administration, to counter much of what Trump did and much of what Trump said as it pertained to the new coronavirus. A Quinnipiac University poll taken in July showed that while 65 percent of Americans trusted information about the pandemic provided by Fauci, 67 percent of Americans *dis*trusted information about the pandemic provided by Trump.[44] Fauci was able, in other words, for months on end to walk a fine line: on the one hand sometimes being carefully critical of the president for the way he was handling the health crisis; and on the other hand, not only escaping being fired (which he technically would have been by his immediate superior, Dr. Francis Collins, director of the National Institutes of Health), but avoiding the most lacerating of Trump's tongue-lashings. (By fall 2020 this rapprochement, of sorts, changed, dramatically, about which more below.)

However, this raises a question: Was it enough for the highly esteemed director of the National Institute of Allergy and Infectious Diseases during this period to be occasionally "carefully critical"? When the pandemic hit, Fauci was a 79-year-old man who had been in his position for well over three decades and who, especially on account of his prominent part in the HIV/AIDS epidemic, was already quite well known and certainly highly respected. Because Fauci's name and even his face was relatively familiar, he was in a stronger position than anyone else, including Drs. Birx and Redfield, to act as an expert, a truth-teller during America's time of trouble. Especially between January and June 2020, when the United States was in dire need of a leader, specifically a medical and scientific expert, who in every way was qualified to fill that role. But did Dr. Fauci do enough? Did he do everything he possibly could to stave off the American disaster that was in consequence of the pandemic? I argue no.

Throughout 2020 Fauci retained his privileged position in the estimation of most Americans. Though his approval ratings dropped later in the year from what they were earlier, he remained more trusted a source than any other, including the president and the CDC.[45] Withal, he raises the question of what should good people do when they are caught in the vise of a bad situation? This question is not new. It is as old as human history, raised again and again when good people are threatened by bad people. Especially when followers – in this case ordinary Americans – are put somehow in peril by bad leaders.

During virtually all of 2020 Dr. Anthony Fauci was a media darling, specifically of mainstream media scrambling to settle on an administration mouthpiece they thought they could trust. But, notwithstanding his impeccable credentials, Fauci was not, at least not early on, always accurate in the information he provided. For whatever reason – insufficient information? political caution? – in February 2020 Fauci gave counsel that was, it turned out, simply wrong. For example, mid-month he said there was no need for Americans to worry about the new coronavirus, for any danger it might pose was "just minuscule." He also said that there was no need to wear a mask – "I don't want to denigrate people who walk around wearing masks," he told one audience, but they should be worn only by sick people. "Put a mask on them, not on yourself," he said. And he pooh-poohed the idea that anyone would worry about, say, getting on a plane. "I was getting calls from people in Sacramento saying, 'Can I get on an airplane to go to Seattle?'" Fauci said. "Like, what? What does that got to do with anything?"[46] Even at the end of the month he told the American people, on NBC's widely watched *Today Show*, that at the moment there was "no need" for them "to change anything" they were doing.[47]

Again, to be clear about masks. The retrospective reason for not recommending them was to avoid people mask hoarding, and to be certain that those who most needed masks, especially healthcare workers, would be able to obtain them. But this is an excuse that will not wash. For it has long been known, well known, that face coverings lessen the likelihood of pathogen transmission. Even during the flu epidemic of 1918 "people understood the utility of this simple intervention, and detailed scientific studies of mask effectiveness were published over a century ago." Similarly, it has long been known that even "homemade cotton masks," or simple cotton kerchiefs or other cotton cloths will serve the same purpose. They will not be as effective as, say, a surgical N95 mask, but they will be somewhat effective at doing what they are supposed to do – at slowing if not stopping contagion.[48]

By mid-March Fauci had modified his message. Having spent weeks in late winter calming the American people, in early spring he was warning especially older adults and people of all ages with underlying conditions, to avoid cruises, flights, and large gatherings. Fauci further volunteered that "we've got a serious problem in New York," and that some models indicated that between 100,000 and 200,000 Americans might die from COVID-19.

Meantime, Fauci, along with Drs. Birx and Redfield, worked with the president behind the scenes to develop guidelines for slowing the spread of COVID-19 – which included shutting down a good part of the country, hence the economy. Trump finally agreed to do this, though he agreed only to 15 days, almost certain not to be long enough. Toward the end of two weeks Fauci and Birx went back to the president, to try to persuade him the shutdown had to be extended. Though Trump finally, reluctantly, agreed, it was around then that the tensions between him and Fauci increased. Not only was the president now obviously unhappy with his expert, Fauci was now obviously unhappy with him. Fauci told the Associated Press that those long White House Coronavirus Task Force briefings – during which he was mostly reduced to being a presidential prop, given a few minutes at most to speak – were "really draining." Then he added, it would "really have been much better" had he been "able to just make a few comments and then go back to work."[49]

Trump and Fauci had, it became obvious, entirely different interpretations of the situation the American people were in, and entirely different ideas on what the American people should be told. A single example: in a late April interview with *Time* Fauci said, "We need to significantly ramp up not only the number of tests, but the capacity to perform them ... I am not overly confident right now at all that we have what it takes to do that." In no time flat Trump took issue. "No, I don't agree with him on that," said the president. "I think we're doing a great job on testing ... We've tested far more than anyone else in the world and within a short period of time you'll be hearing about new tests that ... are going to be incredible."[50]

There were also extreme differences in style between the large, aggressive former real estate developer who played fast and loose with the facts, and the lifelong man of science who was slight and steady, and cautious in his comments. As Trump became increasingly restive, aware of how economically costly the shutdown was, his hostility to Fauci grew. Though the White House dismissed questions about tensions between them merely as "media chatter," pro-Trump "zealots in the far-right media ecosystem" were beginning relentlessly to attack Fauci.[51] In fact, Trump himself retweeted the hashtag, #FireFauci.

In May 2020, the verbal volleying continued. Mid-month Fauci testified before Congress, his comments including a warning against opening the country too quickly and sending children back to school prematurely. The president was not happy. "I was surprised by his answer," Trump told reporters. "To me it is not an acceptable answer." He went on, adding that Fauci "wants to play all sides of the equation," before bragging that next year the economy would be "phenomenal."[52] Perhaps in response to Trump's criticisms of him, perhaps not, one week later Fauci modified his earlier remarks or, at least, he changed what he emphasized. Now he told CNBC that if stay-at-home orders intended to curb the spread of the virus were imposed for too long, they would cause "irreparable damage." "Now is the time," he went on, "depending upon where you are and what your situation is, to begin to seriously look at reopening the economy ... to try to get back to some degree of normal."[53]

Fauci's late May comments did not go unnoticed. A piece in *Forbes* said he was now sounding more "like White House talking points than the voice of candor that we have become accustomed to hearing."[54] But, for the administration it was too little too late. By then it had already muzzled Fauci: it forbade him from making more than occasional appearances on television. The result was that when Trump did something with which Fauci strongly disagreed, he was reduced to taking issue, again, carefully, in print and on social media, instead of on-air, specifically the major networks, where his audiences would have been far larger.

In early June there was this headline: "Fauci Says His Contact with Trump Has 'Dramatically Decreased.'"[55] In mid-June there was this headline: "The White House Has Pushed Fauci Into a Little Box on the Side."[56] And in early July there was this headline: "Fauci is Sidelined by the White House as He Steps Up Blunt Talk on Pandemic."[57] In short, by summer Fauci's access to the president was effectively cut off. Trump had come to see Fauci as a competitor for the nation's attention and affection, which inevitably meant the president wanted to hear nothing the nation's most visible, and widely respected expert on infectious disease had to say. Whatever their relationship had been in the past, it was over.

Trump though was not done. Months later, with two weeks to go before the presidential election, he let loose. In mid-October, the president called the Director of the National Institute of Allergy and Infectious Diseases, "a disaster." Trump then added, presumably for good measure, that "People are tired of hearing Fauci and these idiots, all these idiots got it all wrong."[58]

Which again raises the question: What can good people do when they are caught in the vise of a bad situation? More precisely, what *should* good people do when they are caught in the vise of a bad situation? Could, should, Fauci have done more than he did, different than he did, above all *earlier* than he did to correct for Trump's tragic mismanagement of the pandemic? In July, Fauci was asked about just this issue – specifically as it pertained to the task force briefings at which Fauci was present as Trump gave the American people wrong information. Fauci's response was to get defensive. "I can't jump in front of the microphone and push [the president] down," he insisted.[59] Still, the question remains a nagging one. "I wonder when [Fauci] does have a responsibility to jump in front of a microphone," wrote Hannah Kuchler in the *Financial Times*. In fact, during her interview of Fauci she asked him point blank why he did not speak out against "Trump's wild suggestion that injecting disinfectant could help to treat Covid-19"?

Fauci's reply was he "wasn't there when it happened." To Kuchler this was a "poor excuse" – an opinion with which I agree.[60]

A poor excuse – but given who we are talking about, an honest excuse. Fauci had spent nearly his entire career working within the system, the federal government. This is the mark of a man of reason – not of a flamethrower. Fauci was a reasonable man trapped in an unreasonable circumstance and faced with an unreasonable superior who happened also to be nation's chief executive. Moreover, Fauci had no source of power nor, for that matter, did he have much authority. His institute was relatively small and inconsequential in comparison with, for example, the CDC. Worse, his value as an expert was demeaned and diminished by the president's well-known "contempt for expertise."[61] What Fauci did have was influence. Not, obviously, over the White House – but over large swaths of the American people. When he spoke, they listened. The trouble was that so long as he remained in his post, his capacity to influence was constrained. He was constrained from saying what he wanted when he wanted, and from telling the truth, the whole truth and nothing but.

Should Fauci have risked more? Should he have risked infuriating the president by being more direct, less circumspect, less political? For example, by literally or figuratively jumping in front of that microphone? By creating at one or another point, especially early on, no later than spring 2020, when it might still have mattered, a furor by publicly expressing dismay that the president was refusing to put on a mask, and that the president was refusing to tell the American people that they should be putting on a mask? Should Fauci have been visibly, demonstrably angry, or maybe upset when the president continued, recklessly and relentlessly, to lie when what was called for was the unvarnished truth? Was Fauci simply too polite, too deferential, given with whom he was dealing? Should Fauci have quit his post, escaped from inside the Trump tent to speak truth to power from without? If he had, would he have had more running room, more influence because he was free to say his piece? Or, absent his post, would his influence have been diminished? Recall in any case that there are precedents for quitting in preference to obeying a presidential order. For example, in October 1973 both Attorney General Elliot Richardson and Deputy Attorney General William Ruckelshaus resigned rather than do what they were told to do by President Richard Nixon: fire Special Prosecutor Archibald Cox.

Who can say for certain? This much though we can say. First, Fauci cannot have been content with what happened, with the way the pandemic played out and went from bad to far worse during 2020. Millions of Americans became infected, hundreds of thousands of Americans died. Second, when Fauci chose to stay in the administration rather than quit he knew the price would be high – though not, perhaps, that high. As it turned out, his personal life was upended, and his professional life became more complicated than anything he had previously experienced. Moreover, it turned out that his voice did not carry or, at least, it did not carry as far as he hoped. By the end of the year he had long since been preaching only to the converted – the rest of the American people passed on whatever he had to say. They remained, effectively, out of his reach. Third, Fauci was wed to his job. Even though he had been at it for over thirty-five years, and even though he was almost eighty years old, he was not ready to give it up, not even close. In fact, he said as much to Michael Specter of *The New Yorker*. "Even when [leaders are] acting ridiculous, you can't chide them for it. You've got to deal with them. Because if you don't ... then you're out of the picture."[62] Clearly, being "out of the picture," being fired, was not what Fauci wanted, not something he was prepared really to risk. Finally, though Fauci tried every which way to straddle the line between telling the truth and being a good soldier, so long as he put a premium on keeping his job he had no choice but to favor the latter over the former.

It is no more than conventional wisdom to say that from day one it was the federal government, not the 50 states, that should have made public policy as it pertained to the pandemic. And it is no more than conventional wisdom to say that public policy regarding the pandemic should have been made not largely by politicians but largely by scientists. It never happened. It never happened because Trump cowed not only those who were like-minded but also those who were not. Such as at least some of the five physicians discussed in this chapter – each of whom had sworn to do no harm.

But they did do harm. For however reluctantly or unwittingly, each was an enabler. Each followed the leader, President Trump, allowing him to engage in, and then to persist in behaviors that were destructive. Between January and June 2020 and beyond, none deviated, in public, other than meekly, mildly, and modestly from what the president wanted and intended, from what he directed, no matter how wrong-headed. Each of the five acted in accordance with anticipated behaviors, established practices, and conventional norms. They generally behaved well, and they usually obeyed the person in the position of authority, even when the person in the position of authority was ignorant and corrupt. To look for a single person in the Trump administration – other than the rare as a hen's tooth whistleblower – who dared openly to take on Trump and speak truth to power, is to look in vain.

When Donald Trump contracted COVID-19 in fall 2020, it was revealed that a year earlier he had demanded that the physicians who took care of him for a still undisclosed condition, sign nondisclosure agreements. While it is not known if a year later he did the same, what is known is that the doctor primarily responsible for treating him for COVID-19, Dr. Sean Conley, at Walter Reed National Military Center in Washington, refused to share with the American people anything other than some scanty information, all of which described the president as essentially healthy. Whether or not, as argued a contributor to *The Atlantic*, Conley had a duty to the public not to lie, "by omission or otherwise," it was a dismal affair.[63] Conley was yet another doctor who was an enabler, who prioritized the president's political interest over the national interest. Conley did not, in any case, reveal anything more than did Trump. For example, whether the president had done as he was supposed to do – been tested for the coronavirus on the first day of the presidential debate, some 72 hours before he went to the hospital. A few weeks later, when President Trump was asked, directly, on camera, if he was tested on the day of the debate he replied, "I don't know. I don't even remember."[64]

Epilogue – Enabler Effect

*"The fault, dear Brutus, is not in our stars,
But in ourselves, that we are underlings."*

TRUMP

It is Cassius who speaks these lines to Brutus, in Shakespeare's *Julius Caesar*, as he tries to persuade Brutus of his own agency. Tries to persuade him that if he does not want to be an underling, he does not have to be. He does not have to be his leader's, Caesar's, follower. The same with enablers – certainly with every enabler broadly identified or specifically named in this book. It was not in their stars to enable. It was not their fate to enable. It was their *choice* to enable. To enable a bad leader, an American president, Donald Trump, who was deeply flawed, and who between January and June 2020 and beyond mishandled, mismanaged, and misled on the pandemic.

To be clear one final time, though Trump has been, correctly, faulted for his "colossal failure of leadership," blame for the new coronavirus crisis does not rest entirely on his doorstep.[1] There is blame enough, plenty of blame, to go around. For while this was a colossal, even a tragic failure of leadership, it was at the same time, every bit as much, a colossal, tragic failure of *followership*. Pandemics are understood now to be inevitable. But the "systemic" failures that characterized the spread of the virus were not.[2] Moreover, these failures foreshadowed, were a precursor to, the disastrous presidential transition subsequent to the November election.

The American context into which the new coronavirus was introduced early in 2020 was primed. Warnings about impending pandemics went unheeded. The American healthcare system was badly underfunded. Systemic inequities were leaving certain populations especially vulnerable to chronic and infectious diseases. Americans kept clinging to a "dangerous strain of individualism" – dangerous especially during a crisis that necessitated a communal response. And social media had mutated into "vectors for conspiracy theories."[3] But did human agency play a part in the "systemic" failures? You bet.

Just how bad really was Trump's leadership during first six months of the coronavirus crisis – and beyond? Was it in fact colossally bad? Or was it just somewhat bad? In fall 2020 *New York Times* columnist Ross Douthat wrote that while Trump had hardly distinguished himself during the pandemic, differentiating "between Trump's incompetence and how an average president might have managed is harder, so long as so many peer-country death tolls look like ours."[4] Which raises another question: How to measure America's pandemic performance? By the number of deaths from COVID-19? By the number of people who tested positive for the coronavirus? By comparing America's performance during the pandemic to those of other countries? If so, which ones? Douthat's colleague on the *Times*, David Leonhardt, looked at the same situation at about the same time, but whereas the former saw it as not so bad, the latter saw it as extremely bad, even singularly bad. Marshaling batteries of statistics, Leonhardt wrote in August that one country stood alone "as the only affluent nation to have suffered a severe, sustained outbreak for more than four months: The United States."[5]

Notwithstanding the various caveats, the various comparisons and criteria for comparison, and the numbers, when the pandemic has finally passed, history will not be kind to how America performed. Throughout 2020 and beyond, the evidence continued relentlessly to pile up. In comparison with other countries that ought to have been its peers – Canada, South Korea, members of the European Union – the United States was an embarrassment, a national tragedy. A detailed analysis by the *Financial Times* concluded that as soon as "human-to-human transmission was confirmed and Wuhan went into quarantine a few days later, countries could have prepared for its arrival ... Most did not. In particular, the Trump administration's response will go down as one of the worst national security failures in the history of the US republic, with the virus breaching even the White House and infecting the president himself."[6] Most of the experts concur. The lack of coordination at the federal level especially, and especially early on, in February and March, particularly to facilitate and coordinate testing, was extremely costly. A former director of the CDC, Dr. Tom Frieden, captured the prevailing view, which was that what happened was an "epic failure."[7]

During the first three years of his presidency President Trump set the template for what became a pandemic, degrading the American experiment and diminishing the American experience. Abroad most of America's allies had been alienated, many of its adversaries had been coddled. At home cleavages had been widened and income inequities exacerbated. Problems like healthcare and climate change languished, unaddressed. Coarseness had become commonplace. Falsehoods and fabrications had distorted the political discourse. Then came the virus, the new coronavirus. Now the impact of a president as unethical as he was ineffective was more serious – lives were at stake. President Trump knew the truth. But he lied to the American people about how dangerous the virus was. And he shied away from moving heaven and earth to mitigate the threat.

Trump's aversion to wearing masks and even to seeing others wear masks was an indicator not of his inability to recognize the health crisis, but of his refusal to have the crisis become a political pitfall. In part because of calls taped by Bob Woodward early in 2020, on which Trump could be heard describing the virus and depicting it as serious, we know that the president's pattern of promising the American people that it would "just vanish" was pure theater. Performance art.

There is no way of knowing exactly what would have happened if Trump had acted other than he did. If in January or even February, he had called the nation to arms and fought the coronavirus as the "wartime president" he claimed that he was.[8] But he did not and so the consensus is that as it pertained to the pandemic Trump specifically and his administration generally performed poorly, very poorly. In late summer, Trump was asked by a reporter how he could claim that the virus was under control when every day a thousand Americans were dying. He replied, in part, "It is what it is." Had the president been different the pandemic would have been different: presidential empathy would have done wonders for presidential efficacy. But he was not – he was what he was.

By the end of 2020 Donald Trump had lost the presidential election to Joe Biden. And in the United States the pandemic had become as disastrous and deadly as the worst of the prognostications foretold. But ... let it also be noted that therapeutics for use in cases of COVID-19 were greatly improved, and that vaccines against COVID-19 were on the horizon. Ironically, the unprecedented speed with which vaccines were developed was a major achievement for which the Trump administration did not at first claim credit. The administration's Operation Warp Speed – a public–private partnership charged with facilitating and accelerating the development, manufacturing, and distribution of COVID-19 vaccines, therapeutics, and diagnostics – was a significant contribution to winning the war against the virus.[9] But on the day of big pharma's announcement, specifically Pfizer's, that it (along with BioNTech) was readying a vaccine against the virus that was demonstrably effective – a day that was celebrated by markets worldwide – did Trump seize the moment to blow his own horn? He did not. Instead he stayed hidden within the walls of the White House, enraged by the results of the election. Instead he furiously charged that the news of the vaccine had been delayed by the "medical deep state" to sabotage his chances of beating Joe Biden, and demanded of Alex Azar that he "get to the bottom of what happened."[10] One could reasonably argue that the president's failure promptly to take credit where credit was due – due him, and due his administration – was indicative not only of his being incompetent but of his being irrational.

TRUMP'S TRIBE

Decades ago, political scientist Stanley Hoffmann described French collaborators during World War II as enablers (my word, not his). They were followers who allowed or even encouraged their leaders to engage in, and then to persist in behaviors that were destructive. Hoffmann divided the collaborators into two groups: those who worked with the Germans voluntarily, and those who did so only *in*voluntarily. This is an interesting distinction that, though not directly on point, is nevertheless relevant. For Trump was not a foreign occupier who coerced collaboration. He was an American elected by Americans to serve as president. It was a transactional relationship in which both leader and followers had freely engaged. To be sure, Trump was never the choice of most of the American people. In the 2016 presidential election Hillary Clinton received almost 3,000,000 more votes than he did. But given the system, the electoral college, it was Trump who won the White House. This meant that for at least one four-year term the American people had committed themselves – voluntarily – to following where Trump led. Unless, of course, he was impeached and, additionally, convicted, which he was not.

Like Hoffmann I made a distinction between the president's enablers, in this case one group a subset of the other. There was the large group I named Trump's tribe, and the small group I named Trump's team. Trump's tribe included many millions of Americans who for a constellation of reasons – including, as mentioned, family fealty, group loyalty, ideological affinity, party identity, professional anxiety, political expediency, personal preference, promise of reward or fear of punishment – chose first to follow Donald Trump, and then to continue to follow Donald Trump. They were his base, his party, members of his administration, and his inner circle.

Trump's base was singular for its solidity and solidarity. Even after his dismal performance during the first six months of the pandemic, most of his supporters continued to stand by him. In summer 2020 between 58 percent and 76 percent of voters in nine battle ground states who had cast their ballots for him in 2016 reported their support for the president remained "very strong."[11] And even in fall, despite the turmoil and tumult of the preceding eight months, his overall approval rating continued to hover around where it had been for most of his presidency, in the low 40s. In other words, notwithstanding the health crisis, the economic crisis, and the racial crisis, all of which were now plaguing the country, nothing the president did or did not do, nor anything he said or did not say, nudged most of his followers from where they were four years earlier. To which the 2020 presidential election further attested. Though Biden beat Trump, the incumbent president received the second highest vote tally in American history. More than 74 million people wanted him to secure a second term.

By fall 2020 the question of why Trump's followers continued to follow, notwithstanding all that had happened, seemed newly urgent. For in addition to the three crises just mentioned was a fourth. This one was a political crisis that threatened American democracy itself. Trump's insistence that if Joe Biden won in November it would mean the election was "rigged," a "scam," was a warning – a warning that America's system of governance was more fragile than was thought. Americans had been alerted to the danger by, for example, prize-winning historian Timothy's Snyder's small book, *On Tyranny* (2017); and by the Pulitzer prize-winning journalist Anne Applebaum's slightly heftier one, *Twilight of Democracy* (2020).[12] Both authors cautioned, as did the subtitle of Applebaum's book, that authoritarianism, authoritarians, have a "lure" that is "seductive." To state that the storming of the US Capitol in January 2021, two weeks before Inauguration Day, gives evidence of this is to understate it.

As mentioned in the Prologue, the seminal literature on followership rose out of the ashes of World War II, when in the 1950s, 1960s, and 1970s philosophers, historians, and social scientists sought to explore how Hitler happened. How it happened that Hitler was able to motivate and mobilize the German people to follow him voluntarily and, by the many millions, even eagerly. And how it happened that they continued to follow: into World War II, and then, during the war, killing on Hitler's command and fighting to the end – to Germany's own devastation and destruction.

I am not comparing Trump's base of support to Hitler's base of support. Still, history has lessons to teach about the enduring lure of authoritarianism, about "the allure of toxic leaders."[13] As we have seen, the benefits to followers who constitute a base such as Trump's fall into two groups: those that fill individual needs and those that fill group needs. Applebaum writes, for example, that authoritarianism appeals to people who "cannot tolerate complexity."[14] Who instead want clarity and simplicity, unity, and homogeneity. Especially in a world that moves so fast, changes so swiftly, and feels so tenuous, fractious, and contentious. Our needs as members of groups are different. We seek identity and a sense of belonging and, with a leader like Trump, excitement as part of an experience that is shared. This last was apparent at his rallies – the political equivalent of rock concerts. Throughout his candidacy and presidency, even during the dark days of the pandemic, those rallies were joyous, sometimes raucous gatherings of like-minded supporters, people who were elated by being part of the action and present for the occasion – a tribal ritual with the "great man" at the center. To watch these rallies on television was not, of course, the real thing. But for Trump's tribe, bearing witness on Fox News came close.

The benefits to members of Trump's party, especially to the party elite and to members of his administration and inner circle, were somewhat different. Usually they were more direct, more material. This is not to dismiss the benefits just referenced, such as those provided by group loyalty, ideological affinity, and party identity. But it is to point out that the rewards for being a Trump loyalist to, say, a Republican senator, were usually less visceral and more practical. These included, among others, the political, professional, and financial rewards of getting reelected. Again, this is not to diminish what in some cases were the purely personal pleasures of being proximate to power. Of Senator Lindsey Graham, for example, it was said that every time he met with the president, he "bragged" about it and exhibited a "high school" level of excitement.[15] Thus the benefits of being proximate to power are practical, or pleasing, or both. They in any case explain why many people, most people, are reluctant to give them up. James Mattis, the Secretary of Defense who publicly, proudly, quit Trump's orbit of his own free will, was the exception not the rule.

Three more points about Trump's tribe. First the degree to which many members of his tribe joined the president in one or another alternate universe – one that he had created. Given the gap between what he told the American people about the new coronavirus, and what he told Woodward, it appears that even he did not believe his own tall tales. Moreover, it is not clear that most members of his tribe did. No matter. What did matter is that these alternate universes – figments of Trump's imagination – were important. Essentially there were two, the first beneficent. It was a magical world in which the virus would "disappear," the economic recovery would be "unprecedented," and America would be "great again." This happy place was a nostalgic throwback to an earlier time when America was whiter, when there were good jobs of all kinds aplenty, and when life seemed to many Americans to have been simpler and more secure. The second of Trump's alternate realities was in stark contrast, it was malignant. It was a dark and fearsome place, the United States of America where cities were burning and suburbs were threatened, where people lurked "in the dark shadows," and menaces such as "anarchists" and "looters," "rioters" and "agitators" abounded.[16] It was a world in which the news was "fake," elections were "rigged," impeachment was a "scam," and everything was a "hoax."

The second point about Trump's tribe is the degree to which it was governed by fear. Up to now I have emphasized the benefits to members of Trump's tribe. But leaders can and do, of course, punish as well as reward. There is no question that members of Trump's tribe, especially Republican officeholders, members of his administration, and yes, members of his family, felt fear. Fear of what Trump would do – to them – if they were other than abjectly loyal. Some of this seemed to outsiders to be irrational. For as I wrote earlier, we are not talking here about Russia, where Alexei Navalny was poisoned, almost certainly at the instruction of, or at least with the complicity of, President Vladimir Putin. Still, never let it be said that the fear of being cut off or cut out; of being sidelined or marginalized; of being embarrassed or humiliated; of being defeated or demoted; of being personally, professionally, and politically attacked; of being in some way seriously if not physically hurt, is not real.

Consider what happened to members of the intelligence community. Journalist Robert Draper described how deeply affected they were by President Trump's animosity to any agency he perceived as other than one thousand percent loyal. Loyal not to the American people but, as we have come by now to know, to Trump especially, if not even exclusively. At the Justice Department led by Attorney General William Barr, the administration set out "step by step" to destroy "one of the crown jewels of the American government." And in the Office of the Director of National Intelligence, the same. The "wearing down" of the intelligence community "extended well beyond the dismissal of a few top intelligence officials whom the president perceived to be disloyal." It also meant that those who remained in their posts were "acutely mindful of the risks of challenging Trump's 'alternate facts.'" The 40 current and former intelligence officials, lawmakers, and congressional staff whom Draper interviewed were willing to discuss their experiences only in exchange for anonymity. Why? "Out of fear of reprisal or dismissal." It was, Draper noted, testament to "how profoundly Trump had reordered their world and their work."[17] It was, I would add, testament to how fear was pervasive, ever an arrow in Trump's quiver.

The third point about Trump's tribe is how some were more culpable than others. In the Prologue I made the point that the best way to think about the president's enablers is as along a continuum – depending on their level of engagement. Enablers at a distance, such as Trump's base, were important to his management/mismanagement of the pandemic not because they were directly involved, but because their support of the president was critical to, for example, Republican senators who, in turn, provided Trump with political support – support that was critical to his political survival. It can reasonably be claimed, then, and I do, that virtually every Republican member of the Senate was culpable during the pandemic to the point of being complicit. I would say the same about the previously mentioned cast of characters at Fox News. Scholars of the Holocaust have written about how important to Hitler's rise to power – and to his remaining in power – were members of the German elite. Among them were "well-educated professionals: bankers, professors, doctors, journalists, transport workers, engineers, judges, authors, teachers, lawyers and civil servants."[18] We do not usually associate people who are privileged with an attraction to authoritarianism. But there they were, enablers of Adolf Hitler.

What Applebaum calls "soft dictatorships" do not, in contrast to hard dictatorships (think Hitler or Stalin), require mass violence to stay in power. Instead they rely on the elites just mentioned, those who, for example, run big businesses, the bureaucracies, the courts, and the media, and who are, in return for their reliability, "rewarded and advanced."[19] Significantly, elites like these do more than merely make the trains run on time. For example, Republican senators, governors, and those high up at Fox News were not merely intermediaries between the president and the people, they were interpreters. By following Trump in lockstep during the entirety of his presidency, not only did they bestow on him their seal of approval, they conveyed the message that he wanted to send. It was they who told the American people, sometimes explicitly, sometimes implicitly, what the president wanted them to hear. That he was a great leader who was making America great again. Republican senators, governors, and prominent cogs in Fox's media machine were, then, more than mere bystanders. They were participants – they participated, actively, in Trump's presidency. Their role was to protect and promote the nation's chief executive, however outrageous his mendacity, however obvious his corruption, and however corrosive his impact on American democracy.[20]

TRUMP'S TEAM

I could not in this book name every enabler – there were too many individually to identify. Among those not previously mentioned were other members of Trump's team such as, for example, his secretary of agriculture, Sonny Perdue. Perdue was a Trump crony who never even "pretended to separate his political and personal interests," and who himself hired his subordinates not on the basis of their competence but their loyalty.[21] In spring he told meat processing plants to reopen – despite thousands of their workers already having contracted COVID-19, and despite most of these facilities not yet having complied with government recommendations for increased safety measures.[22] Another enabler was Admiral Brett Giroir, a member of the White House Coronavirus Task Force who was responsible for overseeing the administration's program on testing. Bottom line on him: it is impossible to defend his record. Since February Americans had understood that testing in this country had failed. By May testing was still failing; in fact, it was continuing further to deteriorate.[23]

Of course, some enablers matter more than others. Some whose importance to the president and acquiescence to the president – giving him license to politicize the pandemic – are especially dispiriting. One such was Dr. Robert Redfield, director of the CDC, discussed in the previous chapter. Not for a moment do I question Redfield's good intention. Still, I return to him here for three reasons. First, because he was a physician who had sworn to uphold the highest of professional standards. Second, because he was responsible for running the nation's largest, most prominent, and widely respected healthcare agency. Which meant that he was responsible for protecting not only the CDC, and the thousands of dedicated men and women who work there, but also, by extension, the American people. Third, because what happened to Redfield is a cautionary lesson. *A lesson in the perils of gradualism – of becoming, gradually, over time, day by day, week by week, month by month, an enabler.*

At some point we will know more. But well before 2020 was over we learned that Redfield had tolerated some tampering from the start. All along, throughout the first half of the year and beyond, work at the CDC was interfered with, politicized at the direction of the president. At the same time, Redfield was himself all along personally belittled, professionally demeaned, and politically cowed. We know that Trump ignored Redfield early in the year when the alarm first sounded. We know that Redfield stood by and did nothing, or not enough, when someone who reported to him, Dr. Nancy Messonnier, was punished by the president for doing her job. We know that Trump insulted Redfield in public. Above all we know that Redfield tolerated political interference with scientific practice. Most damagingly, he allowed political hacks to water down the CDC's deeply researched and carefully crafted admonitions and recommendations – entirely for the president's benefit. It was in what the president perceived his political interest to reopen the country as rapidly as possible – to open up the economy, to send children back to school – and to diminish the significance of the new coronavirus, even if that meant bending science to his will by concealing some of the CDC's findings and amending some of its postings.

Redfield accommodated every one of these interests. Moreover, as the year continued the pattern continued. As in summer 2020 when "top White House officials" pressured the CDC to "downplay the risk of sending children back to school."[24] And in September 2020 when one headline read, "C.D.C. Testing Guidance was Published Against Scientists' Objections."[25] And again in October 2020 when it emerged that "The White House Blocked the C.D.C. from Requiring Masks on Public Transit."[26] For all this there are only two possible explanations: either Redfield knowingly acquiesced to what the White House wanted; or what the White House wanted was done without

Redfield even knowing. Either way he was a follower – an enabler – when what he should have been was a leader.

In fairness to Redfield, he was caught between the proverbial rock and hard place. On the one hand, he seems to have assumed, probably correctly, that if he had stood up to the president to the point of being perceived as disloyal or even resistant, he would have been dismissed. On the other hand, his failure from day one to stand up to the White House meant that during 2020 he was increasingly hounded, pressured to do what the administration wanted when it wanted it.

In April, administration propagandist Michael Caputo, a former Trump campaign official who lacked any medical or scientific background, was nevertheless installed at the Department of Health and Human Services. It was his job to align every CDC report with whatever message the White House wanted to send. In fact, it was his job to prevent some of the CDC findings and recommendations even from being released. As director of the CDC, Redfield was Caputo's main target. Either Caputo or a member of his team would call Redfield to demand that he change a report that had already been made public, or to demand that he preclude a report from being made public without prior approval. Frequently, Caputo's underling, Dr. Paul Alexander, was the hatchet man. He would accuse the CDC of writing "hit pieces on the administration," and he would demand that the CDC withhold a report "unless I read and agree with the findings."[27]

None of this is to convey the impression that under Redfield the CDC was entirely supine. It was not. In fact, as time went on, the agency seemed on slightly stronger footing, Redfield presumably having come to realize that unless and until he developed a more muscular response to the administration's belittling and berating, he along with the CDC would be considered complicit. Withal, by fall 2020 Redfield's position had become downright embarrassing, to the point where he was openly rebuked by, among others, one of his eminent predecessors, Dr. William Foege. In no uncertain terms Foege called on

Redfield, publicly, to "stand up to a bully" – to stand up to the president. So, while compromises were sought and occasionally found, Redfield's reticence – his readiness to shut up, his reluctance or even refusal to speak out – made his plight all but inevitable. Early on Trump understood about Redfield that he was more pliable than powerful, an enabler who kept compromising himself, his agency, and the science that supposedly was his calling – all to bend to a leader who was a bully.

The tragedy is that Redfield's willingness to play Trump's game was not the exception but the rule. The CDC director was not atypical but typical of every other Trump team member who stayed silent despite his being by far the worst president in American history. By far the most incompetent. By far the most unethical. And by far the most dangerous. These included not just those who, like Steve Mnuchin, stayed the course, remained in the administration from start to finish, but those who did not. Those like Gary Cohn (Trump's former chief economic advisor), Rex Tillerson, and H. R. McMaster, who had long since left but who still chose to say little or more likely nothing. They chose not to speak out publicly about the president's most grievous flaws – even though they had witnessed them up close and personal. To be sure, some did speak out, but only obliquely, behind closed doors, for example, to Woodward. *But to speak in a whisper is not tantamount to shouting from a rooftop.* Bystanders included Republican senators – Mitt Romney was the single exception – who had a chance to convict Trump after his first impeachment or, at least, to hold a fair hearing, but who did not take it, thereby setting the stage for the calamity that ensued effectively immediately. The calamity that was the pandemic – the pandemic that compromised or destroyed the physical health of many millions, and the financial health of millions more. And, additionally, the calamity that occurred on January 6, 2021: the assault, this time a physical assault, on American democracy.

John Bolton, Trump's former national security advisor, did at one point speak out, describing Trump as a "danger to the republic."

But Bolton did so only after he had left the White House, to promote his book, and not when it might have had an impact, even made a difference, during the first impeachment proceedings.[28] Somewhat similarly, a few former top officials made their feelings known, though again, only indirectly. For example, former Director of National Intelligence, Dan Coats, wrote an opinion piece that appeared in the *New York Times* in September, in which he suggested that a commission be established to ensure confidence in the upcoming election. But he did not say why exactly such a commission was needed now, in 2020, when there never was such a need before. Coats was too genteel, too careful, too cautious, and too conservative to reference the reason – that is, a president who repeatedly threatened to go rogue.[29] Threatened to call the election a fraud unless he won – which is, of course, exactly what happened. Trump lost and he charged the election was rigged.

To be clear: *not every follower followed.* Not every follower was an enabler – nor did every enabler necessarily remain an enabler. There is such a thing as breaking away even from a leader with as great a capacity for inspiration on the one hand and intimidation on the other as Donald Trump.

One such was Olivia Troye who, not long before the November election, started to speak out about her experience working in the Trump administration. Originally Troye was Vice President Pence's advisor for homeland security. But after the White House Coronavirus Task Force was established, she was his top aide in his new capacity as task force leader. For the duration of the period under discussion, therefore, Troye was in the room where it happened, where the president and the vice president managed/mismanaged the pandemic. In an article she wrote for *The New Yorker*, Susan Glasser commented that while Troye was "the first White House staff member who has worked on the coronavirus response to speak out publicly against Trump, the President and the Administration she described were drearily consistent" with what had already been reported. That Trump had blocked the task force from doing what it should have, that he had "derailed" much if not most of what it had tried to do. Glasser asked Troye if she was bothered by the failure of other officials to speak out as she finally had done. Troye replied that speaking publicly was "hard." Then she added that now was not, however, a "time for silence."[30]

After the November election, others came out of the woodwork to admit their decision-making had been flawed. Though few so directly and abjectly as Erica Newland, who had worked in the Justice Department. In an opinion piece that was published in the *New York Times* she wrote she remained in the administration (until 2018) because she believed that "a critical mass of responsible attorneys staying in government might provide a last line of defense against the administration's worst instincts." But after the election she concluded she was wrong. "I now see what might have happened if responsible Justice Department attorneys had collectively – ethically, lawfully – refused to participate in President Trump's systematic attacks on our democracy from the beginning. The attacks would have failed."[31] I agree. At least it was possible they would have failed – especially if people had acted collectively as opposed to alone.

ENABLER EFFECT

To enable a bad leader is to be a bad follower. Full stop. Followers who follow bad leaders by choice are, by definition, enablers. They allow or even encourage their leaders to engage in, and then to persist in behaviors that are destructive. Enablers are not, moreover, junior partners, they are full partners. Bad leaders cannot function without them. So, if bad things happen, bad followers must share the blame – they like their leaders are responsible.

Enablers believe that they do what they do for good reason. Senator Mitch McConnell would maintain that he followed where Trump led as means to an end that he deemed desirable, such as filling the federal courts with like-minded judges. Judges who held opinions that were deeply conservative and reflected his, McConnell's views. John Kelly would say that that he came and remained in the administration – until he was fired – to serve the national interest. And still others of Trump's followers would claim that they are true believers. Mike Pence, Mike Pompeo, and William Barr fall into this category. They believed that they were "in a biblical moment." A moment in which, as Barr once put it, "militant secularists" were destroying America, and "irreligion and secular values [were] being forced on people of faith."[32] If this is the picture you paint in your head, to follow a leader like Trump is not only a good thing to do, it is the right thing to do. For Trump's politics – though not his ideology, as there is no evidence that before he ran for president, he even had one – are in almost every policy area conservative. Whether on abortion or climate change, on race relations or tax policy, on immigration or regulation, on "law and order" or "America First," Trump is on the right not on the left.

I want to be clear: we cannot know for certain how, or even if, history would have been different had key people in Trump's tribe and, especially, members of Trump's team behaved differently. If they had spoken out against, instead of pandering to, surrendering to, a leader who, as it pertained to the pandemic, was demonstrably bad.

But, while we cannot know without question what would have happened had Trump's enablers behaved differently, what we can know without question is what happened in consequence of their behaving as they did. A cascade that began on February 5, 2020, when President Donald J. Trump was acquitted (without hearing witnesses) of the charges brought against him in the articles of impeachment – charges that he had abused his power and obstructed justice. A cascade that continued and then accelerated straight through, from January through June 2020 and beyond. It is no accident that Trump's gross misleading and mismanaging during the pandemic came in the immediate wake of his acquittal by the Senate. He was cleared because he was enabled, and because he was enabled and then cleared, he was empowered. Effectively he was free to do what he wanted when he wanted without constraint. *The path to political calamity was, in other words, as it usually is, a process. Yet another example – if any were needed – of why reining in bad leaders early in their tenures is of paramount importance.* In time, then, the lack of constraint on President Donald Trump, the enablement of President Donald Trump, led inexorably to this. A lethal assault on the nation's Capitol by a furious, ferocious mob of Trump supporters who believed his big lie – that he, not Joe Biden, had won the election. And by February 2021 more Americans dead – over half a million – than was conceivable one year earlier when "COVID-19" was coined.

"The fault, dear Brutus, is not in our stars / But in ourselves, that we are underlings." Nowhere was it written that President Donald Trump's enablers were destined to do what they did. They could have done differently, decided not to enable, decided not to be because they did not have to be, underlings. In which case the American experience of the pandemic would have been different. For history is made not by institutions, but by individuals. By leaders and their followers acting in tandem.

Notes

PROLOGUE — ENABLER

1. Ira Chaleff, *The Courageous Follower: Standing Up to & for Our Leaders* (Berrett-Koehler, 2009), p. 3.

2. Joseph Rost, "Followership: An Outmoded Concept," in Ronald Riggio, Ira Chaleff, and Jean Lipman-Blumen (eds.), *The Art of Followership: How Great Followers Create Great Leaders and Organizations* (Jossey-Bass, 2008), p. 57.

3. Barbara Kellerman, *Followership: How Followers are Creating Change and Changing Leaders* (Harvard Business School Press, 2008), pp. xix and xx.

4. Quotes from Lao Tsu, Confucius, and Machiavelli in Barbara Kellerman (ed.), *Leadership: Essential Selections on Power, Authority, and Influence* (McGraw-Hill, 2010), pp. 3 ff.

5. The quotes are all in Kellerman, *Leadership: Essential Selections*, passim. For a more general discussion of the impact of the Enlightenment on the balance of power between leaders and followers, see Barbara Kellerman, *The End of Leadership* (HarperCollins, 2012), pp. 11 ff. and passim.

6. Theodor W. Adorno, Else Frenkel-Brunswik, Daniel Levinson, and Nevitt Sanford, *The Authoritarian Personality* (Harper, 1950). For more on this seminal volume, see https://en.wikipedia.org/wiki/The_Authoritarian_Personality.

7. The phrase was in Arendt's book titled, *Eichmann in Jerusalem: A Report on the Banality of Evil* (Viking Press, 1963). For more on this controversial work, see https://en.wikipedia.org/wiki/Eichmann_in_Jerusalem.

8. For more on Milgram's work, see https://en.wikipedia.org/wiki/Obedience_to_Authority:_An_Experimental_View.

9. Christopher Browning, *Ordinary Men: Reserve Police Battalion 101 and the Final Solution in Poland* (Harper, 1992).

10. Barbara Kellerman, "Leadership: It's a System, Not a Person!," *Daedalus*, 145 (2016), 83–94 (www.mitpressjournals.org/doi/abs/10.1162/DAED_a_00399?journalCode=daed).

11. Figures in George Will, "The Nation is in a Downward Spiral," *Washington Post*, July 15, 2020.

12. www.cnn.com/2020/06/30/health/us-coronavirus-toll-in-numbers-june-trnd/index.html.

13. Jason Beaubien, "Americans Are Dying in the Pandemic at Rates Far Higher Than in Other Countries," *NPR*, October 13, 2020.

14. www.nytimes.com/2020/07/08/briefing/arizona-mary-trump-facebook-your-wednesday-briefing.html.

15. "Underlying Conditions," *The Atlantic*, June 2020.

16. www.factcheck.org/2020/08/trump's-misleading-covid-19-comparisons-to-other-countries/.

17. Barbara Kellerman, *Bad Leadership: What It Is, How It Happens, Why It Matters* (Harvard Business School Press, 2004).

18. George Parker, Clive Cookson, Sarah Neville, and Sebastian Payne, "The Blame Game," *Financial Times*, July 19, 2020.

19. www.nytimes.com/2020/05/20/us/coronavirus-distancing-deaths.html.

20. https://fortune.com/2020/06/04/us-unemployment-rate-numbers-claims-this-week-total-job-losses-june-4-2020-benefits-claims/.

21. Patricia Cohen, "Another 2.4 Million Jobs Vanish," *New York Times*, May 22, 2020.

22. https://jamanetwork.com/journals/jama/fullarticle/2771764.

23. www.nbcnews.com/politics/meet-the-press/poll-80-percent-voters-say-things-are-out-control-u-n1226276.

24. www.politico.com/news/2020/06/26/trump-retribution-protesters-statues-340957.

25. This paragraph is based on Kellerman, *Bad Leadership*, pp. 32 ff.

26. For further discussion of this phenomenon, see, for example, Kellerman, *The End of Leadership* (HarperCollins, 2012); Mois Naim, *The End of Power* (Basic Books, 2013); and Tom Nichols, *The Death of Expertise* (Oxford University Press, 2017).

I   BASE

1. Tim Alberta, *American Carnage: On the Front Lines of the Republican Civil War and the Rise of President Trump* (HarperCollins, 2019), pp. 213–214.

2. Ezra Klein, *Why We're Polarized* (Avid Reader Press, 2020) p. xix.

3. Klein, *Why We're Polarized*, pp. 135–137.

4. Quoted in Neil Irwin and Josh Katz, "The Geography of Trumpism," *New York Times*, March 12, 2016.

5. Karlyn Bowman, "Who Were Donald Trump's Voters? Now We Know," *Forbes*, June 23, 2017.

6. Sean McElwee, "Who is Trump's Base?," *Data for Progress*, August 21, 2018.

7. Alan Abramowitz, *The Great Alignment: Race, Party Transformation, and the Rise of Donald Trump* (Yale University Press, 2016), pp. 123 ff.

8. Quotes in this paragraph are in Jelani Cobb, "Burning Cities," *The New Yorker*, June 8 and 15, 2020.

9. This paragraph – also the quotes – is based on Rory McVeigh and Keven Estep, *The Politics of Losing: Trump, the Klan, and the Mainstreaming of Resentment* (Columbia University Press, 2019), pp. 76 ff.

10. The book was published by Melville House. The quote is from an article about the book by Christopher Ingraham, "New Research Explores Authoritarian Mind-Set of Trump's Core Supporters," *Washington Post*, October 12, 2020.

11. Kellerman, *Bad Leadership*, pp. 21 ff.

12. Jean Lipman-Blumen, *The Allure of Toxic Leaders: Why We Follow Destructive Bosses and Corrupt Politicians – and How We Can Survive Them* (Oxford University Press, 2005), pp. 29 and 80.

13. https://news.ballotpedia.org/2020/05/06/trump-has-appointed-second-most-federal-judges-through-may-1-of-a-presidents-fourth-year/.

14. Quoted in Alberta, *American Carnage*, p. 504.

15. The quote about Trump's trying to seduce Bush's cohost is from Alberta, *American Carnage*, p. 367. The "tape" paragraphs and other relevant quotes are from https://en.wikipedia.org/wiki/Donald_Trump_Access_Hollywood_tape.

16. Alberta, *American Carnage*, p. 375.

17. All quotes in this paragraph from Alberta, *American Carnage*, p. 381.

18. www.fastcompany.com/3066599/the-worst-design-of-2016-was-also-the-most-effective.

19. www.cnn.com/2020/06/07/politics/trump-base-analysis/index.html.

20. E. J. Dionne, Jr., "Trump's Base is Smaller than he Thinks," *Washington Post*, October 6, 2019.

21. To wit, this event in North Carolina: www.voanews.com/2020-usa-votes/trump-defies-north-carolina-covid-guidelines-large-outdoor-rally.

22. Sheryl Gay Stolberg, "Stanford Study Seeks to Quantify Infections Stemming from Trump Rallies," *New York Times*, October 31, 2020.

23. The quotes are from George Packer, "Head of the Class," *The New Yorker*, May 16, 2016.

24. www.washingtonpost.com/politics/2020/07/13/president-trump-has-made-more-than-20000-false-or-misleading-claims/.

25. Unless otherwise identified, the quotes in this paragraph are from www.newyorker.com/news/letter-from-trumps-washington/the-most-mendacious-president-in-us-history.

26. Timothy Snyder, "The American Abyss," *New York Times*, January 9, 2021.

2   PARTY

1. David A. Graham, "Republicans are Prepared to Go Down with Trump," *The Atlantic*, January 31, 2020.

2. Bob Woodward, *Fear: Trump in the White House* (Simon & Schuster, 2018), p. 5.

3. Michael Barone, "The Normalcy of Trump's Republican Party," *Wall Street Journal*, August 21, 2020.

4. George Packer, "The Corruption of the Republican Party," *The Atlantic*, December 14, 2018.

5. https://en.wikipedia.org/wiki/William_F._Buckley_Jr.

6. The three "insurgencies" were identified by Packer; therefore, my argument in this section follows Packer's.

7. The quotes relating to Republican political elites are from Klein, *Why We're Polarized*, p. 177.

8. This paragraph and the quotes are from Evan Osnos, "The Greenwich Rebellion," *The New Yorker*, May 11, 2020.

9. The quote is from Klein, *Why We're Polarized*, p. 178.

10. Quoted in Klein, *Why We're Polarized*, p. 226. The quote is from a book by Thomas Mann and Norman Ornstein titled, *It's Even Worse Than It Looks: How the American Constitutional System Collided with the New Politics of Extremism* (Basic Books, 2012).

11. www.politico.com/story/2016/11/2016-election-best-insults-230794.

12. John Cassidy, "How Donald Trump Won the G.O.P. Nomination," *The New Yorker*, May 4, 2016.

13. https://cpj.org/reports/2020/04/trump-media-attacks-credibility-leaks/. The following paragraph is based on the same source.

14. www.washingtonpost.com/politics/2020/05/12/how-much-trumps-presidency-has-he-spent-tweeting/,

15. www.pewresearch.org/fact-tank/2020/04/08/five-facts-about-fox-news/.

16. www.theatlantic.com/entertainment/archive/2019/11/how-fox-news-covered-day-1-impeachment-hearings/602020/.

17. In Klein, *Why We're Polarized*, p. 237.

18. www.washingtonpost.com/opinions/2020/02/05/how-rush-limbaugh-made-trump-presidency-possible/.

19. Philip Rucker and Carol Leonnig, *A Very Stable Genius* (Penguin, 2020), p. 349.

20. www.washingtonpost.com/lifestyle/media/the-data-is-in-fox-news-may-have-kept-millions-from-taking-the-coronavirus-threat-seriously/2020/06/26/60d88aa2-b7c3-11ea-a8da-693df3d7674a_story.html.

21. "Peaked online." MIT Sloan research about social media, misinformation, and elections | MIT Sloan.

22. www.washingtonpost.com/graphics/politics/2016-election/campaign-finance/. Also, Reuters, December 9, 2016.

23. Quoted in Michela Tindera, "Here are the Billionaires Backing Donald Trump's Campaign," *Forbes*, April 17, 2020.

24. This paragraph is based on Tindera's informative article.

25. Kate Storey, "Donald Trump Brought Reclusive Marvel Billionaire Ike Perlmutter Out of the Shadows," *Esquire*, December 4, 2018.

26. www.cnbc.com/2020/04/15/robert-mercer-starts-big-money-effort-for-trump-campaign.html.

27. Jeremy Peters, "Sheldon Adelson Sees a Lot to Like in Trump's Washington," *New York Times*, September 22, 2018.

28. www.politico.com/news/2020/02/19/sheldon-adelson-host-trump-fundraiser-116008.

29. www.nytimes.com/2020/03/01/us/politics/bernie-sanders-money.html.

30. The quote is from Alberta, *American Carnage*, p. 112.

31. https://en.wikipedia.org/wiki/Citizens_United_v._FEC.

32. Glenn Thrush, Rebecca R. Ruiz, and Karen Yourish, "Trump's Campaign Coffers Low on Big-Dollar Checks," *New York Times*, August 17, 2020.

33. www.politico.com/news/2020/10/15/trump-outraised-by-biden-in-september-383m-to-248m-429760.

34. www.nbcnews.com/politics/congress/former-gop-rep-says-some-republicans-secretly-disgusted-trump-s-n1093456. This is just one of many reports that indicate that however stalwart the Republican fealty to Trump in public, in private many if not most Republicans saw him differently.

35. Barone, "The Normalcy of Trump's Republican Party."

36. The paragraphs on Governor Mike DeWine are based on Trip Gabriel, "Veering from Trump, G.O.P. Governor Turns Himself into a Household Name," *New York Times*, April 29, 2020.

37. Peter Wehner, "The Downfall of the Republican Party," *The Atlantic*, February 2, 2020.

38. Klein, *Why We're Polarized*, p. xiv.

39. www.nytimes.com/2020/09/07/us/politics/trump-election-campaign-fundraising.html.

40. From the jacket of the book, published by Simon & Schuster.

3   ADMINISTRATION

1. www.theguardian.com/us-news/2017/jan/22/trump-inauguration-crowd-sean-spicers-claims-versus-the-evidence.

2. www.theguardian.com/world/2018/sep/06/donald-trump-inauguration-crowd-size-photos-edited.

3. www.theatlantic.com/magazine/archive/2020/07/trumps-collaborators/612250/.

4. https://foreignpolicy.com/2020/02/14/trump-is-failing-his-dictatorship-test/.

5. Mateo Gold and Anu Narayanswamy, "Six Donors that Trump Appointed Gave Almost $12 million," *Washington Post*, December 9, 2016.

6. The quotes in this paragraph are from Rucker and Leonnig, *A Very Stable Genius*, pp. 12 and 17.

7. Henry Jackson, "Trump's Cabinet by the Numbers," *Politico*, January 24, 2017.

8. Elana Schor, "Trump Administration Still Riddled with Key Vacancies," *Politico*, August 11, 2017.

9. Rucker and Leonnig, *A Very Stable Genius*, p. 35.

10. Quoted in Rucker and Leonnig, *A Very Stable Genius*, p. 45.

11. James Mann, "The Adults in the Room," *The New York Review of Books*, October 26, 2017.

12. The quotes in this paragraph are in Woodward, *Fear*, pp. 226, 227, and 323.

13. Woodward, *Fear*, p. 90.

14. McMaster's book is aptly titled. H. R. McMaster, *Dereliction of Duty: Johnson, McNamara, the Joint Chiefs of Staff, and the Lies That Led to Vietnam* (Harper Perennial, 1998).

15. In Rucker and Leonnig, *A Very Stable Genius*, p. 233.

16. Woodward, *Fear*, p. 263.

17. Rucker and Leonnig, *A Very Stable Genius*, p. 157.

18. Rucker and Leonnig, *A Very Stable Genius*, p. 332.

19. Jeffrey Goldberg, "The Man Who Couldn't Take it Anymore," *The Atlantic*, October 2019.

20. Quoted in Rucker and Leonnig, *A Very Stable Genius*, p. 342.

21. The account in this paragraph and the quote is from Goldberg.

22. "Why Staff Turnover in the White House is Such a Bad Thing – Especially for President Trump," *Harvard Business Review*, April 6, 2018.

23. David Graham, "Trump's White House Turnover is Ahead of Schedule," *The Atlantic*, January 3, 2018.

24. Quoted in Jamiles Lartey and Julia Carrie Wong, "You're Fired! I Quit! The Major Trump Departures," *The Guardian*, April 10, 2018.

25. Kathryn Dunn Tenpas, "Record Setting White House Staff Turnover Continues with News of Counsel's Departure," *Brookings*, October 19, 2018.

26. Rucker and Leonnig, *A Very Stable Genius*, p. 48.

27. www.brookings.edu/blog/fixgov/2020/04/13/and-then-there-were-ten-with-85-turnover-across-president-trumps-a-team-who-remains/.

28. Kathryn Dunn Tenpas, "Why is Trump's Staff Turnover Higher Than the 5 Most Recent Presidents?," *Brookings*, January 19, 2018.

29. Quoted in Rucker and Leonnig, *A Very Stable Genius*, p. 21.

30. www.politico.com/magazine/story/2018/03/06/donald-trump-loyalty-staff-217227.

31. www.washingtonpost.com/outlook/2020/04/07/covid-19-white-house-personnel-fauci-birx-atkinson/.

32. www.washingtonpost.com/politics/praise-for-the-chief–trumps-cabinet-tells-him-its-an-honor-privilege-blessing-to-serve/2017/06/12/ddd3919e-4fa4-11e7-91eb-9611861a988f_story.html?itid=lk_inline_manual_2.

33. Jonathan Lemire, Catherine Lucey, and Zeke Miller, "Life in Trump's Cabinet: Perks, Pestering, Power, Putdowns," *AP*, July 5, 2018.

34. Woodward, *Fear*, p. xix.

35. Quoted in www.theatlantic.com/ideas/archive/2020/06/john-boltons-damning-indictment-of-trump/613168/.

36. Kathryn Dunn Tenpas, "And Then There Were Ten," *Brookings*, April 13, 2020.

37. Lisa Friedman, "Midlevel Staff Stifles Science About Climate," *New York Times*, June 15, 2020.

38. Quoted by Jennifer Senior, "The Trump Administration is Made of Swiss Cheese," *New York Times*, May 11, 2020.

39. April 5, 2020.

40. For more on this see Helene Cooper and Eric Schmitt, "A President's Displeasure Rattles the Pentagon," *New York Times*, June 26, 2020. The quote about the Pentagon is from this piece.

41. Comey and McGahn's relationship to the president is fully documented in Michael Schmidt's book, *Donald Trump v. The United States: Inside the Struggle to Stop a President* (Random House, 2020). Schmidt concluded that McGahn was one of the "few Trump advisers – or members of the Republican establishment, for that matter – who regularly stood up to the president" (p. 5).

42. Pranshu Verma and Michael Shear, "Condemning the President, a Top Aide Resigns," *New York Times*, June 20, 2020.

4 INNER CIRCLE

1. This paragraph and the quotes therein are based on www.politico.com/magazine/story/2017/09/15/donald-trump-isolated-alone-trumpology-white-house-215604.

2. Edwin Fisher, "The Loneliness of Fateful Decisions," in Bandy Lee (ed.), *The Dangerous Case of Donald Trump* (St. Martin's Press, 2017), p. 328.

3. Daniel Lippman, August 19, 2019.

4. www.theatlantic.com/politics/archive/2018/05/trumps-tactics-dont-work-for-everyone/560114/.

5. Rucker and Leonnig, *A Very Stable Genius*, p. 237.

6. www.nytimes.com/2019/04/21/us/politics/michael-cohen-trump.html.

7. Michael Cohen, *Disloyal: A Memoir – The True Story of the Former Personal Attorney to the President of the United States* (Skyhorse, 2020).

8. Julia Joffe, "The Believer," *Politico*, June 27, 2016.

9. Josh Dawsey and Eliana Johnson, "Trump's Got a New Favorite Steve," *Politico*, April 13, 2017. The "my two Steves" quote is also in this piece.

10. Dawsey and Johnson, "Trump's Got a New Favorite Steve."

11. Glenn Thrush and Jennifer Steinhauer, "Stephen Miller is a 'True Believer' Behind Core Trump Policies," *New York Times*, February 11, 2017.

12. The phrase is the title of McKay Coppins's article in *The Atlantic*, May 28, 2018.

13. Amanda Holpuch, "Stephen Miller: Why is Trump's White Nationalist Aide Untouchable?," *The Guardian*, December 4, 2019.

14. Jeremy Stahl, "This Is Still Happening: Stephen Miller," *Slate*, April 22, 2020.

15. www.whitehouse.gov/presidential-actions/proclamation-suspending-entry-immigrants-present-risk-u-s-labor-market-economic-recovery-following-covid-19-outbreak/.

16. Woodward, *Fear*, p. 66.

17. Annie Karnie, "The Untouchable Hope Hicks," *Politico*, July 22, 2017.

18. Rucker and Leonnig, *A Very Stable Genius*, p. 209.

19. "Alternative facts," https://en.wikipedia.org/wiki/Alternative_facts.

20. In *Disloyal*, p. 224.

21. The quoted phrase is from Rucker and Leonnig, *A Very Stable Genius*, p. 115.

22. Darren Samuelsohn, "Trump Sons Run the Business – and Keep Tweeting about their Dad," *Politico*, March 18, 2017.

23. This quote and the one preceding are from Jason Zengerle, "The Next Trump," *New York Times Magazine*, August 30, 2020.

24. David Smith, "Family Values: Why Trump's Children are Key to his Reelection Campaign," *The Guardian*, May 24, 2020.

25. This quote and the one preceding are in Taylor Nicole Rogers, "Eric Trump says Coronavirus is a plot to stop his father's campaign rallies and

will 'magically' disappear after election day," *Business Insider*, May 17, 2020.

26. Smith "Family Values."

27. www.nytimes.com/2020/08/09/business/media/fox-news-ratings.html

28. www.foxnews.com/media/highest-viewership-network-history-msnbc-cnn-2020.

29. An article by Will Yakowicz claimed that casino mogul Phil Ruffin was "Donald Trump's Best Friend" (*Forbes*, April 30, 2020). However, there is no evidence either in the article or elsewhere to sustain the claim, certainly not as it applied to Trump's time in the White House.

30. Quoted in Matthew Shaer, "How Far will Sean Hannity Go?," *New York Times Magazine*, November 29, 2017.

31. Quoted in Shaer, "How Far will Sean Hannity Go?"

32. Olivia Nuzzi, "Donald Trump and Sean Hannity Like to Talk Before Bedtime," *New York Magazine*, May, 13, 2018.

33. Nuzzi, "Donald Trump and Sean Hannity Like to Talk Before Bedtime."

34. www.newyorker.com/news/letter-from-trumps-washington/trump-retreats-to-his-hannity-bunker.

35. Mary Jordan, *The Art of Her Deal: The Untold Story of Melania Trump* (Simon & Schuster, 2020), pp. 42, 43.

36. "Man on a Wire: Mike Pence's Tightrope Act," *Politico*, July/August, 2017.

37. Matthew Nussbaum, "Trump Puts Pence in a Corner," *Politico*, May 14, 2018.

38. Michael Crowley and Maggie Haberman, "Pence Makes Clear There is No Daylight Between Him and Trump," *New York Times*, October 3, 2019.

39. Elaina Plott, "Inside Ivanka's Dreamworld," *The Atlantic*, April 12, 2019.

40. www.independent.co.uk/news/world/americas/us-elections/donald-trump-ivanka-trump-creepiest-most-unsettling-comments-a-roundup-a7353876.html and www.independent.co.uk/news/world/americas/us-politics/trump-ivanka-beautiful-new-hampshire-rally-primary-sanders-a9330241.html.

41. Plott, "Inside Ivanka's Dreamworld."

42. Jordan, *The Art of Her Deal*, p. 31.

43. Quoted by Plott, "Inside Ivanka's Dreamworld."

44. www.cnn.com/2019/07/01/politics/ivanka-trump-donald-trump-jr/index.html.

45. Rucker and Leonnig, *A Very Stable Genius*, p. 93.

46. Glenn Thrush and Maggie Haberman, "Jared Kushner Named Senior White House Adviser to Donald Trump," *New York Times*, January 9, 2017.

47. Josh Dawsey, Kenneth P. Vogel, and Alex Isenstadt, "Kushner's Privileged Status Stokes Resentment in White House," *Politico*, April 1, 2017.

48. Peter Baker, Maggie Haberman, Zolan Kanno-Youngs, and Noah Weiland, "Kushner Puts Himself in Middle of White House's Chaotic Coronavirus Response," *New York Times*, April 2, 2020.

49. Rucker and Leonnig, *A Very Stable Genius*, p. 92.

50. www.thedailybeast.com/cnn-melania-trumps-favorability-rating-falls-by -double-digits.

51. Woodward, *Fear*, pp. 174, 175.

52. The quotes in this paragraph are in Jordan, *The Art of Her Deal*, p. 28.

53. The descriptor of Melania as "mysterious" is from Julie Hirschfeld Davis, Maggie Haberman, and Katie Rogers, "Melania Trump, a Mysterious First Lady, Weathers a Chaotic White House," *New York Times*, August 17, 2018. The word "mysterious" was also used by Mary Jordan who said of Melania that "she works at being mysterious." *The Art of Her Deal*, p. 6.

54. The quote is from Jordan, *The Art of Her Deal*, p. 22.

55. Quoted in Jordan, *The Art of Her Deal*, p. 5.

56. www.cnn.com/2020/03/15/politics/melania-trump-coronavirus/index .html.

5   PREQUEL TO THE PANDEMIC

1. Dylan Byron, "Acting Like Animals During a Pandemic," *Lapham's Quarterly*, May 18, 2020. The paragraphs on La Fontaine are based in part on Byron's essay.

2. https://en.wikisource.org/wiki/The_Original_Fables_of_La_Fontaine/ The_Animals_Sick_of_the_Plague.

3. The quotes in this paragraph and the preceding one, as well as most of the information on which they are based, are from Orhan Pamuk, "What Plague Novels Tell Us," *New York Times*, April 26, 2020.

4. https://en.wikipedia.org/wiki/The_Plague.

5. The paragraphs on Camus are based in part on Liesl Schillinger, "What We Can Learn (and Should Unlearn) from Albert Camus's *The Plague*," *Literary Hub*, March 13, 2020.

6. https://datebook.sfchronicle.com/movies-tv/sf-pandemic-thriller-contagion-ignored-after-2011-is-the-film-of-2020.

7. All the information in this paragraph, and the quotes, including those from Procopius, are from Elizabeth Kolbert, "Pandemics and the Shape of Human History," *The New Yorker*, March 30, 2020.

8. Quoted in Jon Meacham, "The Long View: Pandemics Past," *New York Times Book Review*, May 24, 2020.

9. "The Germs that Transformed History," *Wall Street Journal*, May 23–24, 2020.

10. Quoted in Gina Kolata, "Pandemics End with a Bang, or a Whimper," *New York Times*, May 11, 2020.

11. All the quotes in this paragraph are from Kolbert, "Pandemics and the Shape of Human History."

12. Angel Desai, "Twentieth-Century Lessons for a Modern Coronavirus Pandemic," in *Journal of the American Medical Association Network*, April 27, 2020.

13. Joshua Zeitz, "Rampant Lies, Fake Cures and Not Enough Beds: What the Spanish Flu Debacle Can Teach Us about Coronavirus," *Politico*, March 17, 2020.

14. Andrew T. Price-Smith, *Contagion and Chaos: Disease, Ecology, and National Security in the Era of Globalization* (MIT Press, 2020), p. 57.

15. Price-Smith, *Contagion and Chaos*, p. 62.

16. Zeitz, "Rampant Lies, Fake Cures and Not Enough Beds."

17. Price-Smith, *Contagion and Chaos*, p. 61.

18. Quoted in Zeitz, "Rampant Lies, Fake Cures and Not Enough Beds."

19. Zeitz, "Rampant Lies, Fake Cures and Not Enough Beds."

20. "A Storm for Which We Were Unprepared," reprinted in *The American Mind*, April 13, 2020.

21. Quoted in Liz Schrayer, "Why America Could Become Vulnerable to the Next Major Pandemic," *Time*, February 27, 2018.

22. www.geekwire.com/2020/bill-gates-warned-us-covid-19-like-pandemic-watch-ted-talk-2015/.

23. Nicholas Kristof, "A Colossal Failure of Leadership," *New York Times*, October 25, 2020.

24. Beth Cameron, "I ran the White House pandemic office. Trump closed it," *Washington Post*, March 13, 2020.

25. May 10, 2018.

26. Quoted by Julia Belluz in "Trump vs. 'disease x,'" *Vox*, February 23, 2018.

27. Cameron, "I ran the White House pandemic office."

28. Lisa Monaco quoted by Abigail Tracy in "How Trump Gutted Obama's Pandemic-Preparedness Systems," *Vanity Fair*, May 1, 2020.

29. Quoted by Deb Reichmann in "Trump Disbanded NSC Unit that Experts had Praised," *AP News*, March 14, 2020.

30. Lena Sun, "None of these 195 Countries – the U.S. Included – is fully prepared for a Pandemic," *Washington Post*, October 24, 2019.

31. www.theguardian.com/world/2020/may/10/100-days-later-how-did-britain-fail-so-badly-in-dealing-with-covid-19.

32. Council on Foreign Relations News Release, "U.S. Must Apply Lessons from 'Deeply Flawed' Pandemic Response to Preempt a Deadlier Disaster," October 8, 2020.

33. Quoted in Julia Belluz, "The US doesn't have an emergency fund for health crises like Zika, That's a huge mistake," *Vox*, May 16, 2016.

34. https://hbr.org/2003/04/predictable-surprises-the-disasters-you-should-have-seen-coming. Bazerman and Watkins later published a book of the same title. It should be noted that they list a fifth cognitive bias that relates to how much we do or do not listen to other people. Because the evidence on this is conflicting, I have omitted mention of it here.

35. Some of the ideas in this paragraph are from Robert Meyer and Howard Kunreuther, *The Ostrich Paradox: Why We Underprepare for Disasters* (Wharton School Press, 2017). This entire section, on our psychological unreadiness even to prepare for "predictable disasters," owes a great debt to this splendid summary article: Tim Hartford, "Why We Fail to Prepare for Disasters," *Financial Times*, April 18–19, 2020.

36. Nicholas Christakis, *Apollo's Arrow: The Profound and Enduring Impact of Coronavirus on the Way We Live* (Little, Brown Spark, 2020), p. 84.

6   SEQUENCE OF THE PANDEMIC

1. For a careful chronicle of what happened published in fall 2020, see Christakis, *Apollo's Arrow*, especially chapter 1.

2. For a careful chronicle of "What Went Wrong in Wuhan," see this article: www.ft.com/content/82574e3d-1633-48ad-8afb-71ebb3fe3dee.

3. The timeline presented in this chapter is based in considerable part on Derrick Bryson Taylor, "A Timeline of the Coronavirus Pandemic," *New York Times*, July 8, 2020.

4. Derek Watkins, "It Started Small," *New York Times*, July 5, 2020.

5. Erika Edwards, "Coronavirus Spreads for First Time in U.S., CDC Says," *NBC News*, January 30, 2020.

6. Quoted by Donald McNeil Jr. in "Wuhan Coronavirus Looks Increasingly Like a Pandemic, Experts Say," *New York Times*, February 2, 2020.

7. www.bbc.com/news/business-51612520.

8. The first quote in this sentence is from Watkins, "It Started Small." The second is the title of an article by Lena Sun et al. in the *Washington Post*, February 25, 2020.

9. Vanessa Romo, "Trump Appoints Pence to Lead Government's Coronavirus Response," *NPR*, February 26, 2020.

10. Bob Woodward, *Rage* (Simon & Schuster, 2020), p. xiii.

11. Woodward, *Rage*, p. xix.

12. www.livescience.com/coronavirus-pandemic-who.html.

13. www.talkbasket.net/86665-nba-commissioner-adam-silver-on-resuming -the-season-in-empty-arenas-it-sucks.

14. Matt Apuzzo et al., "Failures on the Diamond Princess Shadow – Another Cruise Ship Outbreak," *New York Times*, March 8, 2020.

15. The article was titled, "America is Broken." It appeared in the March 16–29 issue.

16. *Monthly Labor Review*, US Bureau of Labor Statistics, April 2020.

17. Quote in Caitlin Oprysko, "Trump on a Nationwide Lockdown," *Politico*, March 20, 2020.

18. Michael Rothfeld et al., "13 Deaths in a Day," *New York Times*, March 25, 2020.

19. Michael Shear, "Trump Extends Social Distancing Guidelines through April," *New York Times*, March 29, 2020.

20. Shane Harris et al., "U.S. Intelligence Reports from January and February Warned about a Likely Pandemic," *Washington Post*, March 20, 2020.

21. Josh Margolin and James Gordon Meek, "Intelligence Report Warned of Coronavirus Crisis as Early as November," *ABC News*, April 8, 2020.

22. Associated Press, "China Didn't Warn Public of Likely Pandemic for 6 Key Days," April 15, 2020.

23. The quotes in this paragraph are from www.vanityfair.com/news/2020/0 4/trump-received-coronavirus-warnings-daily-intelligence-briefings-pdb.

24. Eric Lipton et al., "He Could Have Seen What Was Coming: Behind Trump's Failure on the Virus," *New York Times*, April 11, updated May 4, 2020.

25. Stephen Collinson, "Trump Passes the Buck as Deadly Ventilator Shortage Looms," *CNN Politics*, April 3, 2020.

26. Philip Ewing and Barbara Sprunt, "On Coronavirus Trump Walks a Tightrope Between Grim Warnings and Offering Hope," *NPR*, April 6, 2000.

27. Eli Stokols and Noah Bierman, "Trump Stokes Up his Blame Game for the Coronavirus," *Los Angeles Times*, April 13, 2020.

28. Quote in Stokols and Bierman, "Trump Stokes Up his Blame Game."

29. www.theatlantic.com/politics/archive/2020/07/trumps-lies-about-coronavirus/608647/.

30. https://static01.nyt.com/images/2021/01/18/nytfrontpage/scan.pdf.

31. Taylor, "A Timeline."

32. www.washingtonpost.com/politics/2020/07/20/when-trump-was-holding-regular-briefings-his-approval-was-higher-it-wasnt-because-briefings/.

33. Alexandra Berzon et al., "Many Missteps Led to Mask Shortages," *Wall Street Journal*, April 30, 2020.

34. www.nytimes.com/2020/05/05/us/jared-kushner-fema-coronavirus.html.

35. This paragraph is based on Phillip Rucker, Josh Dawsey, Yasmeen Abutaleb, Robert Costa, and Lena H. Sun, "34 Days of Pandemic: Inside Trump's Desperate Attempts to Reopen America," *Washington Post*, May 2, 2020.

36. Quoted in Stephen Collinson, "Trump Sows Division and Confusion as Anxious Country Edges Toward Opening," *CNN Politics*, May 20, 2020.

37. GOP is the abbreviation for Grand Old Party, the traditional nickname for the Republican Party.

38. Burgess Everett and John Bresnahan, "Republicans Praise Trump's Pandemic Response with Senate Majority at Risk," *Politico*, May 6, 2020.

39. www.axios.com/always-trumpers-republicans-axios-on-hbo-f4a866a6-03a8-4632-b92b-47f79607ef01.html.

40. www.washingtonpost.com/politics/2020/07/13/president-trump-has-made-more-than-20000-false-or-misleading-claims/.

41. Quoted in Dan Diamond, "White House Goes Quiet on Coronavirus as Outbreak Spikes Again Across the U.S.," *Politico*, June 10, 2020.

42. This quote and the information in this paragraph are from the article in *The Atlantic* by Robinson Meyer, "The Week America Lost Control of the Pandemic," July 2, 2020.

43. "This is Trump's Plague Now," *The Atlantic*, June 29, 2020.

44. Nigel Chiwaya and Corky Siemaszko, "Covid-19 Cases, Deaths Rising Rapidly Ahead of Election Day," *NBC News*, November 2, 2020.

7 SCIENCE OF THE PANDEMIC

1. The painting by West hangs in the Philadelphia Museum of Art. It is titled *Benjamin Franklin Drawing Electricity from the Sky*.

2. All the quotes in this paragraph are from www.realclearscience.com/blog/2012/02/thomas-jefferson-citizen-scientist.html.

3. Abby Goodnough, "Under Pressure C.D.C. Backs Call to Open Schools," *New York Times*, July 25, 2020.

4. Stephanie Nebehay, "WHO Says New China Virus Could Spread," *Reuters*, January 14, 2020.

5. The quotes – and the description that precedes them – are from Matt Apuzzo et al., "How the World Missed Covid-19's Silent Spread," *New York Times*, June 27, 2020.

6. The quote is Richard Horton's. It is in Anjana Ahuja, "Lunch with the FT," *Financial Times*, April 26, 2020.

7. Apuzzo et al., "How the World Missed Covid-19's Silent Spread."

8. https://abcnews.go.com/US/timeline-cuomos-trumps-responses-coronavirus-outbreak/story?id=69914641.

9. www.usatoday.com/story/news/health/2020/02/17/nih-disease-official-anthony-fauci-risk-of-coronavirus-in-u-s-is-minuscule-skip-mask-and-wash-hands/4787209002/.

10. Quoted in Huo Jingnan, "Why There Are So Many Different Guidelines for Face Masks for the Public," *NPR*, April 10, 2020.

11. https://thehill.com/changing-america/well-being/prevention-cures/502890-fauci-why-the-public-wasnt-told-to-wear-masks.

12. Quoted in Jingnan, "Why There Are So Many Different Guidelines."

13. David Gelles, "Corner Office," *New York Times*, May 3, 2020.

14. www.axios.com/everything-trump-says-he-knows-more-about-than-anybody-b278b592-cff0-47dc-a75f-5767f42bcf1e.html.

15. www.washingtonpost.com/politics/maybe-i-have-a-natural-ability-trump-plays-medical-expert-on-coronavirus-by-second-guessing-the-professionals/2020/03/06/3ee0574c-5ffb-11ea-9055-5fa12981bbbf_story.html.

16. Lisa Friedman and Brad Plumer, "Science Speaks (But the President Rarely Listens)," *New York Times*, April 29, 2020.

17. Christopher Flavelle and Lisa Friedman, "President Acts to Undermine Science Agency," *New York Times*, October 28, 2020.

18. www.theatlantic.com/culture/archive/2020/04/trumps-coronavirus-briefings-dystopia-real-time/610642/.

19. *Wall Street Journal*, May 16–17, 2020 and www.nytimes.com/2020/04/16/us/politics/michael-savage-trump-coronavirus.html.

20. www.usatoday.com/story/opinion/todaysdebate/2020/07/14/anthony-fauci-wrong-with-me-peter-navarro-editorials-debates/5439374002/.

21. Peter Nicholas and Ed Yong, "Fauci: 'Bizarre' White House Behavior Only Hurts the President," *The Atlantic*, July 15, 2020. This paragraph is also based on Philip Rucker, Laurie McGinley, Josh Dawsey, and Yasmeen Abutaleb, "Rancor Between Scientists and Trump Allies Threatens Pandemic Response as Cases Surge," *Washington Post*, July 17, 2020.

22. In Nichols and Yong, "Fauci: 'Bizarre' White House Behavior."

23. www.bbc.com/news/world-us-canada-53587527.

24. Quoted in Rucker et al., "Rancor Between Scientists and Trump."

25. www.cnn.com/2020/02/25/health/coronavirus-us-american-cases/index.html.

26. https://thehill.com/homenews/administration/494187-trump-threatened-to-fire-cdcs-chief-of-respiratory-diseases-in.

27. Sheryl Gay Stolberg, "Whistle-Blower Describes Clashes and 'Cronyism' in Administration Response," *New York Times*, May 6, 2020.

28. Quoted in Amy Ross Sorkin, "Rick Bright and the Pandemic Path Not Taken," *The New Yorker*, May 15, 2020.

29. Edward Luce, "Trump and the Great Coronavirus Meltdown," *Financial Times*, May 17, 2020.

30. www.marketwatch.com/story/this-chart-shows-just-how-badly-the-us-coronavirus-response-has-damaged-americas-reputation-in-europe-2020-06-25.

31. D'Angelo Gore, *Factcheck Posts*, "Covid-19 Cases and Deaths, By the Numbers," *Factcheck Posts*, June 30, 2020.

32. https://fortune.com/2020/07/12/how-is-us-economy-doing-2020-recession-unemployment-rate-benefits-consumer-spending-job-losses-state-by-state-pmi-coronavirus-pandemic/.

33. Derek Hawkins, "Coronavirus Update: Birx Says U.S. has Entered a 'New Phase' of Pandemic as Cases, Deaths, Rise," *Washington Post*, August 2, 2020.

34. For 21 years, between 2000 and 2021, I was a member of the Harvard faculty.
35. Interview with Lawrence Bacow conducted by John Rosenberg in the April 2020 issue of *Harvard Magazine*.
36. The quotes in this paragraph are in Cory Turner and Anya Kamenetz, "When Should Schools Close for Coronavirus?," *NPR*, March 11, 2020.
37. www.whitehouse.gov/briefings-statements/remarks-president-trump-safely-reopening-americas-schools/.
38. https://time.com/5874742/barron-trump-school-coronavirus/.

8   POLITICS OF THE PANDEMIC

1. In contrast to other divisive diseases, such as AIDS, COVID-19 was exceedingly widespread.
2. In my book, *Followership*, I identified five different types of followers, of whom Isolates are one. I defined Isolates in part as followers "who are completely detached." They "do not care about their leaders or know anything about them or respond to them in any way." *Followership: How Followers are Changing Leaders and Creating Change* (Harvard Business School Press, 2008), p. 86. My point is that even as it pertained to the virus crisis, some Americans were Isolates.
3. www.washingtonpost.com/video/politics/22-times-trump-said-the-coronavirus-would-go-away/2020/04/30/d2593312-9593-4ec2-aff7-72c14 38fca0e_video.html.
4. Peter Nicolas, "The Coronavirus Outbreak Could Bring Out the Worst in Trump," *The Atlantic*, February 18, 2020.
5. Quotes from Emily Badger and Kevin Quealy, "Red vs. Blue on Coronavirus Concern: The Gap is Still Big but Closing," *New York Times*, March 21, 2020.
6. Natalie Moore, "Study Finds More Covid-19 Cases Among Viewers of Fox News Host Who Downplayed the Pandemic," *NPR*, May 4, 2000.
7. McKay Coppins, "The Social-Distancing Culture War has Begun," *The Atlantic*, March 30, 2020.
8. Jesse Singal, "The Theory that Explains the Politicization of the Coronavirus," *New York Magazine*, May 8, 2020.
9. Thomas Edsall, "How Could Human Nature Have Become This Politicized?," *New York Times*, July 8, 2020.

10. Both quotes in this paragraph are in Kevin Liptak, "Trump Announces New Face Mask Recommendations After Heated Internal Debate," *CNN*, April 3, 2020.

11. Annie Karni and Maggie Astor, "As Leaders Urge Face Masks, Their Behavior Muffles the Message," *New York Times*, April 22, 2020.

12. Liz Goodwin, "Trump's Refusal to Wear a Mask is Helping Politicize a Crucial Tool for Fighting Virus," *Boston Globe*, May 27, 2020.

13. Anna North, "What Trump's Refusal to Wear a Mask Says about Masculinity in America," *Vox*, May 12, 2020.

14. Mariel Padilla, "Who's Wearing a Mask? Women, Democrats and City Dwellers," *New York Times*, June 2, 2020.

15. Julie Bosman, July 2, 2020.

16. This paragraph including the quotes is from Bosman, "For Many Republicans, an Abrupt About-Face on Masks."

17. Aamer Madhani and Laurie Kellman, "Republicans, with Exception of Trump, Now Push Mask-Wearing," *AP*, June 30, 2020.

18. Peter Baker, "Trump, in a Shift, Endorses Masks and Says Virus Will Get Worse," *New York Times*, July 21, 2020.

19. Bottoms fought back, loudly, and Kemp's suit was soon dropped.

20. www.pewresearch.org/fact-tank/2020/10/29/both-republicans-and-democrats-cite-masks-as-a-negative-effect-of-covid-19-but-for-very-different-reasons/.

21. This paragraph is based Monica Anderson, Skye Toor, Lee Rainie, and Aaron Smith, "Activism in the Social Media Age," Pew Research Center, July 2018. Also see Jelani Cobb, "The Matter of Black Lives," *The New Yorker*, July 27, 2020. Cobb's article first appeared on March 14, 2016.

22. Jack Healy and Dionne Searcey, "Twin Crises and Surging Anger Convulse U.S.," *New York Times*, June 1, 2020.

23. "The Long Reach of Racism in the U.S.," *Wall Street Journal*, June 6–7, 2020.

24. This paragraph is based on Patricia Cohen and Ben Casselman, "For Laid-off Minorities Recovery Looks Distant," *New York Times*, June 6, 2020.

25. Emily Bobrow, "Black, Pregnant, and in Greater Peril," *New York Times*, August 9, 2020.

26. The figures on Hispanics and American Indians are from Christakis, *Apollo's Arrow*, p. 197.

27. This paragraph is based on the *New York Times* article referred to in the text. It is by Nate Cohn and Kevin Quealy.

28. Giovanni Russonello, "A 'Seismic Shift' in the Views on Racism in America," *New York Times*, June 6, 2020.

29. www.theatlantic.com/magazine/archive/2019/06/trump-racism-comments /588067/.

30. For more on why I admire how the American military teaches how to lead see my book, *Professionalizing Leadership* (Oxford University Press, 2018).

31. Tom Gjelton, "Peaceful Protesters Tear-Gassed to Clear Way for Trump Church Photo-Op," *NPR*, June 1, 2020.

32. www.theatlantic.com/politics/archive/2020/06/james-mattis-denounces -trump-protests-militarization/612640/.

33. Helene Cooper, "General Regrets Joining Photo Op Staged by Trump," *New York Times*, June 12, 2020.

34. For somewhat more detail on this see this article about "systemic economic racism": www.newyorker.com/news/news-desk/the-pandemic -has-intensified-systemic-economic-racism-against-black-americans.

35. www.cnn.com/2020/04/21/politics/trump-china-praise-coronavirus- timeline/index.html.

36. Demetri Sevastopulo and Katrina Manson, "Trump Steps Up Anti-China Push with Sanctions against HK Officials," *FT Weekend*, August 8–9, 2020.

37. Stewart Patrick, "When the System Fails," *Foreign Affairs*, July/August 2020.

38. John Bolton, *The Room Where It Happened: A White House Memoir* (Simon & Schuster, 2020), p. 287.

39. www.cnn.com/2020/04/21/politics/trump-china-praise-coronavirus- timeline/index.html.

40. Bolton, *The Room Where It Happened*, p. 315.

41. Quoted in Katie Rogers, "Politicians' Use of 'Wuhan Virus' Starts a Debate Health Experts Wanted to Avoid," *New York Times*, March 10, 2020.

42. Thomas Levinson, "Conservatives Try to Rebrand the Coronavirus," *The Atlantic*, March 11, 2020.

43. www.theguardian.com/us-news/2020/apr/11/republican-tom-cotton- coronavirus-china.

44. Reported by Associated Press in *Politico*, March 3, 2020.

45. Edith Lederer, "China Calls for Solidarity not 'Finger-Pointing' on Virus," APNews.com, April 21, 2020.

46. www.pewresearch.org/global/2020/07/30/americans-fault-china-for-its-role-in-the-spread-of-covid-19/.

47. Laura Silver, Kat Devlin, and Christine Huang, "Americans Fault China for its Role in the Spread of Covid-19," Pew Research Center, July 30, 2020.

9   VICE PRESIDENT, CABINET

1. Peter Nicholas, "Mike Pence's Plan to Save Trump – and Himself," *The Atlantic*, July 8, 2020.

2. www.washingtonpost.com/news/the-fix/wp/2017/12/20/in-cabinet-meeting-pence-praises-trump-once-every-12-seconds-for-3-minutes-straight/.

3. Tim Alberta, "Man on a Wire: Mike Pence's Tightrope Act," *Politico*, July/August 2017.

4. The 2018 quotes are in Matthew Nussbaum, "Trump Puts Pence in a Corner," *Politico*, May 14, 2018.

5. Crowley and Haberman, "Pence Makes Clear There is No Daylight between Him and Trump."

6. The descriptor is in McKay Coppins, "When a Vice President Becomes a Threat," *The Atlantic*, October 4, 2019.

7. Mark Mazzetti, Noah Weiland, and Sheryl Stolberg, "Under Pence, Politics Regularly Seeped into Coronavirus Response," *New York Times*, October 9, 2020.

8. All quotes in this paragraph are in Adam Gabatt, "Mike Pence 'not up to task' of leading US coronavirus response, say experts," *The Guardian*, February 27, 2020.

9. Gabby Orr and Anita Kumar, "A Presidency of Two for Coronavirus: Trump Hands His Sidekick the Job of a Savior," *Politico*, March 6, 2020.

10. Quotes in this paragraph are in Alexander Burns and Maggie Haberman, "'Good Soldier' Pence Walks Line Between Loyalty and His Future," *New York Times*, August 26, 2020.

11. Linda Qiu, "As Cases Surge, Pence Misleads on Coronavirus Pandemic," *New York Times*, June 26, 2020.

12. www.axios.com/off-the-rails-trump-pence-048fcbc8-54dc-43bc-8832-46950ffd6fd5.html.

13. This paragraph including the quotes, from Susan Glasser, "Mike Pompeo, The Secretary of Trump," *The New Yorker*, August 19, 2019.

14. Mattathias Schwartz, "Mike Pompeo's Mission: Clean Up Trump's Messes," *New York Times Magazine*, February 26, 2019.

15. Nahal Toosi, "Mike Pompeo Suddenly Finds His Voice on the Virus," *Politico*, March 31, 2001.

16. Josh Wingrove, "Mike Pompeo Accuses China of Posing a Worldwide Threat for Hiding Origin of the Coronavirus," in *Time*, April 29, 2020.

17. www.washingtonpost.com/opinions/global-opinions/how-mike-pompeo-became-trumps-china-hawk/2019/06/27/a166361e-991a-11e9-916d-9c61607d8190_story.html.

18. The descriptor "unscrupulous sycophancy" was used by Eric Levitz in "American Winner: Treasury Secretary Steven Mnuchin Embodies the Plutocratic Principle that a Crisis is a Terrible Thing to Waste," *New York Magazine*, April, 2020.

19. Jason Zengerle, "Steven Mnuchin's Deal Staved Off Catastrophe. Can He Make Another One?," *New York Times Magazine*, October 4, 2020.

20. Levitz, "American Winner."

21. Daniel Strauss, "Trump Administration Has No Regrets about Reopening Push, Says Mnuchin," *The Guardian*, July 2, 2020.

22. www.brookings.edu/blog/up-front/2020/05/06/the-covid-19-crisis-has-already-left-too-many-children-hungry-in-america/.

23. www.brookings.edu/blog/up-front/2020/07/09/about-14-million-children-in-the-us-are-not-getting-enough-to-eat/.

24. www.cbpp.org/research/poverty-and-inequality/tracking-the-covid-19-recessions-effects-on-food-housing-and.

25. www.nytimes.com/2019/12/12/opinion/trump-bill-barr-.html.

26. Quoted in Jeffrey Toobin, "The Surrender," *The New Yorker*, July 6 and 13, 2020.

27. www.theatlantic.com/ideas/archive/2019/05/barr-misled-the-publicand-it-worked/588463/.

28. Jeffrey Toobin, *True Crimes and Misdemeanors: The Investigation of Donald Trump* (Doubleday, 2020), p. 447.

29. www.nytimes.com/2020/08/18/us/politics/senate-intelligence-russian-interference-report.html.

30. Mattathias Schwartz, "The Advocate," *New York Times Magazine*, June 7, 2020.

31. www.nytimes.com/2019/12/12/opinion/trump-bill-barr-.html.

32. Matt Zapotosky, "Barr Calls Current Restrictions 'Draconian,' and Suggests They Should Be Revisited Next Month," *Washington Post*, April 9, 2020.

33. Zapotosky, "Barr Calls Current Restrictions 'Draconian.'"

34. Matt Zapotosky, "Barr tells prosecutors to 'be on the lookout' for state, local coronavirus orders that may violate Constitution," *Washington Post*, April 27, 2020.

35. https://abcnews.go.com/Politics/wireStory/barr-fire-comparison-virus-lock-slavery-73071003.

36. Schwartz, "The Advocate."

37. Gabriel Sherman, "Inside Donald Trump and Jared Kushner's Two Months of Magical Thinking," *Vanity Fair*, April 28, 2020.

38. Ashley Parker, Yasmeen Abutaleb, and Lena H. Sun, "Squandered Time: How the Trump Administration Lost Control of the Coronavirus Crisis," *Washington Post*, March 7, 2020.

39. Sherman, "Inside Donald Trump and Jared Kushner's Two Months of Magical Thinking."

40. Parker et al., "Squandered Time."

41. The account in this paragraph is based on Lipton et al., "He Could Have Seen What Was Coming."

42. Jeremy Diamond, Jamie Gangel, and Tami Luhby, "White House Officials Are Discussing Plans to Replace HHS Secretary Alex Azar," *CNN Politics*, April 26, 2020.

43. May 21, 2020.

10   SENIOR ADVISORS

1. www.nytimes.com/2020/08/18/us/politics/senate-intelligence-russian-interference-report.html.

2. www.forbes.com/sites/stevenbertoni/2016/11/22/exclusive-interview-how-jared-kushner-won-trump-the-white-house/#6401bc033af6.

3. This is not to say Kushner was entirely without accomplishments. His helping to broker a deal between Israel and the United Arab Emirates and also Bahrain was arguably the most significant.

4. Baker et al., "Kushner Puts Himself in Middle of White House's Chaotic Coronavirus Response."

5. https://en.wikipedia.org/wiki/White_House_Coronavirus_Task_Force.

6. Tom McCarthy, "Jared Kushner and his Shadow Corona Unit," *The Guardian*, April 5, 2020.

7. The first two quotes are in Baker et al., "Kushner Puts Himself in Middle of White House's Chaotic Coronavirus Response." The next two are in Adam Cancryn and Dan Diamond, "Behind the Scenes, Kushner Takes Charge of Coronavirus Response," *Politico*, April 1, 2020. The last two are in McCarthy, "Jared Kushner and his Shadow Corona Unit."

8. The first two quotes are in McCarthy, "Jared Kushner and his Shadow Corona Unit"; the third is in Sherman, "Inside Donald Trump and Jared Kushner's Two Months of Magical Thinking."

9. See for example, Jonathan Allen et al., "Behind Closed Doors, Trump's Coronavirus Task Force Boosts Industry and Sows Confusion," *NBCNews.com*, April 11, 2020. Also see, https://slate.com/news-and-politics/2020/05/this-is-still-happening-jared-kushner-pandemic-czar.html.

10. In McCarthy, "Jared Kushner and his Shadow Corona Unit."

11. Katherine Eban, "How Jared Kushner's Secret Testing Plan 'Went Poof Into Thin Air,'" *Vanity Fair*, July 20, 2020.

12. Andrea Bernstein, "How Jared Kushner is Tackling the White House's Coronavirus Response – Without any Evident Experience," *ProPublica*, April 22, 2020.

13. www.theatlantic.com/politics/archive/2020/08/how-jared-kushner-became-trumps-most-dangerous-enabler/615169/.

14. McCarthy, "Jared Kushner and his Shadow Corona Unit."

15. www.cnn.com/2020/10/28/politics/woodward-kushner-coronavirus-doctors/index.html.

16. Sherman, "Inside Donald Trump and Jared Kushner's Two Months of Magical Thinking."

17. Peter Baker, "Trump and Kushner Engage in Revisionist History in Boasting of Success Over Virus," *New York Times*, April 29, 2020. Kushner's quote is in the same article. For a year-end summary of what happened during the "pandemic's dark winter," and Kushner's role in it see this piece in the *Washington Post*: "The inside story of how Trump's denial and mismanagement led to the covid pandemic's dark winter," *Washington Post*, December 19, 2020.

18. Formally, Mulvaney was Acting Chief of Staff. Among other reasons, he continued at the same time to hold other administration positions.

19. Nancy Cook, "Trump Keeps His Staff in Flux with White House Musical Chairs," *Politico*, May 18, 2020.

20. Nancy Cook and Gabby Orr, "Mulvaney Isolated in West Wing at Critical Moment for Trump," *Politico*, January 11, 2019.

21. Kevin Breuninger, "Media's coronavirus stories trying to hurt Trump, Mick Mulvaney says as he urges public to turn off TV," *CNBC.com*.

22. Alison Durkee, "As Trump Touted the 'Fantastic' Economy, Mick Mulvaney was Selling off His Stocks," *Vanity Fair*, June 20, 2020.

23. www.politico.com/news/2020/04/06/task-mark-meadows-control-crisis-save-presidency-167323.

24. Olivia Beavers, "Meadows Joins White House in Crisis Mode," *The Hill*, March 31, 2020.

25. All the quotes in this paragraph are in Michael Shear et al., "Passing Off Virus Burden, White House Fueled Crisis," *New York Times*, July 19, 2020.

26. This section is based on the account in Shear et al., "Passing Off Virus Burden."

27. Shear et al., "Passing Off Virus Burden."

28. www.washingtonpost.com/politics/trump-struggled-summer-coronavirus/2020/08/08/e12ceace-d80a-11ea-aff6-220dd3a14741_story.html.

29. Maggie Haberman, "Trade Adviser Warned White House in January of the Risks of a Pandemic," *New York Times*, April 17, 2020.

30. Quoted in Haberman, "Trade Adviser Warned White House."

31. Quoted in Haberman, "Trade Adviser Warned White House."

32. Navarro's quote is in Chandelis Duster, "Peter Navarro on his qualifications to disagree with Dr. Fauci on coronavirus treatments: 'I'm a social scientist,'" *CNN Politics*, April 6, 2020.

33. Alan Rappeport, "Navarro Calls Medical Experts 'Tone Deaf' Over Coronavirus Shutdown," *New York Times*, April 13, 2020.

34. The piece was dated July 14, 2020.

35. Sheryl Gay Stolberg, "Slow Response Cost Lives, Ousted Scientist Testifies," *New York Times*, May 15, 2020.

36. The quotes relating to the events of late summer are all in David Lynch et al., "Tactics of fiery White House trade adviser draw new scrutiny as some of his pandemic moves unravel," *Washington Post*, September 2, 2020.

37. www.foxnews.com/politics/peter-navarro-defends-contracts-tactics-white-house.

38. The quotes and the account are in *Rage*, pp. xiii ff.

39. www.washingtonpost.com/politics/matthew-pottinger-faced-communist-chinas-intimidation-as-a-reporter-hes-now-at-the-white-house-shaping-trumps-hard-line-policy-toward-beijing/2020/04/28/5fb3 f6d4-856e-11ea-ae26-989cfce1c7c7_story.html.

40. Lipton et al., "He Could Have Seen What Was Coming."

41. Lipton et al., "He Could Have Seen What Was Coming."

42. This paragraph is based largely on Daniel Lippman and Meridith McGraw, "Inside the National Security Council, a Rising Sense of Dread," *Politico*, April 2, 2020.

43. *Rage*, p. 276.

44. David Nakamura et al., "Matthew Pottinger faced Communist China's intimidation as a reporter. He's now at the White House shaping Trump's hard line policy toward Beijing," *Washington Post*, April 29, 2020.

45. Maggie Haberman, "Hope Hicks to Return to the White House After Nearly Two-Year Absence," *New York Times*, February 13, 2020.

46. www.washingtonpost.com/lifestyle/hope-hicks-job-coronavirus-trump-covid/2020/10/09/e73f97e6-0806-11eb-9be6-cf25fb429f1a_story.html? outputType=amp.

47. Tony Sayegh quoted in Nancy Cook and Meridith McGraw, "Trump Looks to Hope Hicks as Coronavirus Crisis Spills Over," *Politico*, April 27, 2020.

48. Quoted in Cook and McGraw, "Trump Looks to Hope Hicks as Coronavirus Crisis Spills Over."

49. "Alternative facts," https://en.wikipedia.org/wiki/Alternative_facts.

50. https://nypost/com/20/04/20/kellyanne-conway-slams-michigan-going-too-far-with-lockdown/.

51. www.foxnews.com/politics/kellyanne-conway-biden-coronavirus-ignorance-arrogance.

11   SENATORS, GOVERNORS, MEDIA

1. April 20, 2020.

2. The quote is in Andrew Prokop, "Donald Trump's Feud with Mitch McConnell, Explained," *Vox*, August 23, 2017.

3. www.nbcnews.com/politics/congress/mcconnell-reaches-milestone-judges-filling-final-circuit-court-vacancy-n1232011.

4. Glenn Thrush, "Mitch McConnell, Never a Grandstander, Learns to Play by Trump's Rules," *New York Times*, April 14, 2019. Also see Alberta, *American Carnage*, p. 506.

5. Mayer, "Enabler in Chief."

6. www.kentucky.com/news/politics-government/article244715797.html.

7. Toobin, *True Crimes and Misdemeanors*, pp. 430 and 431.

8. Mayer, "Enabler in Chief."

9. https://abcnews.go.com/Politics/inside-john-mccains-amigos-friendship/story?id=57392266.

10. Mark Leibovich, "How Lindsey Graham Went from Trump Skeptic to Trump Sidekick," *New York Times Magazine*, February 25, 2019.

11. Leibovich, "How Lindsey Graham Went from Trump Skeptic to Trump Sidekick."

12. Leibovich, "How Lindsey Graham Went from Trump Skeptic to Trump Sidekick."

13. Seung Min Kim and Burgess Everett, "Trump's On-and-Off Relationship with Graham Hits the Skids," *Politico*, January 17, 2018.

14. Myah Ward, "Graham Contradicts Trump: US 'still struggling with testing on a large scale,'" *Politico*, April 16, 2020.

15. Rebecca Klar, "Graham: Trump Visa Order will have a 'chilling effect on our economic recovery,'" *The Hill*, June 22, 2020.

16. This quote and the remainder of this paragraph is based on www.salon.com/2020/07/02/as-covid-deaths-mounted-lindsey-graham-kept-moving-the-goalposts-for-trump/.

17. www.rollingstone.com/politics/politics-features/lindsey-graham-senate-trump-928948/.

18. Peter Nicolas and Kathy Gilsinan, "The End of the Imperial Presidency," *The Atlantic*, May 2, 2020.

19. Matt Dixon, "What does Gov. DeSantis owe Trump?," *Politico*, March 5, 2020. Also see, Zak Cheney-Rice, "Florida Man – Don't Overthink Ron DeSantis," *New York Magazine*, May 12, 2020.

20. Most of this paragraph and the quotes draw from Ronald Brownstein, "The Two States Where Trump's Covid-19 Response Could Backfire in 2020," *The Atlantic*, April 9, 2020.

21. www.cnbc.com/2020/04/28/trump-and-florida-gov-ron-desantis-to-hold-press-conference-tuesday-morning.html.

22. Kimiko de Freytas-Tamura et al., "Florida Breaks U.S. Record for Most Cases in a Day," *New York Times*, July 12, 2020.

23. www.theguardian.com/us-news/2020/jul/17/florida-coronavirus-ron-desantis-governor-trump.

24. Matt Dixon and Arek Sarkissian, "DeSantis Turns to Hannity for Shelter from Political Storms," *Politico*, July 8, 2020.

25. www.gainesvilletimes.com/news/health-care/gov-kemp-declares-georgia-public-health-emergency-effective-march-14/.

26. www.nbcnews.com/politics/donald-trump/trump-approved-georgia-gov-kemp-s-plan-reopen-early-president-n1191621.

27. www.theatlantic.com/health/archive/2020/08/georgia-brian-kemp-authoritarian/615010/.

28. www.usatoday.com/story/news/health/2020/08/13/georgia-coronavirus-pandemic-school-highest-daily-deaths/3347071001/.

29. Ashley Parker, Amy Gardner, and Josh Dawsey, "Inside the 'nasty' feud between Trump and the Republican governor he blames for losing Georgia," *Washington Post*, December 14, 2020.

30. The information in this paragraph and the quotes are in Brian Stelter, *Hoax: Donald Trump, Fox News, and the Dangerous Distortion of Truth* (One Signal Publishers, 2020), pp. 12 and 295.

31. www.nytimes.com/2020/08/09/business/media/fox-news-ratings.html.

32. Jeremy Peters and Michael Grynbaum, "How Right-Wing Pundits are Covering Coronavirus," *New York Times*, March 11, 2020.

33. www.nytimes.com/2017/12/23/business/media/murdoch-trump-relationship.html.

34. Stelter, *Hoax*, p. 20.

35. The account of Carlson in this paragraph and the quote is from Stelter, *Hoax*, p. 298.

36. www.thedailybeast.com/fox-news-star-tucker-carlsons-journey-from-taking-coronavirus-seriously-to-covid-truther.

37. Joe Berkowitz, "Exposure to Laura Ingraham may be dangerous, new study on Covid-19 misinformation suggests," *Fast Company*, July 17, 2020.

38. This paragraph and the quotes are from Stelter, *Hoax*, pp. 309–310.

39. www.washingtonpost.com/opinions/2020/09/01/trump-is-too-loony-even-laura-ingraham/.

40. Cohen, *Disloyal*, p. 333.

41. Quotes and information in this paragraph and the one preceding are based on Paul Farhi and Sarah Ellison, "On Fox News, Suddenly a Very Different Tune about the Coronavirus," *Washington Post*, March 16, 2020.

42. David Frum, "This is Trump's Plague Now," *The Atlantic*, June 29, 2020.

43. Jeremy Peters, "Alarm, Denial, Blame: The Pro-Trump Media's Coronavirus Distortion," *New York Times*, April 1, 2020.

44. Stelter, *Hoax*, p. 295.

45. "Trump Retreats to His Hannity Bunker," June 26, 2020.

46. Michael Cohen makes this point, correctly, in his book, *Disloyal*, pp. 207 ff.

47. The quotes in this paragraph are from Stelter, *Hoax*, pp. 23, 73, and 97.

48. www.npr.org/local/309/2020/05/04/849109486/study-finds-more-c-o-v-i-d-19-cases-among-viewers-of-fox-news-host-who-downplayed-pandemic. Also see, www.vox.com/policy-and-politics/2020/4/22/21229360/coronavirus-covid-19-fox-news-sean-hannity-misinformation-death,

49. www.pewresearch.org/fact-tank/2020/04/08/five-facts-about-fox-news/.

50. Michael Grynbaum, "Viewership for R.N.C. Dips for All But Fox News," *New York Times*, August 26, 2020.

51. Anne Applebaum, *Twilight of Democracy: The Seductive Lure of Authoritarianism* (Doubleday, 2020), pp. 167 ff.

52. www.thestreet.com/lifestyle/highest-paid-news-anchors-15062420.

53. www.forbes.com/sites/hayleycuccinello/2018/07/16/sean-hannity-celebrity-100/#7affa5352d93.

54. Stelter, *Hoax*, p. 9.

12   MEDICAL EXPERTS

1. www.whitehouse.gov/briefings-statements/statement-press-secretary-regarding-presidents-coronavirus-task-force/.

2. Rucker et al., "34 Days of Pandemic."

3. Sam Levin, "Fauci Says His Contact with Trump Has 'Dramatically Decreased,'" *The Guardian*, June 1, 2020.

4. David Sanger and Maggie Haberman, "Does the Coronavirus Task Force Even Matter for Trump?," *New York Times*, May 7, 2020.

5. Brian Bennett, "The Coronavirus Task Force Reemerges After 2 Months, With Bad News and No President in Sight," *Time*, June 26, 2020.

6. Quoted in Mazzetti et al., "Under Pence, Politics Regularly Seeped into the Coronavirus Response."

7. This paragraph and the quotes therein are from Yasmeen Abutaleb, Philip Rucker, Josh Dawsey, and Robert Costa, "Trump's Den of Dissent: Inside the White House Task Force as Coronavirus Surges," *Washington Post*, October 19, 2020.

8. Lisa Friedman and Brad Plumer, "Science Speaks (But President Rarely Listens)," *New York Times*, April 29, 2020.

9. Amy Ross Sorkin, "Rick Bright and the Pandemic Path Not Taken," *The New Yorker*, May 15, 2020.

10. Unless otherwise indicated, the quotes in this paragraph and the information are in Sheryl Gay Stolberg and Noah Weiland, "Surgeon General, in the Hot Seat, Steps Up," *New York Times*, July 23, 2020.

11. www.usnews.com/news/politics/articles/2020–03-19/surgeon-generals-tv-praise-of-trump-earns-his-star-label.

12. James Fallows, "The Three Weeks that Changed Everything," *The Atlantic*, June 29, 2020.

13. Lipton et al., "He Could Have Seen What Was Coming."

14. The emails are available online. For a summary see Eric Lipton, "The 'Red Down' Emails: 8 Key Exchanges on the Faltering Response to the Coronavirus," *New York Times*, April 11, 2020.

15. https://abcnews.go.com/Health/coronavirus-threatened-invasion-red-dawn-team-save-america/story?id=72000727.

16. Sheryl Gay Stolberg et al., "Key Players in Federal Government's Effort Were Locked in a Feud," *New York Times*, May 10, 2020; and Stolberg, "Whistle-Blower Describes Clashes and 'Cronyism' in Administration Response."

17. Rucker et al., "34 Days of Pandemic."

18. Noah Weiland and Maggie Haberman, "For Dr. Deborah Birx, Urging Calm Has Come With Heavy Criticism," *New York Times*, March 27, 2020.

19. www.nbcnews.com/politics/donald-trump/dr-birx-goes-viral-reaction-trump-s-injection-comments-n1191841.

20. https://time.com/5827448/birx-trump-disinfectant-sunlight/.

21. www.prweek.com/article/1681380/lysol-clorox-respond-trump-comment-injecting-disinfectant.

22. Christakis, *Apollo's Arrow*, p. 165.

23. The quotes in this paragraph are from Michael Shear et al., "Passing Off Virus Burden."

24. Up to this point the quotes in this paragraph are in Sheryl Gay Stolberg, "Coordinator Becomes a Woman Without a Country," *New York Times*, August 7, 2020.

25. Shear et al., "Passing Off Virus Burden."

26. Derek Hawkins, "Coronavirus Update: Birx Says U.S. Has Entered a 'New Phase' of Pandemic as Cases, Deaths, Rise," *Washington Post*, August 2, 2020.

27. www.usatoday.com/story/news/politics/2020/09/16/trump-cdc-director-robert-redfield-confused-vaccine-masks/5720828002/.

28. Luce, "Trump and the Great Coronavirus Meltdown."

29. For more on Redfield during those early weeks, see Woodward, *Rage*, pp. 212 ff. The quote is on p. 220. It seems clear, though he is not so listed, that Redfield was one of Woodward's sources. (Woodward, famously, does not name his sources.)

30. Woodward, *Rage*, p. 252. Woodward shies away, though, from making the point that I make here.

31. For more on the testing mess in summer, see Sheryl Gay Stolberg, "'Clarification' from C.D.C. on Who Needs a Test Adds to the Confusion," *New York Times*, August 28, 2020. Also see Apoorva Mandavilli, "C.D.C. Reverses Its Testing Guidelines for Those Exposed to Someone Infected," *New York Times*, September 19, 2020. Also see David Willman, "The CDC's failed race against Covid-19: A threat underestimated and a test overcomplicated," *New York Times*, December 28, 2020.

32. Abby Goodnough and Sheila Kaplan, "C.D.C.'s Dr. Robert Redfield Confronts Coronavirus, and Anger," *New York Times*, March 13, 2020.

33. Brianna Ehley, "CDC Chief Says He Isn't Being Muzzled," *Politico*, May 21, 2020.

34. Dan Diamond, "White House Goes Quiet on Coronavirus as Outbreak Spikes Again across the U.S.," *Politico*, June 10, 2020.

35. Lena Sun and Joel Aschenbach, "CDC Chief Says Coronavirus Cases May Be 10 Times Higher than Reported," *Washington Post*, June 25, 2020.

36. www.npr.org/2020/07/08/888898194/trump-blasts-expensive-cdc-guidelines-for-reopening-schools.

37. www.nytimes.com/2020/09/18/us/politics/trump-cdc-coronavirus.html.

38. Rebecca Ballhaus et al., "A Demoralized CDC Grapples With White House Meddling and Its Own Mistakes," *Wall Street Journal*, October 15, 2020.

39. Noah Weiland et al., "Political Appointees Meddled in C.D.C.'s 'Holiest of the Holy' Reports," *New York Times*, September 13, 2020. Also see Noah Weiland, "Emails Describe Long Campaign to Muzzle Doctors at the C.D.C.," *New York Times*, September 19, 2020.

40. Weiland ct al., "Political Appointees Meddled."

41. Noah Weiland, "How the C.D.C. Lost Its Voice Under Trump," *New York Times*, December 17, 2020.

42. Ed Yong, "Anatomy of an American Failure," *The Atlantic*, September 2020.

43. www.nytimes.com/2020/08/31/opinion/cdc-testing-coronavirus.html.

44. www.forbes.com/sites/andrewsolender/2020/07/15/amid-white-house-attacks-polls-show-dr-fauci-remains-nations-most-trusted-voice-on-covid-19/#452e286a1ee2.

45. www.statnews.com/2020/09/10/trust-cdc-fauci-evaporating/.

46. The mask line is in Woodward, *Rage*, p. 246. The next quote is in Jayne O'Donnell, "Top Disease Official: Risk of Coronavirus in USA is 'Minuscule'; Skip Mask and Wash Hands," *USA Today*, February 17, 2020.

47. www.today.com/video/dr-fauci-on-coronavirus-fears-no-need-to-change-lifestyle-yet-79684677616.

48. The quotes in this paragraph are from Christakis, *Apollo's Arrow*, pp. 103 and 104.

49. www.businessinsider.com/fauci-white-houses-long-coronavirus-briefings-are-really-draining-2020-4.

50. Morgan Chalfant, "Trump Says He Disagrees with Fauci on Testing Capabilities," *The Hill*, April 23, 2020.

51. Tom McCarthy, "Trump and Fauci: America's Future Hangs on This Delicate Relationship," *The Guardian*, April 19, 2020.

52. Katie Rogers, "Trump Pointedly Criticized Fauci for His Testimony to Congress," *New York Times*, May 13, 2020.

53. Berkeley Lovelace, Jr., "Dr. Anthony Fauci Says Staying Closed for Too Long Could Cause 'Irreparable Damage,'" cnbc.com, May 22, 2020.

54. www.forbes.com/sites/sethcohen/2020/05/23/did-anthony-fauci-get-out-foxed-why-his-reversal-on-reopening-is-so-troubling/#310ce2b92e93.

55. Levin, "Fauci Says His Contact with Trump Has 'Dramatically Decreased.'"

56. Jonathan Allen, *NBC News*, June 24, 2020.

57. Yasmeen Abutaleb et al., *Washington Post*, July 11, 2020.

58. www.nytimes.com/2020/10/19/us/politics/trump-fauci-covid.html.

59. Woodward, *Rage*, p. 353.

60. "Lunch with the FT – Anthony Fauci," *Financial Times*, July 11–12, 2020.

61. The phrase is Michael Specter's in "The Good Doctor," *The New Yorker*, April 20, 2020.

62. Specter, "The Good Doctor."

63. www.theatlantic.com/health/archive/2020/10/sean-conley-trump-covid-coronavirus/616630/.

64. www.axios.com/trump-coronavirus-test-presidential-debate-8762825f-2f9e-4118-9c18-83f824afc9a1.html.

EPILOGUE — ENABLER EFFECT

1. It was the veteran epidemiologist Larry Brilliant who used the phrase "colossal failure of leadership." Quoted in Nicholas Kristof, "A Colossal Failure of Leadership," *New York Times*, October 25, 2020.

2. "U.S. Must Apply Lessons from 'Deeply Flawed' Pandemic Response to Preempt a Deadlier Disaster," Council on Foreign Relations Task Force Report, October 8, 2020.

3. Both quotes in the paragraph are in Yong, "Anatomy of an American Failure."

4. Ross Douthat, "Could Trump Have Saved More Lives?," *New York Times*, September 6, 2020.

5. "U.S. Is Alone Among Peers in Failing to Contain Crisis," *New York Times*, August 7, 2020.

6. Tom Mitchell, Sun Yu, Xinning Liu, and Michael Peel, "China and Covid-19: What Went Wrong in Wuhan?," *Financial Times*, October 17, 2020.

7. Quoted in Christakis, *Apollo's Arrow*, p. 116.

8. www.politico.com/news/2020/03/18/trump-administration-self-swab-coronavirus-tests-135590.

9. https://en.wikipedia.org/wiki/Operation_Warp_Speed.

10. www.washingtonpost.com/politics/2020/11/11/trump-angry-about-pfizer-vaccine/.

11. www.cbsnews.com/news/trump-supporters-reluctant-2020-campaign/.

12. Snyder's book is: *On Tyranny: Twenty Lessons from the Twentieth Century* (Tim Duggan, 2017); Applebaum's book is as referenced in the text earlier.

13. Jean Lipman-Blumen, *The Allure of Toxic Leaders: Why We Follow Destructive Bosses and Corrupt Politicians – and How We Can Survive*

Them (Oxford University Press, 2005). My most extensive work on bad leadership/followership are the books, *Bad Leadership* and *Followership: How Followers are Creating Change and Changing Leaders* (Harvard Business School Press, 2008).

14. Applebaum, *Twilight of Democracy*, p. 16.
15. Anne Applebaum, "History Will Judge the Complicit," *The Atlantic*, July/August 2020.
16. www.nytimes.com/2020/09/01/us/politics/trump-conspiracy-theory-thugs-plane.html.
17. Robert Draper, "Unwanted Truths: The Untold Story of President Trump's Battle with the Country's Intelligence Agencies," *New York Times Magazine*, August 16, 2020.
18. Paul Bartrop and Eve Grimm, *Perpetrating the Holocaust: Leaders, Enablers, and Collaborators* (ABC-CLIO, 2019), p. xxvi.
19. Applebaum, *Twilight of Democracy*, pp. 25, 26.
20. A sentence somewhat similar is in Applebaum, *Twilight of Democracy*, p. 26.
21. Applebaum, "History Will Judge the Complicit."
22. www.msnbc.com/topics/agriculture.
23. www.theatlantic.com/health/archive/2020/08/how-to-test-every-american-for-covid-19-every-day/615217/.
24. Mark Mazzett et al., "White House Pushed C.D.C. on School Risk," *New York Times*, September 29, 2020.
25. www.nytimes.com/2020/09/17/health/coronavirus-testing-cdc.html. This article is itself a revelation, fully supporting the points I make in this section.
26. www.nytimes.com/live/2020/10/09/world/covid-coronavirus#the-white-house-blocked-the-cdc-from-requiring-masks-on-public-transit.
27. All the quotes in this paragraph are in: www.politico.com/news/2020/09/11/exclusive-trump-officials-interfered-with-cdc-reports-on-covid-19-412809.
28. www.nytimes.com/2020/06/21/us/bolton-trump.html.
29. This point was made by Susan Glasser in "'It Was All About the Election': The Ex-White House Aide Olivia Troye on Trump's Narcissistic Mishandling of Covid-19," *The New Yorker*, September 18, 2020. Also see, www.nytimes.com/2020/09/17/opinion/2020-election-voting.html.

30. Glasser, "'It Was All About the Election.'"

31. Erica Newland, "'I'm Haunted by What I Did' as a Lawyer in the Trump Justice Department," *New York Times*, December 21, 2020.

32. The preceding quotes are in Applebaum, "History Will Judge the Complicit."

Index

Access Hollywood tape, 89
Adams, Jerome, 136, 154, 239–240
Adelson, Sheldon, 47
administration of Donald Trump
    Alex Azar, 186–188
    demographics, 57
    dysfunctionality of, 57–58
    early signs of
        crowd size lies, 55
        inaugural address, 54–55
    family involvement, 56
    Hope Hicks, 207–208
    H. R. McMaster, 60–61
    James Mattis, 61–62
    John Kelly, 61
    Kellyanne Conway, 207–208
    loyalty tests, 64–67
    Mark Meadows, 196–199
    media savviness importance, 57
    Mick Mulvaney, 195–196
    Mike Pence, 171–176
    Mike Pompeo, 176–179
    military appointees, 56
    Peter Navarro, 199–201
    Rex Tillerson, 59–60
    Robert O'Brien, 201–202
    Sonny Perdue, 271
    Steven Mnuchin, 179–181
    subordinate subservience, 67–70
    turnover, 61–64
    wealth of, 56
    William Barr, 181–186
advisors. *See* senior advisors, Trump
African Americans, 159
Age of Enlightenment, 130–132
Allure of Toxic Leaders, The, 25
alternative facts, 77–78, 207
American preservationist, 22
anti-elite Trump supporter, 22
Applebaum, Anne, 266, 270
Atkinson, Michael, 68

Atlas, Scott, 237–238
authoritarianism
    of base supporters of Trump, 24–25
    democracy and, 266–267
    soft dictatorship and, 270–271
    of Trump, 24–25, 266–267
Azar, Alex, 186–188

Bacow, Lawrence, 146–147
bad leadership/followership categories
    ineffective, 15
    unethical, 15
Bannon, Steve, 73
Barr, William, 181–186
Barrack, Tom, 72–73
base supporters of Trump
    COVID-19 and, 32
    deference to authoritarianism, 24–25
    defined, 22
    demographics, 22–23, 33
    devotion of, 19–21, 31–33
    and economic disenfranchisement,
        24
    ethnicity of, 22–23
    polling of, 265–266
    relationship to truth, 33–34
    types of, 21–22
Bethrothed, The, 94
birtherism, 160
Birx, Deborah, 121, 145, 197–198,
    242–246
Black Death, 96–98
Black Lives Matter, 158, 159–160, 185–186
Bolton, John, 201–202, 274
Breitbart media, 43, 73
Bright, Rick, 143–144, 201, 238
Browning, Christopher, 7
bubonic plague, 96–98
Buckley, William F., 37
Bush, Billy, 28
Bush, George W., 102–103

Camus, Albert, 95–96
Caputo, Michael, 273
CARES Act, 180
Carlson, Tucker, 151, 226
Centers for Disease Control, 103, 110, 132, 136–137, 246–251, 271–274
China and COVID-19
    Matthew Pottinger and, 203–204
    Mike Pompeo and, 165–166, 176–179
    mismanagement by, 118
    politicization of, 163–164
    Robert Redfield and, 247–248
    travel restrictions from, 200
    World Health Organization, 109–111
Citizens United ruling, 48
Clinton, Bill, 29
Clinton, Hillary
    dislike of, 30
    presidential vote tally, 265
    Trump lewdness and, 28
Coats, Dan, 69, 275
Cohen, Michael, 73–74
Comey, James, 63, 69
Coming Plague, The, 101
Conley, Sean, 259–260
Contagion (film), 96
containment zone (COVID-19), 113
Conway, George T. III, 78
Conway, Kellyanne, 77–78, 207–208
coronavirus. See COVID-19
Corwin, Steven, 136–137
COVID-19
    administration personnel affected, 78, 208
    American dismal response to, 262–263
    base supporters of Trump and, 32
    failure of United States government to contain, 12–14
    Fox News and, 223–233
    Jared Kushner and, 86
    leadership of Trump during, 8–9
    Lindsey Graham and, 216–217
    Melania Trump and, 89
    Operation Warp Speed, 264
    race and, 158–163
    shifting responsibility management, 197–198
COVID-19 politics
    culture war, 152–153
    global, 163–167

masks, 153–158
    polarization of, 147–153
COVID-19 timeline
    April 2020, 118–121
    January/February 2020, 109–113
    June 2020, 126–129
    March 2020, 113–117
    May 2020, 121–126
cruise industry, 114–115
Cuomo, Andrew, 113

Daniels, Stormy, 73–74
Defense Production Act, 141, 199–201
democracy and authoritarianism, 266–267
Democratic Party
    culture war (COVID-19), 152–153
    as panDEMic party, 227
demographics
    administration of Donald Trump, 57
    base supporters of Trump, 22–23, 33
    mask-wearing, 155–156
DeSantis, Ron, 218–221
DeWine, Mike, 49
Diamond, Jared, 97–98
disaster preparedness
    cognitive biases and, 106–107
    leadership for, 107
disengaged Trump supporter, 22
donors, political
    Bernie Sanders, 47
    Citizens United ruling, 48
    difference between Republican and Democratic individual, 47–48
    Isaac Perlmutter, 46
    Robert and Rebekah Mercer, 46
    Sheldon Adelson, 47
    Stephen Ross, 46
    wealth of Trump, 45–49

Ebola virus, 103
economy
    COVID-19 and, 144–145, 181
    racial disparities in, 159
    reopening guideline tension, 124–125
    unemployment rise, 124–125
enabler effect, 276–278
enablers, defined, 1, 16
enablers of Trump
    administration, 54–70
    fealty of, 16

enablers of Trump (cont.)
  fear of, 268–269
  inner circle, 71–89, 171–188
  levels of, 10–12, 269–270
  pandemic response team, 150–151
  political base supporters, 19–35
  relationship to truth of, 268
  Republican Party, 36–53
  scientific community, 138–139, 144
  types of, 10–12
Enlightenment, The, 5
Esper, Mark, 69
evangelical Christians and Trump,
      29–30
exponential myopia, 107

fables, plague, 93–94
fake news, 120
Fauci, Anthony
  cautious nature of, 104
  hydroxychloroquine, 140
  Lindsey Graham and, 215
  mask-wearing, 136
  pandemic resource allocation, 105
  Peter Navarro and, 200–201
  slow pandemic response of, 111
  target of criticism, 139–140
  Trump enabler, 251–260
  Tucker Carlson and, 226
fiction, plague, 94–96
15 Days to Slow the Spread, 117
Floyd, George, 158
followership
  attraction to bad leaders, 25–26
  bad categories, 15
  defined, 3
  history, 4–7
  and leadership of Trump, 9–10, 261–262
  who do not follow bad leaders, 275–276
Fox News
  COVID-19 spread, 151
  demeaning of other media coverage, 43
  Laura Ingraham, 43
  primary media Trump enabler, 223–225
  Republican Party and, 42–43
  Rupert Murdoch, 225
  Sean Hannity and, 80–82, 228–232
  Tucker Carlson, 226
Franklin, Benjamin, 130–131
free marketer Trump supporter, 22

Frieden, Thomas, 141
Frist, Bill, 101–102

Garrett, Laurie, 101–102
Gates, Bill, 102
Gingrich, Newt, 38
Giroir, Brett, 271
Goldwater, Barry, 37
governors, Trump enablers
    Brian Kemp, 221–222
    Ron DeSantis, 218–221
Graham, Lindsey, 213–217

Hanks, Tom, 114
Hannity, Sean, 80–82, 151, 228–232
Harvard University pandemic decision-
      making process, 146–147
Hicks, Hope, 76–77, 205–207
Hitler, Adolf, 6–7, 266–267
Hoffmann, Stanley, 265
Horton, Richard, 135
hydroxychloroquine, 140, 227

impeachment of Donald Trump
  acquittal of, 277–278
  Lindsey Graham and, 215–216
  Mitch McConnell and, 212
  Republican fealty during, 50–51
Ingraham, Laura, 226–228
inner circle of Trump
  inner ring, 83–86
  lack of, 71–74
  levels of, 74
  middle ring, 78–83, 171–188
  outer ring, 74–78
inner ring of inner circle, Trump enablers,
      83–86

Javanka, 83–86
Jefferson, Thomas, 131
Johnson, Boris, 119
Jordan, Mary, 88–89

Kadlec, Robert, 240–242
Kaine, Tim, 28
Katrina (hurricane), 106
Kelly, John, 61
Kemp, Brian, 157–158, 221–222
Kolbert, Elizabeth, 96
Kushner, Jared

in administration, 56
campaign role, 190
claims of false pandemic success,
    193–195
inner circle of Trump, 83–86
mismanagement by, 192, 193
pandemic supply chain control, 123–124
shadow COVID-19 task force, 190–192
unsavory background of, 189–190

La Fontaine, Jean de, 93–94
leadership
    bad, 34–35
    bad categories, 15
    change of followers as supporters, 4–7
    disaster preparedness, 107
    of Donald Trump, 8–9, 263–264
    societal need for, 25–26
leadership history
    follower history, 4–7
    in Germany during World War II, 7–8
    relationship with enablers, 2–3
Limbaugh, Rush, 43–44
Lincoln Project, 78
Lipman-Blumen, Jean, 25
loyalty tests, 64–67

mainstream media and Trump
    bypassing with Twitter, 42
    destruction of credibility of, 42
    Fox News, 42–43
Manzoni, Alessandro, 94
mask shortage, 123
mask-wearing
    demographics, 155–156
    differing recommendations about
        wearing, 136
    in Florida, 221
    Jerome Adams and, 240
    politics of, 153–158
    reasons for, 253
    Trump not enforcing, 127
Mattis, James, 61–62, 161–162
McCain, John
    Lindsey Graham and, 213–214
    Trump lewdness and, 28
McConnell, Mitch
    enabler of Trump, 209–213
    mask-wearing and, 157
    Trump lewdness and, 28

McGahn, Don, 69
McMaster, H. R., 60–61
Meadows, Mark, 196–199
media Trump enablers
    Fox News, 223–233
    Laura Ingraham, 226–228
    Rupert Murdoch, 225
    Sean Hannity, 228–232
    Tucker Carlson, 226
medical Trump enablers
    Anthony Fauci, 251–260
    Deborah Birx, 242–246
    Jerome Adams, 239–240
    Robert Kadlec, 240–242
    Robert Redfield, 246–251, 271–274
    Sean Conley, 259–260
    White House Coronavirus Task Force,
        234–238
Mercer, Robert and Rebekah, 46
Messonnier, Nancy, 111, 142–143, 238
middle ring of inner circle, Trump enablers,
    78–83, 171–188
Milgram, Stanley, 7
military
    defiance of Trump, 32, 161–162
    Trump appointees, 56
Miller, Stephen, 75–76
Milley, Mark, 162
Mnuchin, Steven, 69, 179–181
Mueller report, 182
Mulvaney, Mick, 195–196
Murdoch, Rupert, 225

National Basketball Association (NBA), 114
national shutdown guidelines, 117
Navarro, Peter, 139, 199–201

Obama, Barack, 102–103
O'Brien, Robert, 201–202
On Tyranny, 266
Operation Warp Speed, 264
Ordinary Men: Reserve Police Battalion 101
        and the Final Solution in
        Poland, 7
outer ring of inner circle, Trump enablers,
    74–78

Pamuk, Orhan, 94–95, 118
pandemic. See also COVID-19
    future preparations for, 104–108

pandemic (cont.)
  politics
    COVID-19, 147–153
    global, 163–167
    mask-wearing, 153–158
    prequel to, 93–96
    race and, 158–163
    school closures, 147–148
  scientific community
    academic input to, 145–148
    Age of Enlightenment, 130–132
    failure to speak truth to power,
      141–145
    global observations, 133–137
    politics of, 150
    slow response to, 135–136
    Trump and, 137–141, 144
pandemic history
  ancient, 96–99
  bubonic plague, 96–98
  Ebola virus, 103
  pandemic of 1918, 99–101
  recent, 99–104
  smallpox, 98–99
  Spanish flu, 99–101
Pence, Mike
  inner circle of Trump, 82–83, 171–176
  masks, 156
  Trump lewdness and, 28
  White House Coronavirus Task Force,
    112, 173
Perdue, Sonny, 271
Perlmutter, Isaac, 46
Perry, Rick, 56
pestilence. See bubonic plague
Plague, The, 95–96
politics
  COVID-19, 147–153
  global pandemic, 163–167
  race and, 158–163
politics and polarization
  and base loyalty, 20–21
  Fox News and, 227, 229–230
  and Republican fealty, 51
Pompeo, Mike, 165–167, 176–179
Pottinger, Matthew, 203–204

race and COVID-19, 158–163
Rage, 202, 247, 309

Red Dawn emails, 242
Redfield, Robert, 110, 122, 132, 246–251,
    271–274
reopening guideline tension
  Florida, 220–221
  in Georgia, 221–222
Republican Party and Donald Trump
  culture war (COVID-19), 152–153
  fealty of, 49–53, 125–126
  Fox News, 42–43
  history of, 36–41
  mask-wearing and, 156–158
  media coverage, 41–44
  Rush Limbaugh, 43–44
  wealth of, 45–49
Ross, Stephen, 46
Rubio, Marco, 50

Sanders, Bernie, 47
Scavino, Dan, 140
school closures, 147–148, 219
scientific community
  academic input to, 145–148
  Age of Enlightenment, 130–132
  failure to speak truth to power, 141–145
  global observations, 133–137
  politics of, 150
  slow response to pandemic, 135–136
  Trump and, 137–141, 144
Scientific Revolution, 130
senator Trump enablers
  Lindsey Graham, 213–217
  Mitch McConnell, 209–213
senior advisors, Trump, 72, 189–208
Sessions, Jeff, 63
shifting responsibility management of
    COVID-19, 197–198
Silver, Adam, 114
smallpox, 98–99
Snyder, Timothy, 266
soft dictatorship, 270–271
Spanish flu, 99–101, 133
state authority handoff, 197–198
state response to COVID-19
  bids against each other for
    equipment, 120
  hospital overwhelm, 116–117
  increase in caseload, 127–128
  opening up guidelines, 124–125

tension with federal, 115–116, 197–198
    William Barr and, 184–185
staunch conservative Trump supporter, 22

Taylor, Mary Elizabeth, 70
Tea Party, 38
Tillerson, Rex, 56, 59–60
Troye, Olivia, 275–276
Trump, Donald
    anti-science bias of, 103–104, 131–132,
        137–141
    authoritarianism of, 24–25, 266–267
    bad leadership of, 8–9, 263–264
    Bill Clinton and, 29
    children of, 79–80
    China and, 163–164
    confidence of, 25–26
    COVID-19 treatment, 259–260
    impeachment of, 50–51
    lewd comments by, 28
    marriages of, 88
    mask-wearing, 155, 157
    outsider image of, 26–27
    pandering to base fears, 23–24
    presidency of
        accomplishments of, 26
        administration, 54–70
        bad leadership, 34–35
        base support during, 31–33
        enemy punishment, 52
        loyalty tests, 52
        military defiance against, 161–162
        policies, 52
        polling of, 51
        rallies, 30
        relationship to truth and, 33–34
        senior advisors, 72, 189–208

shifting responsibility management
    of COVID-19, 197–198
staff turnover, 61–64
tumultuous nature, 30–31
unqualified to be, 126
worst in history, 274
racism of, 160–161
relationship to truth and, 52, 55,
    120–121, 268
temper of, 57–58
unconventional anti-establishment
    nature of, 27–28
Trump, Donald, Jr., 56, 79–80, 157
Trump, Eric, 56, 79–80
Trump, Ivanka, 56, 83–86
Trump, Melania, 87–89
Twilight of Democracy, 266
Twitter, 42

unemployment statistics, 124–125

Vindman, Alexander, 69

whistleblower complaint, 143–144
White House Coronavirus Task Force
    acquiescence of, 127
    briefings, 122–123
    enablers of Trump, 234–238
    Mark Meadows and, 198
    Mike Pence and, 112, 173
    real purpose of, 138–139
Woodward, Bob, 202, 247
World Health Organization, 110, 134
World War I and Spanish flu, 99–100
World War II
    history of followership in, 6–7
    leadership system in Germany, 7–8